THE LIBERATION OF GUAM

THE LIBERATION OF GUAM
21 July–10 August 1944

Harry Gailey

PRESIDIO

Library of Congress Cataloging-in-Publication Data

Gailey, Harry A.
  The liberation of Guam, 21 July–10 August 1944.

  Bibliography: p. 219
  Includes index.
  1. World War, 1939–1945—Campaigns—Guam.
I. Title.
D767.99.G8G35   1988   940.54'26   88–9960
ISBN 0-89141-324-3

Printed in the United States of America

CONTENTS

Introduction

On 10 December 1941 a major Japanese invading force landed on Guam and within hours the small, hopelessly outnumbered garrison of U.S. Marines and Navy personnel had surrendered. This event, masked by the Japanese air assault on Pearl Harbor and subsequent invasions of the Philippines, Malaya, and the East Indies, nevertheless was significant. The capitulation of the governor, Navy Capt. George McMillan, confirmed the loss of the first American territory to an enemy in World War II. It was, in a sense, a fitting climax to over forty years of neglect of the island, its population, and defenses by the government in Washington. Despite Guam's strategic location in the Central Pacific and its potential as a major naval base, almost nothing had been done to provide even minimal defenses. By the time American defense planners had awakened to its value, it was much too late. By contrast the Japanese, although not creating the fortresses of their mandated islands that some alarmists believed, had been busy in the late 1930s in making them secure from attack. Guam's sister island in the Marianas, Saipan, in 1941 was already a major military and air base. Even though in subsequent years the Japanese did not utilize fully the defensive potential of Saipan, Tinian, and the recently captured island of Guam, they had by mid–1944 enough men and materials in the Marianas to ensure that any invasion would be very costly.

The surrender of Guam after minimal resistance ushered in

1

two and one-half years of Japanese occupation. The native Guamanian population, although its petition for citizenship had consistently been ignored, remained loyal to the United States with very few exceptions. In the early stages of the occupation at great risk to themselves, they sheltered American military personnel. The Japanese authorities, dedicated to establishing not only Japanese rule but the dominance of their culture, reacted at times brutally toward the Guamanians. The random and largely senseless cruelty increased after large numbers of Japanese army troops were transferred to the Marianas. By late 1943, as the Japanese planners belatedly began to shore up their defenses in the Central Pacific, the lot of the Guamanians worsened and they could only pray for an early liberation. Although required by the authorities to learn Japanese patriotic songs in school, the children also made up their own forbidden songs. A verse from one poignantly expressed the hopes of the general population for deliverance. Both children and adults sang:

> Oh, Mr. Sam, Sam
> My dear Uncle Sam
> Won't you please come
> Back to Guam?

There was never serious doubt in the minds of the naval planners who were responsible for the Central Pacific theater of operations about the military importance of the Marianas. Although neglected before, once the war began the strategic value of these islands became obvious. Located slightly more than one thousand miles from the Japanese home islands, their capture could further advance the radius of action of the American fleet and air units in their attempts to cut the Japanese vital supply links southward. Further, gaining control of the Marianas fitted well within the context of pre-war naval planning which had envisioned an offensive westward across the Central Pacific in case of war with Japan. The only dissenting voice against such a policy was raised at General MacArthur's headquarters in Australia. He favored bypassing many of the projected targets in the Central Pacific. MacArthur wanted the men and materials diverted to the Southwest Pacific to be utilized in a unitary thrust up the coastline of New Guinea to recapture the Philippines. The decision in favor of the dual approach toward Japan was made by mid–1943 although General MacArthur continued to press his ideas until the Pearl Harbor conference with President Roosevelt in July 1944.

In all these discussions about the Marianas, the recapture of Guam did not take precedence. Instead, Saipan, the most heavily defended of the islands, was always the prime target. Unlike the planned invasion of the Philippines, little was mentioned about the duty of American forces to liberate the Guamanians from their oppressors. If this was ever a reason, it does not appear in any of the documents pertaining to the invasion or the memoirs of those who made the strategic and tactical decisions. These men did not confuse military objectives with humanitarian or political concerns although these could have provided a counter-argument to MacArthur's single-thrust concept.

The Central Pacific theater was fundamentally a naval concern. The vast distances separating the island objectives made this a logical choice. Although Army and Air Force units were used to a much greater degree than the general public ever suspected, they were directed by Adm. Chester Nimitz and his naval staff at Pearl Harbor. The shock troops utilized to carry out the many amphibious assaults were men of the various units of the Marine Corps. By the end of 1943 there were three full Marine divisions and a number of separate raider units available for action in the Pacific.

There were two reasons why Admiral Nimitz and his subordinates preferred to use Marines rather than Army units. One obvious one is that the Marines were elite troops especially trained for amphibious operations. The second, less publicized, reason is that the Navy controlled the Corps and therefore in all landing operations the Naval commander was in charge until the troops were actually on the beach. Even the transfer of control at that point was disputed by some admirals. Most notable in this respect was Adm. Kelly Turner who believed he should continue to command land operations from his flagship. However cooperative an Army general might be, any serious disagreements between him and his Naval counterpart could not be easily dealt with.

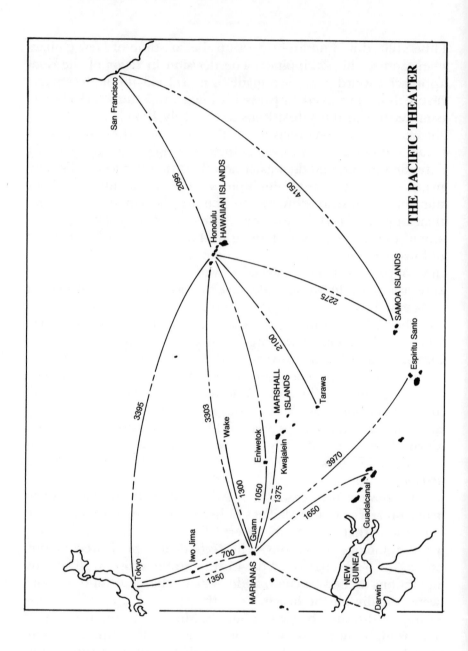

This fact became painfully obvious during the battle for Saipan when Gen. H. M. Smith of the Marine Corps summarily removed his Army subordinate, Gen. Ralph Smith, on very questionable grounds. Thus it was only natural for the Marine Corps to be assigned the primary role in the conquest of the Marianas. Its units had performed every task assigned them—securing Guadalcanal, assaulting Tarawa, invading Bougainville, operating on Cape Gloucester, and taking atolls in the Kwajalein and Eniwetok group. Now in the largest set of amphibious invasions yet undertaken, three Marine divisions and a brigade were scheduled to invade the Marianas. The main effort was to be directed at Saipan where the 2nd and 4th Marine divisions supported by the Army's 27th Division would invade on D day, 15 June 1944. Almost simultaneously, the 3rd Marine Division and the 1st Provisional Brigade were to assault the western beaches of Guam on W day, 18 June.

There were two negative factors in the planning for this operation. The first is the lack of detailed, accurate intelligence information on the size or disposition of Japanese units on Saipan and Guam. This deficiency was particularly true of Guam. Despite the fact that Guam had been an American possession for over forty years, there was minimal knowledge of even the road or communications networks. The second and most obvious negative factor, however, is the understated arrogance with which the plans for the operation were created. It was true that by the projected date of the invasion American naval and air power were supreme in the Central Pacific. But there was nothing in the actions of the Japanese in previous encounters to support the idea that the conquest of these vital islands would be easy. Yet the senior planners had allocated only one reserve division which they believed would not really be needed and they hoped could be diverted to seize Tinian. The rosy picture of a relatively quick seizure of Saipan was dashed by the same type of calculated, fanatical resistance which had characterized all Japanese defense efforts. The Army's 27th Division had to be hurriedly committed because of this heavy opposition and because the main elements of the Japanese fleet chose to fight it out with Admiral Spruance's Fifth Fleet.[5] These two factors forced a reassessment of the plans for liberating Guam. Fortunately for the Marines awaiting the signal to invade, reality intruded upon the thoughts of the senior commanders. They decided not to attempt a landing with no reserve force and only a minimal time for the pre-invasion bombardment. Admiral Spruance postponed the planned assault and the Marine units were transported back to Kwajalein to await the arrival of their backup, the Army's 77th Division.

This delay, however wearing on the Marines confined on board ship, proved a blessing. The Navy had time to thoroughly work over all suspected targets on Guam, particularly those on or adjacent to the beaches. When the Marines finally landed they were still met with considerable fire from artillery and mortars untouched by the fierce air and naval bombardment. Nevertheless, their lodgement had been assured by the long, concentrated naval support fire. Once ashore the Marines sustained heavy losses. They were not fully aware of how precarious was their position and were in great danger of losing their footholds. Had the Japanese commander chosen to commit the bulk of his western defense forces early, the Marines might have lost their tenuous footholds on the beach. His hesitation and later sanctioning of the disastrous *banzai* attacks made possible the relatively speedy conquest of Guam despite its natural defenses. Commitment of the Army's 77th Division gave the attackers numerical as well as technical superiority which the Japanese could not match. Nevertheless, the liberation of Guam was costly. The Marines once again redeemed with their blood the over-optimism of their leaders. It was also discovered that Army units, despite the opinions of some, could perform as well as their Marine counterparts. The Guam campaign was not without its faults but, in retrospect, it was an excellent example of cooperation between the various branches of the service in achieving the common goal of defeating the enemy as quickly and as expeditiously as possible.

The Saipan operation in conjunction with the successful battle of the Philippine Sea has overshadowed the liberation of Guam. The bombastic actions of Gen. H. M. Smith were more newsworthy than the quiet competence of his counterpart, Roy Geiger, who commanded the Southern Landing Force attacking Guam. These factors partially explain why little note has been taken of the actions there more than forty years ago. Aside from the official

Marine Corps and Army histories, nothing substantial or critical has been written about the Guam campaign. And this is strange considering the large number of books and articles which have appeared detailing other Marine Corps' assaults. Yet the actions begun on 21 July 1944 resulted in the liberation of American territory and the freeing of more than 20,000 Guamanians, most of whom retained even in the bleakest of times their faith in the United States.

Soon after the island had been declared secure it became the nerve center for the Pacific Fleet and the Twentieth Air Force whose activities contributed so much to the eventual destruction of Japan. The liberation of Guam, then, was no small event and has deserved better from historians of the Second World War. The following chapters are an attempt in a small measure to rectify this oversight and to restore the Guam operation to its proper place in the chronicles of the Pacific War.

CHAPTER I
Guam: The Early Days

Guam, the largest of the islands of the Central Pacific east of the Philippines, was first visited by Europeans in the spring of 1521 by the starving crews of Magellan's ships. The native people, the Chamorros, paddled their canoes out to his ships, swarmed aboard, and began to take whatever they could lay their hands on. They were particularly interested in items made of iron which they appeared to know and value. This incident caused Magellan to name the island Ladrones, the island of thieves. Eventually this uncomplimentary name was applied to the entire chain of what are today called the Mariana Islands. After ridding himself of his guests, Magellan paid them back by firing cannon into a Guamanian village and then ransacking it for food and supplies which made possible the continuation of his voyage.[1]

A further expedition in 1526 provided the Spanish with more information about the islands, but it was not until 1565 that Miguel López de Legazpe formally annexed the island for Spain. His expedition which had begun in Mexico was later to be very important in the establishment of Spanish hegemony over Micronesia because it was Legazpe who discovered the northern trade winds which blow continually eastward. This prevalent wind pattern which he encountered north of Saipan enabled relatively safe, easy passage along roughly the 40th parallel between the Philippines and the Alta California coast. Very soon there

9

was a small garrison posted on Guam, and Spanish galleons stopped from time to time on the way to and from the Philippines.

At first, relations between the Chamorros and the Spanish were good since trade, however slight, was to the benefit of both. However, over a century passed after the Legazpe expedition before Guam became anything but a minor way-stop in the Central Pacific. Then the Society of Jesus in 1668, with the support of Queen Mother Mariana, established a mission on Guam. The Jesuits labored with little success to bring Christianity to the natives of Saipan and Tinian also. The leader of these early Christianizing endeavors was Father Diego Luis de Sanvitores who renamed the islands the Marianas in honor of the queen who had been responsible for authorizing the activities of the Jesuits in the islands despite the opposition of her son, Charles II, and the governor of the Philippines.[2]

The good relations which prevailed during the first years of Spanish contact with the natives soon changed. The Jesuits insisted that the Chamorros change their social behavior and conform to Christian practices under threats by the missionaries and the small Spanish garrison. Armed clashes between the Chamorros and soldiers became frequent, and by the early 1670s, there was open war between the two groups. Violent confrontations continued in an intermittent fashion until 1690 when a series of military forays mounted by the Spanish from the Philippines finally ended the fighting and brought the Marianas firmly under their control. By that time the majority of the Chamorros had been killed. Estimates indicate that before the arrival of the Spanish the Chamorros in all the islands numbered at least fifty thousand. At the close of the long series of wars there were probably no more than a tenth of that number. The rest had been killed in the war or by Spanish reprisals or by the most dread scourge of non-European populations—smallpox. At the close of the eighteenth century the native population of the Marianas had declined to perhaps as few as two thousand. Long intervals of peace, intermarriage, and miscegenation between the Chamorros, Filipinos, Spanish, and other Europeans produced the modern Guamanian population. By the time of the American occupation in 1898, the native population of Guam had reached approximately ten thousand persons.[3]

Events in Europe in the latter eighteenth century greatly affected the future of Guam. The Jesuit order, by its activism, had alienated its aristocratic supporters with the result that the order was outlawed. The Spanish governor in the Philippines, upon learning of this action, removed all the Jesuit missionaries from the areas under his control. They were eventually replaced by Augustinian missionaries who were not as zealous as their predecessors in forcing the Chamorros to work at the European-style agriculture which the Jesuits had introduced. With time, the harvests became poorer and the once flourishing herds of cattle declined in number. The Chamorro population during the nineteenth century never suffered from famine, but most villages existed in a state of semi-hunger.[4]

The relative isolation of Guam from contact with the outside world increased during the last hundred years of Spanish control. The governor and the small number of Spanish residents might not see a Spanish ship for years. Mexican independence in the early 1800s almost completely removed Guam's direct ties with Spain since most of the ships bound for the Marianas began their voyage in Mexico. In the latter nineteenth century the Spanish government began subsidizing a bimonthly steamship service to Guam. However, this ship did not always arrive when scheduled. The Spanish governor of Guam in June 1898 hastened to send a welcoming party to greet Capt. Henry Glass of the American warship USS *Charleston*, blissfully ignorant of the fact that war had been declared between the two countries two months before.[5]

Despite Spain's attitude of neglect toward its possessions, other European states in the last quarter of the nineteenth century had become increasingly interested in acquiring new territories in the Pacific. This new Pacific imperialism, paralleling the scramble for Africa and European incursions into Southeast Asia and China soon resulted in most of the unclaimed islands being divided between the competitive European powers. Although Germany and Britain were in the forefront of this imperialism, certain important segments of the American public had shown interest in acquiring Pacific territory even before the Spanish-American War.

The small stopover islands of Howland, Baker, and Midway were acquired in the 1850s. The exotic and valuable China trade, the continuous presence of American whalers in Pacific waters, and the newfound missionary zeal of many Protestant churches all played a role in creating the basis for later American imperialism. Perhaps the best example of this late development of Manifest Destiny was the overthrow of the Hawaiian monarchy in 1893 by American businessmen who imagined that their zeal would be matched by that of President Grover Cleveland. Disappointed in not being immediately annexed, these entrepreneurs had to wait until the onset of the Spanish-American war for annexation.

The government's position throughout most of the nineteenth century was a skeptical one, despite the zeal of some American leaders, doubting the value of any of these Pacific islands, and passing up many opportunities to gain footholds there. These scattered and potentially valuable islands included the Marquesas, Ryukyus, Fiji, Makin, and Samoa.[6] The United States became a Pacific power not because of any deep appreciation of the strategic or economic advantages that could accrue to it, but because of its semicomic diplomacy which brought on a confrontation with Spain over Cuba. This offered expansionists such as Theodore Roosevelt, undersecretary of the Navy, the opportunity to widen American influence throughout the world. Hawaii was hastily annexed, as were Wake Island and Samoa. Commodore Dewey, faithful to his orders, took his small, modern squadron to Manila Bay and destroyed the ancient Spanish fleet, thus opening the way to the eventual conquest of the Philippines.

Guam was captured almost as an afterthought in the context of American operations in the Pacific. On his way to the Philippines, Capt. Henry Glass, commander of the USS *Charleston* and three troopships, was ordered to proceed first to Guam to secure the island. On 20 June 1898, the Americans arrived in Apra Harbor and, much to the surprise of the Spanish governor, demanded the surrender of the garrison within half an hour. The fifty-four Spanish and sixty Guamanian soldiers were disarmed, the American flag raised, and a salute fired from the *Charleston*. This was the only gunfire during the entire operation. On 22 June, Captain Glass and his small convoy left Guam for the Philippines, taking with him all the Spanish officials with the exception of one José Sisto. Glass did not even leave behind any Americans to govern the island, a position that Sisto filled until relieved by Cdr. Edward Taussig who arrived on Guam on 23 January 1899 to take legal possession of the island according to the treaty of peace with Spain.[7]

After the capture of Guam and Manila, Washington could see little value in expanding the conquest over neighboring Spanish islands which were so weakly defended that all could have been had with little difficulty. Even after hostilities in the Spanish-American War had ended, there was only a minimum debate in Washington over annexation of any Central Pacific islands. It was obvious from Spain's weakened diplomatic position that the United States could have had all or any part of the Spanish Pacific empire. The experts in the Navy were divided over any possible use of Guam or even the Philippines. The major use proposed for Guam was first as a base for the Pacific cable and perhaps later as a coaling station. The responsible naval officers, including the recent war hero Admiral Dewey, believed that a coaling station on Guam as well as ones on Samoa, Luzon, and Hawaii would be sufficient to meet the Navy's needs for the China trade as well as for any future Pacific war.[8] The terms presented to the Spanish in Paris in July 1898 thus asked for only one island in the Marianas. In September, President McKinley's instructions to the American commissioners indicated that he intended Guam to be that island.

Later the discussions between American peace commissioners and their Spanish counterparts included the possibility of the cession of all or parts of the Caroline Islands. Germany, however, had declared a protectorate over the Brown, Marshall, and Providence islands in 1886, and in early 1898, its Foreign Office indicated a very definite interest in the Carolines. German representatives concluded a secret agreement with Spain in September for the eventual purchase of Kusaie, Ponape, and Yap, subject to approval by the United States. The lack of both concise knowledge of the Central Pacific islands and of specific plans by the Navy to use them ultimately meant that the American peace commissioners in Paris did not pursue their acquisition with any fervor. Except for the use of one Spanish island in Micronesia for a naval coaling station, the most interest shown in this vast area was by the missionaries who were concerned with "civilizing" the natives. Ultimately the peace commissioners concluded that Germans could do this as well as Americans, and decided to support their ambitions.[9] There is little doubt that had the United States government wished at that time, it could have demanded and received all the Mariana and Caroline islands. This would have ultimately denied the Japanese access to these islands during the period between the two world wars. However, anything beyond this is pure speculation. The reality was that of all these islands, only Guam was considered by the United States government to be important enough to retain, and this was only because of its planned use as a coaling station and because some naval officers believed in its potential as a defensive bastion in the Central Pacific.

Almost immediately after the end of the Spanish-American War, recommendations were made to Congress to build up the defenses on Guam and to complete the necessary work to make it a coaling station. There was an urgent need to dredge the harbor and provide a breakwater. In 1904, a survey board headed by Capt. John Merry spent four months on the island and recommended major harbor improvements, a coaling station, and a naval base, all suitably protected by large-caliber guns.[10] Other high-level recommendations were made to create on Guam a Gibraltar in the Pacific. But all such views remained in the realm of conjecture since the United States government in the period prior to the First World War was hard pressed to fund what they considered more important defense projects elsewhere.

The island's importance as a cable link was diminished with the invention of radio. A small wireless station was established on Guam in 1906 which served the basic communication needs of the military. The major purpose of acquiring the island in the minds of many naval officers had been the need for a coaling station. However, the main trans-Pacific routes to the Orient bypassed Guam, and it soon became obvious that other areas were more suitable for providing coal than was Guam.

The government provided for Guam reflected the ambivalent attitude toward the island and its people taken by the McKinley and subsequent administrations. Since it appeared that the only use which could immediately be foreseen for the island was as a coaling station for the Navy, it seemed logical to continue it under direct Naval administration. The type and quality of administration depended largely upon the personality and policies of the individual commander since little direction was given by Washington during the long period prior to the Japanese attack on Pearl Harbor. Some administrators like Capt. Richard Leary who arrived in August 1899 ran the island as they would a ship, disdaining any advice from the inhabitants and demanding only to be obeyed. For example, it was Leary who deported all the Spanish priests and stopped religious instruction in the schools. Others were more concerned with the general welfare of the Guamanians and sought to provide more services for the people while listening to the complaints of their leaders about their anomalous position within the American empire. Capt. William Maxwell established the Bank of Guam in 1915; the first good roads were built before World War I to link Agana with adjacent military areas; and, despite the destruction wrought by tropical storms, the economy was bolstered by small but important expenditures by the Navy. Conditions of life for the Chamorros, who were still village based, became consistently better. This growing prosperity can be measured in many ways, not the least being the increase in population. Estimated at slightly more than ten thousand persons in 1899, the population had reached twenty-two thousand by 1941 with approximately half of these resident in the Agana area.[11]

Desiring better cooperation with the local Guamanian leaders, Capt. Ray Smith in 1917 convened the first Guam Congress. This organization proved to be of considerable assistance in local affairs. One of the major preoccupations of the congress was first in defining citizenship of the island, and later in attempting to secure outright American citizenship. However, a number of governors in the 1920s were unconcerned with such questions, and the Coolidge and Hoover administrations were not in a mood to change the *status quo*. Eventually, in 1930 Gov. Willis Bradley issued a proclamation defining the basic requirements for Guamanian citizenship. In 1936, when the Senate passed the enabling legislation, it appeared that qualified Guamanian citizens were finally going to be recognized as United States citizens. However, the naval hierarchy opposed the legislation and the House of Representatives refused to act. Further moves to grant United States citizenship to Guam's citizens were not successful. Thus when World War II began, the people of Guam were constitutionally in the same position as they had been at the turn of the century.[12]

Debates, public or private, over such issues as citizenship played a secondary role to the key question of what to do with the island. Conversion of the Navy to oil made the possession of the island as a potential coaling station unnecessary and the development of radio reduced the importance of Guam as part of a worldwide communications network. There remained only one overriding reason for major expenditures on the island—its geopolitical location which could make it a major factor in any conflict in the Pacific.

For over forty years a succession of naval leaders proposed that Guam be converted into a major base which would allow the Pacific fleet much more flexibility in case of war. The island's location and its natural defenses appeared to make it a logical choice for such a bastion.[13] However, all such proposals by naval experts or civilian authorities concerned with defense were negated by two factors. One was the expense involved in building a major harbor and providing the necessary facilities to service a large fleet. During the quiescent period following World War I, government priorities placed defense spending toward the bottom of the list of priorities. Any major improvement on Guam had to compete for money with dozens of other projects, most of which a parsimonious Congress refused to fund. Matters became even worse after the onset of the Depression. The second cause for ignoring the recommendations of the Navy for the improvement of Guam as a military base concerned the diplomatic presumptions held by policy makers during World War I and the two decades following.

The First World War changed irrevocably the balance of power in the Pacific. Even before 1914, the Japanese had taken command of trade in the Marianas and Carolines. This growing economic dominance had brought warnings from some observers of the increased danger to the American position in the Philippines.

These fears, chiefly among senior naval officers, were increased when in October 1914, Japan startled even its ally Britain by occupying the German-held islands in the Marshalls, Carolines, and Marianas. The Japanese diplomats hastened to reassure the United States that these actions were dictated by Japan's role in the war and did not represent a desire for more territory in the Pacific nor did its actions against Tsingtao indicate territorial aggrandizement against China.[14]

Despite the fears expressed by a few in Washington, little was done officially in 1914, when the situation was still fluid, to protest the Japanese actions or to indicate that the United States considered the occupation of these islands to be temporary. Secretary of State Kellogg did lend his support to those in Congress who wanted to improve Guam's defenses as a check to possible future Japanese encroachment in the Central Pacific. Opposition within the government and demands for increased military expenditure elsewhere particularly after 1917 dictated that nothing was done to fortify Guam or to put the Japanese on notice that their continued control of much of Micronesia was not assured. Division among the naval experts also contributed to the inertia. Some of the most important came to consider that the locus of any future naval engagement in the Pacific would occur far to the north of Guam.[15] The reality was that Micronesia played a very small role in the war and by the time of the opening of the Peace Conference in Paris in 1919, Japanese opinion had solidified in regard to ultimate possession of their wartime conquests. Their officials saw the continued occupation of the ex-German areas as extremely important economically and strategically. It would have been nearly impossible to evict the Japanese from them without seriously disturbing diplomatic harmony in the postwar years. The decision to create a mandate system under the League of Nations and to award the conquered Pacific islands to Japan appeared to most allied statesmen as the best solution to a relatively unimportant but vexing problem.

The question of what to do with Guam nevertheless remained. The consensus among naval experts had not altered from that held in 1900. If anything, they were even more in favor than before of fortifying the island and making it into a strong naval base since they now viewed Japan as a potential enemy without a base in the Western Pacific. Any war with Japan would mean the immediate loss of the Philippines. Despite such fears, the American representatives to the Washington Naval Conference in 1921 agreed to Article XIX of the treaty which called for nonfortification of the Pacific islands. The Japanese had been very concerned about the possibility that Guam would become a major naval base and thus act as a check upon the free action of their fleet in the Western Pacific. They could cease worrying. Article XIX, taken together with the naval limitations, reduced considerably the power of the United States in the area.[16] Although in 1931 the Japanese violated the Washington Pact by invading Manchuria, the United States government continued to act as if the treaty was still binding until it formally ended in December 1936. Thus Guam, despite its obvious attractiveness as a check to possible Japanese advances, remained defenseless. It was actually in better condition to resist an invasion in 1921 than it was twenty years later.

Despite the grandiose plans of some naval planners during the 1930s, the reality was far different. The one development that focused attention on the American "specks" in the Pacific was the inauguration of air service between the United States and the Orient. The first Pan American clipper landed in Apra Harbor, Guam, in the fall of 1935. Regular weekly service was established the following year, and the arrival of the large seaplane became a regular fixture, linking the island more closely with the outside world. However, this was a commercial development which although aided by the cooperation of the Navy did not need any additional military commitment anywhere to ensure its success.

The worsening world situation in the latter 1930s should have resulted in the improvement of America's Pacific bases. This, however, did not happen. Partially it was because of the continuing Depression which focused Congress's attention on domestic issues, but the lack of general preparedness for a future war was also the result of the deep commitment to isolation by a large portion of the American public and its leaders. Although the Navy was the favored service and had not suffered the same degree of disarmament as had the Army, it also was ill prepared for a major modern conflict. Those in the Roosevelt administration who wanted rearmament had to be very careful with this politically unpopular idea. Thus only three major ships were laid down after 1934. One was the aircraft carrier *Ranger,* and Congress in 1936 authorized the building of the fast battleships, *North Carolina* and *Washington.* The senior naval authorities hoped that by 1942 the Navy could reach the size authorized by the Washington treaty twenty years before.

American strategic planning during the 1930s was categorized in various plans developed from 1924 through 1938, code-named ORANGE. These envisioned that a future war with Japan would see the United States operating alone and that the war would ultimately be decided by naval forces. The plans called for the movement of a large portion of the fleet westward from Pearl Harbor to an advanced base in the Philippines, preferably Manila Bay. From there Japanese trade routes could be cut and, because Japan depended largely upon imports, this interdiction of its trade would bring an early end to the war. The proposed strategy also called for the occupation of some of the Japanese mandated islands in the Marshalls and Carolines and perhaps even the Ryukyus. In all these plans the Marianas were hardly considered since they lay to the north of the proposed line of attack, which was westward from Hawaii. The solidification of the ORANGE plans was but another reason why, despite opinions to the contrary by some senior naval officers, the buildup of Guam's military facilities was given such a low priority during this period.[17]

To anyone who had followed the high-level discussions over Guam and the Central Pacific islands in the period after their acquisition, the years after 1938 must have appeared as *déjà vu.* Once again the question of building a large, secure naval base west of Hawaii was raised, only now with more urgency. The most comprehensive report on United States defense in the Pacific and recommendations for its improvement were made to Congress on 1 December 1938. The committee responsible for this report was chaired by RAdm. Arthur Hepburn, former commander in chief of the United States fleet.[18] Not surprisingly, the committee, reflecting the basic ORANGE strategy, looked upon the Philippines as the central fixture for American defense in the Western Pacific. Contrary to previous planning, however, Guam was considered important as a base to protect the Philippines adequately from attack. The Hepburn board wanted to have a fully equipped and operational fleet based on Guam which would have the facilities capable of maintaining at least a major part of all types of ships of the Navy assigned to the Pacific.

Although the senior admirals—Leahey, Stark, and later Kimmel—continued to support the board's recommendation as a goal, the Navy did not ask Congress to appropriate funds for such a grandiose undertaking. Rather, as a part of the military request package for 1939, it asked for $5 million. These funds were to be used to build a breakwater, dredge the seaplane takeoff area, and make minor improvements in the facilities for handling aircraft. It was pointed out to Congress that most of these improvements would benefit Pan American Airways, the commercial air company, more than the military. Despite such modest requests, Congress in 1939 and again in 1940 debated the totality of the Hepburn Report. The same arguments pro and con which had been formulated in other debates were once again dusted off and used. The requested appropriation did not really have a chance since it was linked by isolationist members of Congress to what was believed to be President Roosevelt's desire to embroil the United States unnecessarily in foreign adventures. Former President Hoover stated succinctly the isolationist argument about Japan when he noted that Japan's interests lay to the west toward Asia and that the United States had little to fear from Japanese expansion since it was protected by "a moat" of six thousand miles and "no airplane has yet been built that can come one-third the way across the Atlantic and one-fifth of the way across the Pacific with destructive bombs and fly home again."[19]

There was also an aura of appeasement in the Congress; some stated that fortifying Guam would be an unnecessary provocation to Japan since the island was less than 1,400 miles from the Japanese home islands. Some warned that while Japan could have no logical designs on the United States, the proposed buildup of the Pacific fleet indicated a desire of the Navy to attack Japan. In February 1939, Representative J. M. Robinson of Kentucky, in a speech in the House, stated:

> Japan, Italy and Germany had all assured us time and again that they have no designs whatever against the United States. Japan, more than 7,000 miles from our shores and with a navy only two-thirds as large as ours, could make no successful attack on the Hawaiian Islands or continental United States.[20]

With such attitudes in Congress and a pacifistic public, President Roosevelt and the Navy did not push hard in 1939 for the funds requested for Guam, and the appropriation request was defeated in the House of Representatives. It was not until the spring of 1941, with World War II going badly for Great Britain in all theaters and relations with Japan worsening, that Congress finally passed a $4.7 million appropriation to accomplish basically what had been planned two years before.

To place this amount in context, the Guam appropriation was only one-half of that allocated to Samoa. However slight the sum for defense in all the Pacific voted in the spring of 1941, there was a noticeable difference in the attitudes of many former isolationists in Congress. The advent of the war in Europe and continued Japanese depredations in China had altered opinions. This was also reflected in the alteration of the ORANGE plans in April 1941 to include the possibility of a war with Germany as well as Japan. These modifications were code-named RAINBOW and restated in definite terms the goals outlined in the strategic position paper prepared by Col. Albert Wedemeyer in July 1940 for President Roosevelt. The basic presumption, which would guide American policy throughout World War II, was that the main enemy would be Germany and thus most of America's war effort should be directed against its defeat. The plans for the Pacific remained relatively unchanged except to factor in joint cooperation with the British. Basically these plans called for a holding action, retaining the key bastions of Singapore, Malaya, Java, and the Philippines. Within such a perimeter offensive actions would be undertaken to secure more bases in the Marshalls and Carolines. Once again, the planners had considered the Marianas to be of little value and had not assigned a high priority to spending the small Congressional appropriations available for improving Guam's facilities.[21]

As the relations between Japan and the United States worsened during the fall of 1941, the decision was made to write off Guam. Reflecting this realistic attitude, Admiral Stark in August 1941 wrote his subordinate at Pearl Harbor, Admiral Kimmel, stating his assessment of the situation in the Central Pacific:

> We are in complete agreement about developing Guam and bolstering the defense of the Philippines. . . . I fear, however, that it is pretty late to start on Guam anything more than we already have in hand. We will make all the progress we can, remembering that "Dollars Cannot Buy Yesterday."[22]

Last-minute attempts were made to strengthen Midway and Wake islands, but Capt. G. J. McMillan, Guam's governor, knew that in the event of hostilities, even with its great natural defenses, Guam could not be held. He was also aware that war between the United States and Japan would come soon because on 4 December he was ordered to destroy all secret and confidential publications.[23] All dependents had already been evacuated from the island in October.

The possibility of any meaningful defense of Guam in 1941 was considerably less than it had been immediately after World War I. Then there had been five- and six-inch guns located on the high ground around Agana with ranges up to nine thousand yards. In 1919, the Navy had decided to bolster the defenses by siting fourteen-inch coastal defense guns there. These were never installed, and after the Washington Naval Conference, the five- and six-inch guns were removed and shipped to Hawaii. Other than the rifles of the garrison, the entire defensive capability of the island consisted of several .30 caliber machine guns on Cabras Island and one fixed machine gun for anti-aircraft defense on Agana Height.

In 1921, a small Marine air detachment had been posted to Guam and there were plans to dredge the harbor to improve the landing area for seaplanes and to build hangars and service facilities at Orote Point. These had not been completed when the Washington treaty was signed and the decision was made to stop further construction. The size of the Marine garrison was 550 men at the beginning of 1931, but only 207 remained by the end of the year; all aviation personnel were also removed. The numbers of Marines available to the governor for the defense of the island never again exceeded 200 men.[24]

At the time of the attack on Pearl Harbor, there were six Marine officers, one warrant officer, and one hundred and eighteen enlisted men at the barracks at Sumay, and an additional officer and twenty-eight Marines doing police duty in various parts of the island. The Marine garrison was commanded by LtCol. William K. MacNulty. There were also eighty Guamanians of the Insular Force Guard, an organization which had been formed earlier in the year. Members of this force were in government service and received one-half the pay of corresponding ranks in the Navy. They had been organized and given infantry training in order to supplement the local militia, an all-volunteer unpaid force that had no equipment except a few obsolete rifles. In addition, there were 271 naval personnel divided between those whose duties were primarily administrative and those who made up the complement of the few ships in the harbor.[25] There were four of these—one old decommissioned harbor oiler and three small patrol craft. One, the *Penguin,* had anti-aircraft guns, the only weapons larger than .30 caliber available to the defenders.

By contrast the Japanese had assembled a formidable force in the Bonins in early November whose first task was the capture of Guam. This was the South Seas Detachment, a brigade-sized army unit of approximately 5,500 men. In addition there was the 5th Defense Force, an elite naval landing force of 500 men on Saipan who would also land on Guam. The Japanese had assigned twenty planes based on Saipan to soften up the defenses of Guam prior to the actual landings.

MajGen. Tomitara Hori who had earlier been alerted to the probability of war with the United States was informed early in the morning of 8 December that the Greater East Asia War had started and he immediately alerted all elements of his command to execute the invasion of Guam.[26] At about the same time that General Hori was informed of the beginning of the war (0545), Captain McMillan received a dispatch from Adm. Thomas Hart commanding the Asiatic Fleet alerting him that hostilities with Japan had begun. Less than three hours later he had direct confirmation of that when the first planes from Saipan made their initial bombing run on Agana.

For two days these air attacks against the all-but-defenseless island continued, causing considerable damage to the harbor facilities as well as to many buildings in the coastal towns. On the morning of 8 December, three planes strafed the *Penguin* off Orote Point. With a leaky boiler, the old ship could do only five knots per hour. Its single anti-aircraft gun with no range finder was no match for the Japanese aircraft. Ens. Robert White was killed and two crewmen seriously wounded. This attack convinced the *Penguin*'s commander to scuttle the ship. Planes also strafed a number of native villages. On the night of 8 December, some Saipan natives landed on a northern beach. They were an advance party who were to act as interpreters when the Japanese actually landed. Arrested and under questioning, they pinpointed the beach near Agana where the Japanese main force proposed to land. Although this was discounted by the Americans, the information later proved to be correct.[27]

A civilian worker on Guam, James O'Leary, noted in his diary the events of the first two days. Not knowing what to do and without guidance, the civilians scattered into the bush and eventually O'Leary found himself with ten or twelve others in the hills near the reservoir. From there he watched the Japanese land on the morning of 10 December. He wrote:

A signal light flashed the arrival of the landing party and the fuel pier blew up immediately. Bombers arrived and destroyed the remaining objects in Apra harbor. Warships also began to arrive from all directions. About 1:30 P.M., Tiny Lucke and Lieutenant Morgan and a Pan Air Group headed in to surrender. With much misgivings, we followed suit to the Marine Barracks. We were met and escorted by soldiers who fingered their bayonets as if they meant business. After a thorough search of our meager belongings we were taken to the recreation hall to sleep.[28]

There was little fighting and in most cases the Americans surrendered in a similar anticlimactic fashion. The one major clash took place around the plaza at Agana where most of the Insular Force was deployed. A few seamen and Marines who had been on police duty were also there. Just before dawn approximately four hundred men of the Japanese Special Landing Force stormed ashore on the beach pointed out earlier by the Saipan captives. They quickly advanced into the center of the city where they were pinned down by rifle and machine-gun fire from the Americans and Guamanians. Men of the Insular Force acquitted themselves well in the brief exchange of gunfire. One member, Peter Cruz, who with an unarmed ammunition carrier manned one of the machine guns located in the northeast corner of the Plaza recalled:

> I had one of the six .45 caliber pistols . . . I unhitched the pistol belt and gave it to Ben, telling him to use the pistol only to keep the Japanese occupied while I reloaded the machine gun.
>
> You can realize how I felt during those tense moments. There we were, none of us having fired a machine gun, and we knew definitely that the enemy was coming and that we had to face him. I prayed and prayed like I never prayed before. I was scared, knowing that if I weren't in the Guard I wouldn't have had such responsibility.[29]

Cruz need not have worried about his courage or that of the other Insular Guardsmen. He and his partner fired the .30–caliber machine gun until it jammed and then like most of the Guard who were still alive, tried to escape. Most of the losses suffered by the United States' forces occurred during this action in the plaza, although six sailors were killed on the beach near the Agana power plant. In all the fighting, twenty-one American service personnel and civilians were killed and an undetermined number were wounded. The Japanese, although successful in their assault on the plaza, suffered many more casualties.

Within minutes of the first assault, the main body of the Japanese, the South Seas Detached Force, began landing below Agat. The Japanese approached the Marine positions on the Orote Peninsula, but no contact was made before Captain McMillan decided to surrender. Shortly after 0600, a cease-fire was ordered. Cdr. D. T. Giles and the Japanese commander of the Special Landing Force, Captain Hayashi, proceeded to Government House to discuss terms of surrender. While these terms were being considered, many of the defenders were brought in front of the palace. Here the last American casualty of the invasion occurred. A Marine, Pfc. John Kauffman, who suffered from a nervous disorder which caused his face to twitch, was killed when a Japanese soldier believing that the Marine was making faces at him took this as an insult and reacted by bayoneting the hapless Marine to death.[30]

A few minutes after the cease-fire had been arranged, Captain McMillan, the governor, was forced to undergo an unnecessary indignity, probably to symbolize the Japanese victory. McMillan later reported:

> The leader of the squad of Japanese who entered my quarters required me to remove my coat and trousers before marching me into the Plaza, where officers and men were being assembled, covered by machine guns.[31]

A brief discussion of the surrender terms followed between Captain McMillan and Hayashi. Obviously the governor had no leverage and had to accept the inevitable. He signed the document at 0700 on 10 December. In view of the treatment meted out to the civilian population later in the occupation, it is interesting to point to one section of the surrender text which stated:

> I McMillan, have been assured by you Captain Hayashi, that the civil rights of the population of Guam will be respected and that the military forces surrendered to you will be accorded all the rights stipulated by international law and the laws of humanity.[32]

Even before McMillan officially turned over the government of Guam to the Japanese, the American flag had been lowered from the flagstaff at Government House. Thus forty-two years of undistinguished rule came to an end. Few could suspect at the time what the cost would be to restore it once again.

CHAPTER II
The Japanese Occupation

Japanese intelligence on the size of the garrison on Guam and the amount of resistance to be expected was faulty, for they overestimated both. Vice Admiral Inoye, commander of the Fourth Fleet at Truk, had entrusted the operation to Rear Admiral Goto and supplied him with more than five thousand men of the South Seas Detachment. The conquest of the island took only a brief time; within a few days the Guamanians were totally controlled by their new masters. Although the rugged interior of the island could have been used as a base for extended guerrilla operations, there was no organized resistance offered the Japanese during the two and one-half years of their occupation although there were many cases of individuals resisting their conquerors, and those who cooperated did so reluctantly or under threats to themselves or their families.

The foremost example of resistance offered the conquerors was the collusion of many Guamanians in hiding six Americans who had refused to surrender. Al Tyson, L. W. Jones, Albert Yablonsky, L. L. Krump, C. B. Johnston, and George Tweed, all Navy enlisted men, had slipped away into the forested central part of the island. From the very beginning Guamanians of all classes provided food, clothing, and shelter for the Americans. After meeting together briefly, they decided to break up into groups, each being cared for by different families generally in the immediate interior from Agana. There were probably over

29

fifty Guamanians involved in the delicate cat-and-mouse game with the Japanese. The danger in providing such assistance was very real since the Japanese came to look upon the continued freedom of the Americans as a blight on their honor and, by the fall of 1942, they had decided that every effort should be made to capture and kill the fugitives. They used every form of intimidation, including torture, to obtain information. Eventually on 11 September, Jones, Yablonsky, and Krump were captured in the bush area approximately ten miles east of Agana. Their captors beat them, made them dig their own graves, and then bayoneted them to death.

Fate caught up with Tyson and Johnston the next month when a strong patrol of fifty Japanese acting on reports moved to a ranch near Oka, just north of Agana, and forced the Guamanian owner on threats to his life and family to reveal where the Americans were hiding. Both men were killed resisting capture. This left only George Tweed. He was never captured despite increasing efforts by the Japanese authorities to locate him. He owed his survival in part to good fortune, but more to the courage of large numbers of Guamanians who viewed Tweed as a living symbol of the United States. As long as he lived there was proof of an American presence on the island. The Japanese tortured and killed a number of Guamanians including the island's most popular priest, but Tweed survived and was rescued by the Navy during the preliminary bombardment in July 1944.[1]

Despite the unconscionable treatment of the American escapees and those who were suspected of sheltering them, the Japanese authorities accorded relatively humane treatment to most of the islanders early in the war. A number of factors were responsible for this. The most obvious is that the Japanese were winning. Their military were not desperate for food, men, or material, and although secretly they despised soldiers who surrendered, their senior officers made clear to the captured Americans that as long as they assisted "the Japanese in every possible way by working to build up the defenses of Asia" their lives would be guaranteed. They were warned that any questionable action on their part would mean execution.[2] On 10 January 1942, all the American prisoners were transferred from the naval hospital and local buildings to transports which took them to Japan. There their treatment was much harsher than it had been on Guam.

A further set of reasons for the relatively good relations between the Japanese and Guamanians concerns the military personnel who administered the island until 1944. When the South Seas Detachment left in mid-January 1942 to reinforce the garrison at Rabaul there were no army troops left on the island. Instead, the administration was under naval control. The Japanese navy in most areas proved themselves to be more competent administrators and more civilized in their dealings with subject peoples than were their army counterparts. During the early stages there were never many military men on the island. Throughout the first year and one-half of their occupation there were fewer than two hundred sailors on Guam, members of the 54th Keibitai, a naval guard unit.[3] Most of these were located near the chief city, Agana, on the western coast. Therefore, at first there was a minimum number of military to use to intimidate directly the local populations in the numerous small villages throughout the island.

However, from the beginning of their occupation some of the Japanese troops betrayed the same unreasoning cruelty toward the citizens of Guam that marked their relations with subject peoples everywhere during World War II. During the initial landings, a Japanese squad had fired on a jitney bus loaded with civilians. Rushing the bus, they bayoneted all those still alive, a total of thirteen persons.[4] The Japanese enlisted soldiers showed their preference for the bayonet over and over again, particularly against unarmed civilians. The officers, of course, were addicted to using their swords, and later in their occupation would be guilty of a number of atrocities with this weapon against the Guamanians.

Much has been made of the potential defensibility of Guam, but in order to fully understand this one must look carefully at the island which the Japanese occupied in December 1941. It is the largest of the fifteen islands of the Mariana chain of Central Pacific islands which are positioned in a 400-mile arc extending over seven degrees of latitude. From Ritidian Point in the north to the extreme southern coastline is a distance of thirty-four miles. The island's shape is irregular; its width varies from three and one-half miles between Agana Bay in the west and Pago Bay on the east coast to a maximum of almost eight miles in the extreme north and south. Its 228-square-mile area is more than the combined area of all the other islands in the Mariana chain. Guam is the largest of all the Pacific islands between Japan and New Guinea, and is 3,300 miles west of Hawaii, 1,700 miles east of Manila, and 1,650 miles northwest of Guadalcanal.

Guam's size is only one factor that made it potentially the most defensible of all the islands of the Central Pacific. Coral reefs varying in width from thirty yards to almost one-half mile surround the entire island. These relatively unbroken reefs, particularly adjacent to the western beaches, are covered even at high tide by only two to three feet of water. These beaches, from Tumon Bay in the north to Facpi Point in the south, provide the best approach for any invader. Even here they are very narrow and in some places the land rises sharply within a few yards of the waterline.

The northern coastal area from Tumon Bay on the west coast to Fadian Point on the east is dominated by sheer cliffs rising directly from the narrow beaches. Some of these are over 500 feet high. Inland the northern part of the island is a limestone plateau dominated by four heights. In the extreme north there is Mt. Machanao (576 feet), in the east Mt. Santa Rosa (840 feet), and Mt. Mataguac (620 feet), while the southern edge of the plateau is anchored by Mt. Barrigada (640 feet). A bluff line approximately 200 feet high extends from Mt. Barrigada westward across the island marking the southern limit of the plateau. The northern part of the island was only lightly populated in the 1940s since the heavy vegetation precluded any but bare subsistence agriculture. In most places the plateau was covered by a heavy tropical rain forest of large trees, intertwined vines, and tangled undergrowth making movement through the area difficult under the best of circumstances, but ready-made for small-unit defensive action.

A narrow band of lowland extends across the island from Agana Bay to Pago Bay on the east coast. There are several springs in this area and a large swamp lying immediately inland from Agana. A small river runs from the swamp westward into the bay. This marshy area is adjacent to Apra Harbor and blocks off an easy approach to the Orote Peninsula. The peninsula itself is mainly coral limestone, and the seaward approaches are protected throughout much of its perimeter by steep cliffs.

The southern part of the island is where the bulk of the rural Chamorros lived. Its topography is complex and varied. A high ridge paralleling the east coast is the most notable feature. The western slopes are fairly steep; however, the highlands slope more gradually toward the ocean on the west, making it easier to advance into the interior from the coastline. The ridge is anchored in the north by a series of peaks—Mts. Macajna, Chachao, and Tenjo—while in the south is Mt. Lamlam, the highest point on the island with an elevation of 1,334 feet. The plateau east of the ridge has been heavily eroded and there are numerous small streams flowing through a series of valleys and ravines. Most of the southern plateau, although covered with sword- and bunch-grass and scrub forest was agriculturally the most productive part of the island. The many rivers that rise in the highlands are easily fordable by infantry although the banks of some are too steep for untracked vehicles.[5]

One factor that also supported the defense forces and is largely ignored by observers of Pacific campaigns is the weather. It is hot during most of the year with an average daytime mean temperature of eighty-seven degrees. In addition, the humidity is very high, particularly before the onset of the rainy season which normally begins in July and lasts until November. During this four-month period, on an average one can expect rain in varying amounts almost every day. Two-thirds of the annual rainfall total of ninety inches falls during this time. Since there were only a few miles of asphalt paved roads in 1941, most of the island's roads became nearly impassable during the heavy rains. Typhoons, although not an annual occurrence, did strike Guam from time to time with devastating results. The typhoon of 1900 all but destroyed the coconut production on the island. Guam had not fully recovered from the devastating effect of another typhoon when the Japanese landed.[6]

A further important factor which had to be considered by the American planners for the invasion of Guam was that during

the typhoon season there are unusually high tides, making landings on the westward beaches more hazardous than at other times.
The geography and meteorological data would lead to one conclusion by military planners: if at all possible, do not plan an invasion
of the island during the four-month period after June.

The Japanese policy toward Guam during the first months
of their occupation was ambivalent. They wanted, if not the active
cooperation of the Guamanians, at least to minimize resistance
to their plans for the island. Aside from the damage caused by
their planes, the island's facilities were intact. During the two
days prior to their landings no serious attempt had been made
by the American troops to destroy even the most obvious items
of strategic value. Thus the island's water tanks, power plant,
cold storage plant, and all the bridges were undamaged. The
harbor and its facilities were relatively untouched by the bombings.
So the Japanese had a firm base on which to construct a viable
economic system which would provide crops not only for the
Guamanians and Japanese on Guam, but also for export. Their
methods, however, were heavy handed, and instead of convincing
the Guamanians to cooperate freely, the authorities alienated the
citizens of the island long before the war turned against Japan.
They confiscated land and eventually reduced many of the island's
farmers to the level of slaves working in the rice fields and later
in preparing defense positions. All automobiles were confiscated
and given to the Japanese administrators or their sympathizers.
Residents of Sumay were ordered to evacuate their homes and
the schools were closed until late 1942.

The conquerors also changed the name of the island to *Omiya-
jima* (Great Shrine Island) and the name of the capital from Agana
to *Akashi* (Bright Stone). When the schools were reopened, they
were run by Japanese administrators and teachers who followed
a prescribed Japanese-style curriculum. In November 1942, two
Japanese priests were brought in to replace the foreign priests
who had been expelled earlier in the year. It soon became obvious
that Monsignor Fukahori and his assistant were either willing or
helpless agents of Japanese imperialism rather than spiritual
guides to the devout Guamanians. The behind-the-scenes struggle
between Fukahori and the Guamanian priest, Jesus Duenas, was

an indirect but important cause of the latter's subsequent torture and beheading by the Japanese.[7]

There was no concerted effort by the Japanese to build up the defense of Guam during the first two years of their occupation. They apparently viewed the island as only another of their Central Pacific holdings. The American public during World War II believed that the Japanese had spent the previous twenty years fortifying their mandated territories. We know that this was untrue. They had done very little to make their possessions in the Marshalls, Carolines, and Marianas defensible. Their near paranoia against outsiders visiting these islands during the 1930s actually hid the truth. Their Central Pacific islands were no small-size Gibraltars, but rather were important to Japan then because of the foodstuffs they could provide for the poor home islands.[8] Guam was to be no different, and as long as the war exceeded even the expectations of the Japanese High Command, there was no need to change this basically passive attitude. However, very soon in the war Japan extended itself far beyond its capabilities. Their early successes led the Japanese leaders to believe they could continue the war on a half-dozen fronts and adequately supply their forces from a minimal economic base along supply lines many thousands of miles long.

In retrospect it appears that there was no sudden revelation to the Japanese High Command that the strategy and tactics that had been so successful during the first six months of the war would not produce victory. Rather it was a slow process, but by mid–1943 it was apparent that Japan stood on the defensive on every front. They had been checked along the Indian frontier, they were stalemated in China, had lost decisive sea battles at Midway and near Guadalcanal, had been stopped in New Guinea, and been forced to abandon Guadalcanal. The United States had rebuilt its Navy, adding to it many more new ships, particularly aircraft carriers. The Japanese fleet had adopted a defensive strategy after Admiral Yamamoto's death. The Americans had earlier taken the offensive in the Solomons and New Guinea, and then in November 1943, they struck at Tarawa and Makin in the Gilberts. By early 1944 the American fleets built up around the fast carriers could go anywhere in the vast Pacific and would meet with little resistance. Kwajalein and Eniwetok fell, and the Fifth Fleet in February 1944 dealt a devastating blow to the main Japanese Central Pacific bastion at Truk.

Against this backdrop of growing American strength the decision was made to weaken the Japanese garrisons in Manchuria and at home in order to reinforce the key islands in the Pacific. The Japanese, with their concern about possible Russian intervention in Manchuria, had waited too long because even more deadly than the surface vessels of the Third or Fifth fleets were the American submarines. By the time that the Japanese army began embarking troops at Pusan for the Marianas and Carolines, these American submarines dominated the shipping lanes to those islands.

In October 1943, Japanese Imperial Headquarters decided to relocate the veteran 13th Division from central China to the Marianas. An advanced detachment of approximately three hundred men was all that was sent to the Pacific since later it became necessary to use the division for the spring 1944 campaign in China. No action was taken immediately to find a replacement for the 13th Division in the Marianas. It was not until early in 1944 that the 29th Division, a part of the Kwantung Army in Manchuria, was reorganized into a Regimental Combat Team (RCT) type of division and was ordered to the Central Pacific. The first troops of the division's three regiments, the 18th, 38th, and 50th, left Liaoyang on the first stage of their long journey to the Marianas. In addition, the Japanese formed the 6th Expeditionary Force from the 1st and 11th Divisions, also of the Kwantung Army, and dispatched it to Guam under the command of MajGen. Kiyoshi Shigematsu. The 5,100 men of the Expeditionary Force after a long but uneventful journey arrived at Agana on 20 March. In order to have more flexibility, the Japanese commander on Guam divided this unit into the 48th Independent Mixed Brigade (IMB) consisting of 2,800 men and the 10th Independent Mixed Regiment (IMR) of 1,900 men.[9]

The voyage of the 29th Division was not so peaceful. The troop convoy, four ships guarded by three destroyers, was caught northwest of Saipan by American submarines which torpedoed two of the transports. One of these, the *Sakito Maru*, carrying

the 18th RCT, sank. Over 2,200 of the 3,500 men on board including the regimental commander were drowned. Also lost were a
number of tanks and most of the regiment's equipment. The
survivors, rescued by the convoy's escorts, were later landed on
Saipan. The unit was reorganized and two of its battalions sent
on to Guam, but this unit proved of marginal value in the defense
of that island since there was not enough spare equipment to
completely equip the force. The decision was made to land the
50th RCT on Tinian, so the only troops of the division which
would be available for the immediate defense of Guam were the
38th RCT. Division headquarters and the 38th landed on 4 March,
and the division's commander, LtGen. Takeshi Takashina, took
over from the navy the responsibility for the defense of Guam
and Rota.[10]

A possible confusion in command developed just before the
American invasion when LtGen. Hideyoshi Obata, commander
of the 31st Army responsible for the defense of the Marianas,
Bonins, and Carolines, arrived on Guam. He had been in Koror
in Palau on an inspection trip when he learned of the imminent
invasion of Saipan. He left immediately to return to his headquarters there, but could get only as far as Guam. The defense of
Saipan devolved upon LtGen. Yoshitsugu Saito, and Obata remained in an ambivalent position on Guam. General Takashina,
although very proper in informing his superior of his plans, remained in tactical command until he was killed on 28 July. At
that point General Obata assumed control of an already lost
campaign.[11]

The naval force, the 54th Keibitai, which had garrisoned Guam
since December 1941, was also reinforced during the early months
of 1944, and by mid-year there were almost 3,000 naval combat
troops whose senior officer, Capt. Yutaka Sugimoto, relinquished
command of the island to General Takashina. In addition, there
were two naval construction battalions with a total of approximately 1,800 men, many of whom were utilized later as combat
troops. There were also approximately 2,000 men of the naval
air force. Originally there were eighty bombers and eighty fighters
based on two airstrips. The Japanese had belatedly begun construction on one of these near Sumay on the Orote Peninsula in Novem-

ber 1943 and on two others in early 1944 of which the one at Tiyan became operational at mid-year. Unfortunately for the Japanese, they had no aircraft to use in opposing the invasion. These all had been lost either in dogfights over Guam, or shot up on the ground or in supporting the Japanese defenders at Biak in May. Although the actual number of men available to General Takashina is not known for certain, the total strength of 18,500 men estimated by the intelligence officer of the III Amphibious Corps appears to be relatively accurate.[12]

With the arrival of more Japanese and with the army now in command of the island, the living conditions of the Guamanians worsened. All schools were closed and all religious services forbidden. With thousands of Japanese soldiers on the island, there soon developed an acute food shortage. The Japanese seized any surplus and allowed the natives only a bare subsistence ration. They increased their demands on the local population to work either on food production or on helping prepare the island's defenses. The majority of the men conscripted were used to help rush the airfield at Tiyan to completion. As the bad news from Saipan became known in June 1944, the Japanese hurried their coastal defense preparations. The Guamanians were made to dig gun pits, trenches, and put in place dummy guns along the high ground fronting the beaches where the landings were expected. The Japanese forced the people living in areas designated primarily for military use to move from their homes and be reestablished in concentration camps in the interior, where the crowding and neglect by the Japanese took a heavy toll. Food was in short supply, medical supplies all but non-existent, and sanitation inadequate. These factors combined to kill hundreds of Guamanians, mostly old people and the very young.

By the time of their liberation, which did not come for some Guamanians until early August, those who lived through the occupation were in desperate straits. One observer, an infantryman of the 77th Division, described the sight of almost two thousand liberated natives who passed through American lines near Mt. Tenjo. He remembered that all appeared half-starved and disease ridden, "the infants with swollen bellies and fleshless arms." The sight of such a pathetic cavalcade of victims of Japanese brutality did nothing to limit the loathing and hatred most American servicemen had for the Japanese.[13]

Such actions could perhaps be excused by the demands of war. The Japanese commanders on Guam knew by March 1944 that there was a high probability that the island would be invaded. Even with Guam's natural defenses, General Takashina knew that he would be facing an enemy who had far greater support strength than he had available. He and his staff were desperate to complete as much of the planned-for defenses as soon as possible and therefore conscripted the natives to help them. However, there can be no valid excuse for wanton, almost casual brutality. Lack of sufficient food and hard forced labor is one thing, but the Japanese were guilty in 1944 of atrocities of the worst type, in many cases directed against defenseless men and women who had unknowingly incurred the wrath of some Japanese soldier. The maltreatment of civilians increased in intensity during the first weeks of July, just days before the American invasion. There were dozens of summary executions during this period, one of them being Father Duenas who had fearlessly opposed the Japanese brutalities. He was beaten, subjected to the water treatment, and finally beheaded on 12 July.[14]

There were also cases of blatant mass murders which could have availed the Japanese of nothing except to satisfy a blood lust. For example, a group of approximately thirty young men and women from Agat and Sumay were taken to a cave near Fena and there machine-gunned. The worst of the massacres occurred in Merizo in the south where the Japanese on 15 July took two groups of approximately thirty men and women each into separate caves. Of the first group, fourteen survived; all persons in the second were murdered. One of the survivors, Manuel Charfauros, later reported graphically what had happened to his group. They had been rounded up and ordered into the cave ostensibly to spend the night. When they were settled in, the Japanese officer threw grenades and then led his men to the entrance of the cave, pausing long enough to strike Charfauros a number of times with his sword. It is instructive in the context of the Japanese atrocities to quote at length Charfauros' remembrance of that evening. He recalled:

. . . Certain that I was dead, the officer dropped the sword. Then picked up half a dozen handgrenades and threw them one after another into the cave. There were confused sounds of explosions, cries and groans, and a man staggered to the entrance begging for mercy. The officer paused, took out his bayonet and said: "Maila" (come).

"Please have mercy and excuse . . . ."

The officer said again: "Maila."

As soon as the man revealed himself at the entrance, there was a thud and the victim dropped—beheaded.

Then another man, Jose Acfalle, came begging also for mercy and the officer repeated: "Maila."

When Acfalle too reached the entrance, the officer thrust at his throat with the sword and the man dropped, but not dead. Seeing the sword he had leaned swiftly backwards and was struck on the shoulder. He lay still where he dropped and played dead. A third man, not so fortunate, was also beheaded at the entrance.[15]

The officer then ordered his soldiers into the cave to kill anyone left alive.

In retrospect it is obvious that the Japanese senior commanders were indifferent to the conditions they imposed on the Guamanians and did nothing to curb the sadistic behavior of some of their junior officers and enlisted men. Without excusing this negligence and cruelty, one can sympathize with the military problems faced by Generals Obata, Takashina, Shigematsu, and their staffs. The Imperial High Command had decided that the Marianas were the first line of defense of the homeland and all the islands in the group were to be held at any cost. Yet the means of carrying out these instructions were not available. The decision to reinforce the garrisons on Saipan, Tinian, and Guam had come so late that the defenders had less than three months to prepare. There were critical shortages of cement, reinforcing steel, lumber, and a wide range of needed hardware items which limited the kinds of fortifications that could be built.

Saipan was considered the key island; more troops were present there than on all the other islands, and its fortifications had been started earlier. There were also more tanks and artillery available to General Saito and Admiral Nagumo, the Saipan commanders, than Takashina had to defend the larger island of Guam. The value of Saipan to the High Command in Tokyo can be seen in their decision to bring out the bulk of the Japanese fleet to challenge the powerful U.S. Fifth Fleet off Saipan. The ensuing crucial naval engagement of the Philippine Sea not only sealed the fate of the Japanese defenders of Saipan, but meant that Japan's once powerful surface and naval air forces were lost and the entire Central Pacific region became an American lake. By the time of the American landings there on 21 July 1944 the Japanese had already suffered "the Marianas Turkey Shoot" and Saipan and Tinian had been lost. Takashina and his subordinates in the weeks between the landings on Saipan and the invasion of Guam knew that in spite of the added amount of time given them for preparation, their situation was hopeless. However, the loss of these northern islands made the Japanese angry and determined to hold out as long as they could and to exact as heavy a toll as possible of the invaders.[16]

General Takashina, convinced that any landing would be made along the western beaches from Facpi Point to Tumon Bay, concentrated most of his force there. The defense of the long coastline of the southern, eastern, and northern sectors was assigned to only three understrength battalions. Takashina divided the western approaches into two sectors. The area from Facpi Point to Agat Bay including the Orote Peninsula was under the command of Colonel Suenaga who had at his disposal two battalions of infantry from the 38th Division, one battalion of the 10th IMR, and a company of the 9th Light Tank Regiment. Guarding Orote Peninsula and the airfield near Sumay was the Naval 54th Keibitai. The rest of the island was commanded directly by Major General Shigematsu, the bulk of whose forces were located near the coast and inland in the area north of the Orote Peninsula to Agana. These included three battalions, the 320th, 321st, and 322nd, of the 48th IMB guarding directly the beaches from Agana to Tumon Bay. In reserve in the hills behind these beaches were three more battalions of infantry and one light and one heavy tank company.[17]

Although most of the large naval guns available on the coast had not been given the type of protection they needed before the American invasion, there had been considerable improvement in the general defenses after the arrival of the army command in March. Takashina had sited a formidable array of large-caliber guns, some of which had reinforced concrete revetments and ammunition storage bunkers. There were three 150mm guns on Chointo Cliff, four 120mm dual-purpose defense guns just east of Agana, three short 200mm guns above Tumon Bay, one at Asan Point and another at Agana Bay. In all, the Japanese had at least nineteen 200mm, eight 150mm, twenty-two 105mm, and six 75mm coastal defense guns in various placements throughout the island.[18]

The army units relied primarily on 75mm artillery of which they had eighteen 75mm guns and forty 75mm pack howitzers. They also had fourteen 105mm howitzers and one hundred guns of lesser caliber, the majority of which were antitank guns. In addition, the Japanese units had five hundred eighty 7.7 machine guns.[19] The Japanese army field artillery was not awesome in number or caliber, but certainly would have been adequate if the early stages of the battle had gone the way General Takashina and his staff had planned.

The preliminary bombardment in mid-June 1944 and the long bombardment before the actual American invasion on 21 July aided the Japanese in pinpointing the areas where the landings would take place. Therefore, General Takashina began moving the 10th IMR from the south to the Yona area so that it could act as a further mobile reserve for the units directly involved in repulsing the Americans on the Asan beaches. The interval of over a month between the first heavy bombardment in June when the Marines were scheduled to land and the final W day gave the Japanese time to shore up their defenses in the threatened area. The naval construction battalions and the Guamanians who had been conscripted were overworked trying to bolster the defenses in the areas near the beaches and airfields which the Japanese suspected would be prime targets. Supply dumps were constructed in some interior areas, but Takashina and his subordinates felt that they could waste little valuable effort in attempting to create some kind of inland defenses which would take advantage of the natural terrain features. Of particular significance was the work done at the neck of the Orote Peninsula. There the Japanese constructed a series of trenches and foxholes supported by pillboxes, machine-gun nests, and artillery in order to deny easy access to this key peninsula.[20] Much of this work was done under intermittent aerial attack by U.S. Naval planes from Task Force 58 after 11 June, and these were joined by the two carrier divisions of Task Force 53 on 6 July to deliver continuing systematic attacks on all strategic areas.

It is difficult to ascertain how good General Takashina's dispositions were prior to the invasion. The placement of his available troop strength appears to have been excellent, as was his anticipation of the actual landings. He maintained his armor in reserve at the most critical points. In the months before the invasion he had increased the number of machine gun positions by 141, added 51 artillery, and 36 medium anti-aircraft emplacements.[21]

Gen. Lemuel Shepherd, commander of the 1st Marine Provisional Brigade, was later very critical of Takashina's use of artillery during the first few days after the landing, and stated that he and his staff expected much heavier concentrated artillery fire against the beachheads. His comment was that the Japanese tended to use their guns to more effect by establishing alternative positions but lost much effectiveness by their habit of using single guns to fire on targets rather than concentrated fires of many guns.[22] This criticism, however relevant, tended to ignore the devastating effect that the long preliminary bombardment had on the retaliatory potential of the Japanese. Not only were most of their large-caliber coastal defense guns destroyed, but their communications network, so vital for action by combined units, was badly disrupted.

The major tactical fault with the Japanese defense plan for Guam lay in their general and specific ignorance of the potential of their enemy; this was a fault common to all the Japanese commanders in the Pacific. Even very senior commanders such as General Obata were not fully informed by the Imperial High Command of the superiority of the United States naval and air forces in any sector of operations by 1944. These island commanders could believe, therefore, in the absence of contrary evidence, that a particular defense plan was valid when in reality for it to be successful an adequate air and naval force would be necessary. Not only were Japanese army commanders left in the dark concerning the inferiority of their adjunct support forces, but many had no idea about the specifics of their enemy. It is doubtful whether General Takashina had ever attended detailed briefings on the positive and negative aspects of Japanese tactics on New Guinea, Guadalcanal, Tarawa, Eniwetok, or Kwajalein. Lacking such shared information, each Japanese island commander was being called upon "to reinvent the wheel," not suspecting that what he considered a new design had already failed elsewhere.

Finally, the Japanese were generally unaware of the superiority of most American weapons over their own. Two examples will suffice to illustrate this point. The first concerns armor and its utilization. Japanese light and medium tanks, while adequate to overawe Chinese civilians in the mid–1930s, were by 1944 obsolete death traps which could be taken apart by an infantryman with a bazooka. The American Sherman tank with its 75mm gun was far superior to any Japanese tank, yet Japanese commanders persisted in using their armor as if their equipment was on a parity with that of their enemy. The other example of how costly ignorance of the enemy's weaponry was for the Japanese concerned the flame thrower. Although individual commanders on different islands had general knowledge of this weapon, they did not have the details of its many uses or the specifications of the latest models. Therefore, they built their fortifications on the basis of inadequate knowledge and the individual Japanese soldier paid dearly for that ignorance.

To a certain extent, Japanese tactics developed and changed during the course of the war. During the invasions of Biak and Peleliu later in 1944, the Japanese commanders did not order *banzai* charges; rather they tried to limit their offensive operations and force the American troops to attack against well defended natural positions. But on both Saipan and Guam, the Japanese commanders threw the bulk of their strength into what were futile suicide attacks. The tactics followed by every Japanese commander of an island bastion through mid–1944 remained the same—defeat the enemy on the beaches and push the survivors back into the sea. The fact that such plans did not work seems to have been hidden from those Japanese officers responsible for designing the defenses. General Saito had tried the standard tactics on Saipan at the same time that General Takashina was preparing to defend Guam. Although there was continual communication between the two islands through June, Takashina did not modify his plans or alter his troop dispositions. The Japanese defenders of Guam believed they were ready. Six days before the invasion the troops in the Agana sector received confirmation of their major objective. They were to "seek certain victory at the beginning of the battle . . . to utterly destroy the landing enemy at the water's edge."[23] The Japanese unit commanders believed they were capable of this task. Within less than a week they discovered how flawed their battle plan had been.

CHAPTER III
Planning

Japan was ill prepared for a war against the United States, a fact recognized by almost all of its senior naval officers and even a few army leaders. It has become conventional wisdom to view the Japanese leadership during the fall of 1941 as panting for a war which would confirm their superiority in the Far East and the Pacific. According to such an interpretation, only a few far-sighted Japanese warned against hostilities. Chief among these was Admiral Yamamoto who thus emerges as a tragic figure, protesting the follies of his countrymen yet preparing for the devastating attack against Pearl Harbor. Although the reports of Admiral Yamamoto's attitudes are in the main correct, he was not alone. The naval leadership had long protested against the forward policies recommended by the army senior officers who were blinded to the realities of Japan's situation by the successes in China. On the eve of war, the navy leaders and many civilians in the government simply felt that they had no choice. The actions of the United States had placed them in a dilemma from which there was no ready means of escape. Adm. Osami Nagano, Chief of the General Staff, in a meeting of an Imperial Conference in September 1941, put the situation in very clear terms:

> It is agreed that if we do not fight now, our nation will perish. But it may well perish even if we do fight. It must be understood that national ruin without resistance would be ignominy.

In this hopeless situation, survival can be accomplished only by fighting to the last man. Then, even if we lose, posterity will have the heritage of our loyal spirit to inspire them in turn to the defense of our country.[1]

The pessimism expressed by Admiral Nagano two months before the war began was confirmed by the autumn of 1943. Despite its early fantastic success in all theaters of operations, Japan's conquests had been halted everywhere. These very successes led to a weakening of Japan because its leaders, emboldened by their victories, did not concentrate their efforts on the major task at hand, the defeat of the United States in the Pacific. The Japanese tried to conduct offensive operations on four major fronts with the result that they were not completely successful in any. They dissipated men and material in these futile efforts, leaving the United States and its productive capacity untouched.

For the Pacific area, two confrontations stand out in marking the growing weakness of Japan. The first is the battle of Midway in which a large portion of Japanese carrier strength was lost. Still with overwhelming superiority in ships and men, Yamamoto chose to turn back rather than risk his capital ships and transports against American air power. The second landmark leading to the defeat of Japan was their loss of initiative in the South Pacific. Here, in twin victories, the Allies in New Guinea and in the Solomons halted the Japanese short of Australia. By the conclusion in early 1943 of the sea, air, and land battles centered on Guadalcanal, the Japanese had passed their high-water mark, though this was unrecognized at the time, and were soon to be forced on the defensive.

One reason why it did not appear in 1943 that the Japanese had lost their chance of winning even limited objectives was because President Franklin D. Roosevelt and his chief advisors had decided before the war that the major objective of the United States should be the defeat of Germany.[2] Thus even during the dark days following Pearl Harbor, the bulk of equipment being turned out by American defense plants necessary for fighting a modern war was sent to Britain and Russia. This definition of priorities only became firmer after the United States began to build up its own forces in England. Gen. Douglas MacArthur was not alone of the Pacific commanders in complaining that the Pacific area received men and equipment only after a survey of European areas indicated that they could be spared.

By the time of the offensive operations against the Gilbert Islands in the fall of 1943, the United States forces were dominant despite the unfavorable priorities given the Pacific theater. The relatively low level of priority given to the defeat of Japan certainly postponed its eventual defeat, but the reality was that even with this attitude on the part of the American leaders, the Japanese were not able to match the United States' buildup in the Pacific either in ships, planes, or men. The Japanese naval staffs had not moved quickly enough to expand their carrier striking forces. Belatedly they began a hurried construction program which by the end of 1943 added the carriers *Shinyo, Kaiyo, Chiyoda,* and *Chitose* to the Combined Fleet. But the reality facing Admirals Koga and Toyoda was that the loss of four fleet carriers at Midway was not replaced by the time of the Marianas operation. In the meantime, the United States had added a host of new ships to the Pacific Fleet. The backbone of the new carrier-oriented Third and Fifth fleets commanded by Admirals Halsey and Spruance, respectively, were the new 27,000–ton, 32–knot fast carriers of the *Essex* class and the first of the new 11,000–ton *Independence* class which had reached Pearl Harbor by mid–1943. By this time the United States had built six carriers (CV), two light carriers (CVL), and sixteen escort carriers (CVE) in addition to four fast battleships and twelve cruisers. During the same period Japan had produced only two carriers, two light carriers, two escort carriers, one battleship, and three cruisers. When Admiral Mitscher led the devastating neutralization strike against Truk in February 1944, his Task Force 58 numbered six fleet and six light carriers escorted by a huge fleet of battleships and lighter supporting craft.[3]

The Japanese air arm was also inadequate to the task assigned it. The aircraft with which Japan entered the war remained the backbone of its naval and army air forces. Not until near the end of the war were a considerable number of new and higher performance aircraft available. By comparison, the United States had totally replaced its first-line aircraft. By mid–1943 Navy *Hell-cats, Avengers,* and the Marine *Corsairs* were far superior to anything available to American pilots two years before. An even more rapid development had occurred in the equipment used by the Army Air Force where *Lightnings, Thunderbolts,* and *Mustangs* came to control the sky in the Southwest Pacific theater. A comparison of pilots available to the antagonists by 1944 reveals an even greater disparity not only in numbers, but in quality. Japanese policy had kept their first-line pilots in combat almost continuously with few rotations to safer training billets. In time almost all their excellent pilots were lost without being able to pass on their skills to a new generation. The severe pilot losses sustained by the navy at Midway were only partially replaced when the naval high command committed a large part of its most skilled pilots to the air battles over the Solomons. The losses sustained by the Japanese in the southern theater during the first six months of 1943 could never be replaced. By the time serious considerations were given to the conquest of the Marianas, the ability of the Japanese to give naval and air support to these islands had been eroded to the point where they were practically nonexistent unless the Imperial High Command wished to commit to a final battle the last of their major fleet units, and even these were outnumbered and outgunned by Admiral Spruance's forces.

Adm. Ernest King, Chief of Naval Operations, was never satisfied with the priorities established by the president and his advisors. Almost alone of the most senior commanders, he disagreed with the Europe-first doctrine, and although he gave his support to that strategy once the decisions had been made, he never ceased to press for more supplies and men for the Pacific theaters. As early as January 1943 he was arguing that "the Marianas are the key of the situation because of their location on the Japanese line of communication."[4] However, even in the broader field of strategy in the Pacific, Admiral King could not be certain that his ideas on defeating the enemy would be accepted. Largely because of geography, the Navy had inherited the major role in the Central Pacific region, and there his chief lieutenant, Adm. Chester Nimitz operating from Pearl Harbor, had directed many of the earlier successes against the Japanese navy. The Naval high command was in agreement that the easiest approach to Japan was, following the outlines of the old ORANGE plans, to move directly westward and then northward, island-hopping across the Pacific.

General MacArthur and his staff in Australia were in open competition for men and materiel of all types with those whose responsibilities lay in the Central Pacific. However, more than just a scramble for always scarce supplies was involved. MacArthur believed that the situation in the Pacific theater by mid–1943 had significantly altered the basis on which the ORANGE plans had been predicated. He argued that advancing westward across the Central Pacific in a series of dangerous amphibious operations would gain very little until troops could be landed in the Philippines. His counterproposal was that the major effort should be to move in a series of well-calculated stages up the north coast of New Guinea, occupying Hansa Bay, Hollandia, Geelvink Bay, and the Vegelkop Peninsula. This strategy also presumed the capture of the major Japanese staging and air base of Rabaul on New Britain. Once these objectives had been gained, he then proposed the occupation of Halmahera or the Celebes and then finally the Philippines. If MacArthur's suggestions to the Combined Chiefs were accepted, then the Central Pacific theater would become secondary and the Navy would be reduced to a supportive role whose primary task would be ensuring the safety of the Army and Marine units in the Southwest Pacific zone of operations.

In May 1943 President Roosevelt and Prime Minister Churchill and their staffs met in Washington to lay out the broad outlines of allied strategy. This TRIDENT Conference confronted among many other problems that of the conflicting recommendations concerning the Pacific. As would be the case in most of the subsequent meetings of the Combined Chiefs, their decision was a compromise. While not specifically approving the invasion of the Marianas, they made the capture of the Marshalls and Carolines one of the primary objectives for the coming year. Approval of MacArthur's goals in New Guinea made it clear that at least for the time being there would be a two-pronged drive against the Japanese strongholds in the Pacific. This dual strategy was further confirmed by the Combined Chiefs at the QUADRANT Conference in August 1943 when Admiral Nimitz was ordered to seize bases in the Gilberts as a preliminary to further offensive moves in the Marshalls. The Combined Chiefs also ruled against MacArthur's plan to capture Rabaul. This stronghold would be bypassed.[5]

MacArthur and his staff in Brisbane had not yet accepted the dual strategy nor would they be entirely happy with the higher level decisions until MacArthur had met with President Roosevelt at Pearl Harbor in July 1944. Despite the criticism of the strategy emanating from Australia, Nimitz proceeded to carry out the planned occupation of Tarawa and Makin in the Gilberts in November 1943. This was followed by the endorsement of King's long-range strategy at the SEXTANT meeting in Cairo of the Combined Chiefs the following month. Admiral King had gained an ally in his arguments for the systematic seizure of island bases from which ultimately to strike at Japan itself. Gen. Henry Arnold, Chief of the Army Air Force, as early as the Quebec meeting had argued for the need for island bases from which the newly developed superbomber, the B–29, could operate. The first missions of these giant aircraft had originated in India and their attacks against targets in Burma had been more of a shakedown operation than ones designed to cripple the Japanese. Although not happy with the prospect, Arnold planned to build a series of air bases in China from which to strike at Japan itself. He made it clear that the logistical problems alone made China a poor selection for the B–29 bases. After Quebec, the Air Force leaders became open supporters of the Navy's plan for the seizure of the Marianas. Bases there would be supplied more easily, be away from possible Japanese capture, and be well within the 1,500–mile range of the B–29s.

At the Cairo conference, the Combined Chiefs finally negated MacArthur's suggestions for one front and endorsed the two-front concept. Specifically, the goals established for Admiral Nimitz were the seizure of bases in the Marshalls in January and in the Carolines in May, and the capture of Truk in July. MacArthur's general plans and schedule for his advance up the north coast of New Guinea were also approved, as was the capture of Kavieng and Manus islands. MacArthur's goal, the landing in the Philippines, was scheduled for the end of 1944. Nimitz's main objective was to be the Marianas whose invasion was tentatively set for 1 October.[6]

On 27 December 1943, Admiral Nimitz issued his campaign plan, code-named GRANITE, for operations in the coming year in conjunction with MacArthur's attacks. This called for the reduction of the Japanese positions on Kwajalein on 31 January, then the seizure of Kavieng by MacArthur's forces on 20 March and of Manus Island the following month. These attacks would be followed by the invasion of Eniwetok in May and finally the assault on Truk on 15 August. Only after these strongpoints had been seized would there be an assault on the Marianas. The dates projected for these invasions were 1 November for Saipan and Tinian, and 15 December for Guam.[7] The proposed one and one-half months separating the two operations were actually much more realistic than what was later scheduled. However, developments in early 1944 changed this timetable and the planners went from a cautious schedule to one which in retrospect was far too ambitious.

The Japanese fleet had sustained severe losses, particularly of carriers, during the fall of 1943 in support of operations in the Southwest Pacific. Having failed earlier to win decisive victories over main elements of the United States fleet, Admiral Koga adopted a defensive posture and ultimately ordered most of the Combined Fleet from Truk to Koror in the Western Carolines, and his successor then moved it to Tawi Tawi in the southern Philippines. Admiral Nimitz and his staff were not yet aware of the weakness of the Japanese naval units in the Central Pacific and therefore some of the planners working on details of the assault on the Marshalls assumed the worst. Both Admirals Spruance and Turner opposed Nimitz's plan to abandon the idea of seizing Maloelap and Wotje first. Instead Nimitz proposed going directly to the heart of the Marshalls and taking Kwajalein and the adjacent islands of Roi and Namur. Despite the protests of his subordinates, Nimitz's ideas were adopted with only the minor modification of seizing Majuro, from whence air cover could be better provided for the forces attacking Kwajalein.

The capture of Kwajalein, Roi, and Namur was easier than expected. The newly formed 4th Marine Division seized the northern islands in the atoll while the Army's 7th Division captured Kwajalein Island with very few casualties. Emboldened by the ease of neutralizing the Marshalls, Admiral Nimitz decided on a further bold move.[8] Once again, against the advice of some of his senior staff, he decided to advance the attack on Eniwetok from the original date of 1 May to 17 February. Despite the pressures generated on his Naval and Marine Corps staffs, a suitable plan was developed within a few weeks, the transport found, and Marine and Army units brought together for the attack. As Nimitz and Spruance had suspected, the various atolls at Eniwetok were quickly overrun despite stubborn Japanese resistance.[9]

The great question before the Eniwetok invasion concerned Japanese strength at Truk, the so-called Gibraltar of the Pacific. Nimitz decided to attempt to neutralize Truk at the same time that the Marines and Army units assaulted Eniwetok. To accomplish this, Admiral Mitscher's Task Force 58 based at Majuro sortied out toward Truk at the same time that a Navy covering force was protecting the landing. Admiral Spruance also led a major surface force centered on the fast new battleships *Iowa* and *New Jersey* south of the archipelago in order to intercept any ships that might escape Mitscher. The planes of TF58 struck repeatedly on 17 February at the ships in Truk lagoon, the airfield, and shore-based installations. They even continued the bombing during the night using radar. The results of the two-day strike were the destruction of more than two hundred aircraft as well as nineteen cargo vessels and five tankers. Although Admiral Koga had previously removed most of the fleet from Truk, the Japanese still lost fifteen naval vessels, including two cruisers and four destroyers.[10]

After this attack Truk no longer was a major factor in the Central Pacific War. Eniwetok was protected and ultimately the attack proved a major factor in the isolation of Rabaul far to the south. The negation of Truk combined with the Army's and Marines' capture of the key positions in the Marshalls dictated a speeding up of Admiral Nimitz's schedule for the Marianas operation, code-named FORAGER. This was reflected in a joint staff study for FORAGER issued on 20 March. The tentative date for the invasion of Saipan which was considered the most important of the islands was then targeted for 15 June. The study envisioned an almost simultaneous attack upon Guam.[11]

The guide by Admiral Nimitz's staff issued on 20 March, although changed later in minor particulars, remained the key document in preparing for the Marianas operation. It placed Adm. Raymond Spruance, Commander of the Fifth Fleet, in overall command and assigned Vice Admiral Turner to the position of commander of the Joint Expeditionary Forces (TF51). Admiral Nimitz added to his already proven team by appointing LtGen. Holland M. Smith, the commander of V Amphibious Corps located in Hawaii, as overall ground forces commander. His title was Commander Expeditionary Troops (TF56) and he would also serve directly as the commander of those units landing on Saipan. Admiral Turner's area of practical command was also Saipan as he, too, served a dual role as Northern Attack Force Commander (TF52). The Saipan invasion which was considered the most important would be carried out by two Marine divisions, the 2nd and 4th, each reorganized according to a new table of organization. All Marine divisions were authorized 17,465 men instead of the previous 19,965.[12] These Marine divisions were to be supported directly by Army artillery and amphibious units. The Army's 27th Division which had helped garrison Hawaii since early 1942 was to act as Expeditionary Troops Reserve. This meant that its commander, MajGen. Ralph Smith, and his staff had to prepare for the eventuality of landing at a number of places on three different islands.

The invasion of Guam was to be entrusted to another commander, the Southern Attack Force (TF53) under the direction of RAdm. Richard L. Conolly. The ground force scheduled for the actual assault on Guam was the newly renamed III Amphibious Corps commanded by Marine MajGen. Roy Geiger. When the planning for the assault was made, III Amphibious Corps was hardly stronger than the 3rd Marine Division which would be the major unit in the assault. The division which had been activated in September 1942 reached the Pacific in January 1943. Some of its Special Troops had been used against Vella Lavella and Rendova in the Solomons while the rest had undergone regular and continuous training in New Zealand and later Guadalcanal.

On 1 November 1943 most of the men of the division underwent their first combat landing at Cape Torkina on Bougainville. There for two months the 3rd, 9th, and 21st Marine regiments along with their artillery, tank, and other attached units fought through almost impassable jungle against a largely unseen but tenacious enemy. By the time they handed over the enclave they had carved out to the Army, they had secured the final beach line, inflicted very heavy casualties on the Japanese, and without sustaining heavy losses had become a veteran combat unit. The last regiment of the division left Bougainville by the end of December.

Returning to Guadalcanal, Gen. Allen Turnage and his staff immediately began to plan for the invasion of Kavieng Island west of New Ireland. The assault was scheduled for the end of February 1944. This was a part of General MacArthur's plan to neutralize Rabaul and the Bismarck Archipelago. The success of air and naval actions in the Bismarck Sea convinced MacArthur that it was not necessary to occupy Kavieng. Although the division was actually loaded for the assault, it was returned to Guadalcanal. Later elements of the division occupied Emirau without taking any casualties. It was after this action that Turnage was alerted to begin the planning and preparation for Guam.[13]

By late spring of 1944 the staff of the 3rd Marine Division had to overcome a few problems inherent within the units. A large number of men were afflicted by tropical diseases and some of the regiments were still waiting for replacements to bring them up to authorized strength. These technical problems could be dealt with quite easily. This was, however, not the case with the other constituent part of III Amphibious Corps. This, the 1st Marine Provisional Brigade, had only been formed on 22 March, composed of the 4th and 22nd Marine regiments. Its commander, BGen. Lemuel Shepherd, assumed command of the unit on 16 April, a mere two months before the projected landings on Guam. The 4th Marines had just been put together from the various Raider battalions that had been formed earlier to act as shock troops. The decision to reorganize Marine units had included the phasing out of the Raiders because General Vandegrift had concluded that there was no further need for this type of unit. As he stated later, he feared that these Raider battalions actually were divisive to the Corps because they fostered the concept of elitism.[14]

General Shepherd had very real problems in blending together such disparate elements into a cohesive unit in a very short time. Fortunately the majority of the men in each unit were already combat veterans. One problem that caused great anxiety was the lack of trained officers for Brigade Headquarters. General Shepherd who had once commanded the 9th Marines remembered:

> . . . I had tried to get some officers from the 3rd Division for my staff and headquarters company since no allowance had been made for any Brigade Headquarters personnel when the brigade was formed. I knew the 3rd Division was overstrength in officers and requested several be transferred to the brigade. The reply was negative. "Can't do it, can't spare a man."[15]

This was one of the sources for the friendly rivalry between the two Marine units on Guam. General Shepherd recalled with satisfaction how the 1st Provisional Brigade on Guam had reached the link-up point before the 3rd Division and he sent the message, "I am here, where are you?"

A further problem for General Geiger to contend with was the physical condition of many of the men of the 22nd Marines who had contracted filariasis, probably during the unit's stay in Samoa. Combined with wounds, transfers, and normal rotation, this disease forced the replacement of over 1,800 men in the 22nd Regiment in less than two months, while Corps and Brigade were developing tactical plans for the invasion.

Adding further to Geiger's many problems was the scattered nature of his command. When alerted to begin planning for the invasion, his headquarters was located at Noumea, the 3rd Division and most of the attached units were on Guadalcanal, the 22nd Marines were in the Marshalls, and the 4th Marines had just occupied Emirau.[16] These latter units would not be available on Guadalcanal for training until late April.

There was no specific unit designated to immediately back up the Guam assault. The presumption by the planners was that the Saipan operation would not be too difficult and that the Army's 27th Division perhaps would not be needed and could possibly be used to assault Tinian. Anything that might go wrong either on Saipan or Guam could be handled by the forces available. Another division was designated as a long-term reserve. This was the Army's 77th Division which was shifted from the U.S. west coast to Hawaii in March. The earliest date that it could be ready for use in assisting any of the other combat units in the Marianas was twenty days after the Saipan assault had begun.[17]

One factor stands out in any analysis of the preparations for the Marianas operation—its hurried nature. Correlated with this is the overly optimistic projections of the ability of the Marine units to gain a quick decision over the Japanese defenders of the three main islands. This overconfidence of the planning staffs remains inexplicable even if one considers the belief held by many senior Marine commanders, particularly Gen. H. M. Smith, of the invincibility of the Marines. At no time during the recapture of any of the islands had the Japanese meekly surrendered. Rather, despite all odds, they had usually preferred to fight on to the death. During all the planning sessions no one in authority apparently questioned the assumption that Saipan and Guam could be taken simultaneously with only one untested Army division in immediate reserve. Although Admiral Spruance was concerned that the still powerful Japanese fleet in relative hiding at Tawi Tawi might make a sortie against the Marianas invaders, there were no detailed plans of what to do if such an event were to rob the invaders of their major naval support and air cover. Later this lack of contingency planning caused a minor panic on Saipan when Admiral Spruance pulled out his covering fleet in order to engage the Japanese main force naval units in the second battle of the Philippine Sea. The over-optimistic attitudes of Nimitz, Spruance, Turner, H. M. Smith, and their staffs concerning Japanese resistance on Saipan would eventually force postponement of the invasion of Guam to a date more realistic than that originally designated in FORAGER.

All this was in the future, and for Admiral Conolly and General Geiger, their responsibility in the spring of 1944 was to abide by the overall strategic plan enunciated by Nimitz and to fashion tactical plans to achieve those objectives. General Geiger flew to Pearl Harbor and there staff planners from III Amphibious Corps met with Admiral Conolly's representatives in late March to begin fashioning the tactical plan for the Guam invasion which was code-named STEVEDORE. By 3 April, General Smith had approved the tentative plan and the next day this was in turn accepted by Admirals Spruance and Turner.

During the first week in April, Admiral Conolly flew to the Solomons and he and his staff moved into the same area as General Geiger's headquarters at Tetere and the major details of Naval and Marine cooperation were worked out. The Naval planners remained on shore at III Amphibious Corps headquarters until 27 April when Admiral Conolly's flagship the *Appalachian* arrived and took them on board. Later in May, MajGen. H. L. Larsen, the designated Guam base commander, and part of his staff arrived at Geiger's headquarters and thus were able to coordinate their plans directly with those who were developing the details of the invasion. Simultaneously with the work at Corps headquarters, Generals Turnage and Shepherd and their planners were putting the finishing touches on the tactical plans for the 3rd Division and the 1st Brigade. For all practical purposes, the operating plans for Corps, Division, and Brigade had been completed by mid-May although air and naval support annexes were added in the following two weeks. On 17 May, the tentative date for the Guam assault was established as 18 June, three days after the first Saipan landings. The landing date at Saipan was given the code name D day while that at Guam was designated W day.[18]

Although Guam had been a possession of the United States for over forty years, and a few officers had direct previous service there, very little was known about the island. In February 1944 the Office of Naval Intelligence compiled a 345-page study of the island and distributed it to the requisite commands, but this comprehensive study was based on information gathered prior to the Japanese occupation in 1941. General Geiger's request to send in small patrols by submarine to contact Guamanians to find out more up-to-date information was denied.[19] Two basic maps were available. One was an air and gunnery target map with a super-imposed grid comprising eleven sheets with a scale of 1:20,000 and the other was a smaller 1:62,500 map which was used by Corps for planning purposes. The 1:20,000 map was the basic map circulated to all headquarters for tactical planning and was used to construct the larger scale plaster relief maps used for briefing sessions. The Marine Corps also sent many rubber terrain maps from the United States. These were even more inaccurate than the other maps and charts, but because of their portability they were provided to each transport for the instruction of the assault troops.[20]

The planners relied heavily on these maps and upon aerial photographs. The first photo reconnaissance of Guam occurred on 25 April, and others were made at regular intervals during May and June. Various difficulties precluded the planners in the most critical stages of their tasks from having complete up-to-date pictures of the island. Not until the task force was ready to leave for the invasion was there a good mosaic ready for examination. Toward the end of April, the submarine USS *Greenling* returned to Pearl Harbor with good oblique photos of the western beaches and also observations of the tides and depth soundings. Despite all the information that became available to higher headquarters in May, the trickle-down process ensured that lower echelons did not have adequate maps or photos of their landing sites until after the invasion had begun.

General Shepherd in his After Action Report, although generally positive concerning the invasion, nevertheless confirmed the paucity of good information even at brigade level. He complained of the inaccuracy of both aerial photos and maps. The latter were of too small scale; they did not show adequately the topography or vegetation. He stated that the major topographical details were shown incorrectly, particularly in the vicinity of Agat where very few of the small hillocks, twenty to forty feet high, appeared on the maps. Further, he reported:

The road net shown, having been compiled from obsolete data, was very incomplete and in many cases inaccurate. Minor roads constructed by the enemy were not shown and in some cases there were errors in roads constructed by us prior to the occupation of the island by the Japanese.[21]

One need only point to General Shepherd's understatements concerning planning tactical manuevers in a beach assault operation with inadequate information to realize that the planners of the Guam invasion were hoping that American firepower and Marine bravery would overcome their lack of knowledge.

Inadequate maps and aerial photographs obviously hampered the planners and assault troops, but by far the most potentially dangerous miscalculations concerned the numbers of Japanese and types of units present on Guam. The III Amphibious Corps' Operations Plan which established the guidelines for the Guam invasion was issued on 11 May and was based upon intelligence information gathered and presented to General Geiger and his staff in March and April. According to these estimates, the Japanese had fewer than ten thousand combat troops on the island. There was in the intelligence reports a hint that some units of the Japanese 29th Infantry Division might be on Guam, but the educated guess was that the bulk of the division would not be present and therefore could be discounted as a threat to the American landings. If these figures were correct, then the optimistic views of Gen. H. M. Smith and his staff are more understandable. They believed that the two Marine units scheduled for the assault would be adequate to the task even without a reserve force specifically assigned which could be utilized without reference to the events on Saipan. Of course these early estimates were terribly wrong. General Takashina had almost twice the number of men that were reported in the estimate.

It was indeed fortunate for the success of the Guam operation that the stubborn defense of Saipan and the sortie by the Japanese fleet forced the deployment of the Corps' reserve, the 27th Division, there. Japanese documents captured on Saipan indicated that there were 18,000 army and navy personnel on Guam. Belatedly, the senior planners decided on 29 June that the original plans had to be modified to the extent of having another division in immediate reserve.[22] The postponement of W day for almost a month allowed the Army's 77th Division to be available for backup to the initial Marine assaults. The extra time also gave the Navy a chance to bombard the island over a much longer period than the original plans had envisioned. These two factors more than anything else ensured the success of the American invasion. It is not far-fetched to imagine the heavy casualties that the Marines would have taken had Takashina's coastal artillery and defense posts not been blown away by the long naval bombardment. Without adequate reserves immediately available, General Geiger's forces would undoubtedly have been in a very precarious position had they landed on the initial W day of 18 June.

The nature, as well as structure, of command had great influence on the course of the war in the Central Pacific. The most important fact is that operations in this arena was almost exclusively a Naval responsibility. Unlike the Southwest Pacific, Army commanders, much to their dismay, played a subordinate role. Although LtGen. Robert Richardson commanded all Army ground and air units in the Central Pacific, he was a subordinate of Admiral Nimitz. This relegation of Army units to a secondary position caused considerable friction which a lesser personality than Admiral Nimitz would not have been able to contain. For all his diplomacy, he was not able to mask the fact that the spearhead of American conquest of the Japanese-held islands was the Marine Corps with Army units relegated to reserve or supporting actions. There were many reasons for choosing Marine units for the most difficult tasks. They were composed of elite troops especially trained for amphibious operations, and their midrange officers were without peer in the command of infantry units through the regimental level. The resentment harbored by General Richardson and other Army commanders concerned the relative lack of training of Marine Corps general officers in handling divisional and army-sized units. However debatable this charge might be, it was certainly the most serious accusation levelled at LtGen. Holland Smith, the senior Marine commander in the Pacific, for his handling of the Saipan campaign, particularly after his relief of MajGen. Ralph Smith.[23] Army commanders suspected that another reason for their secondary position in the planning for action in the Central Pacific was that the Navy could control senior Marine officers better than they could their Army counterparts for the simple reason that the Marine Corps was a part of the Navy.

This did not mean that Marine commanders meekly accepted

Navy overrule. Although Gen. H. M. Smith's major publicized controversy was with the Army, his continuing battles were with the Navy, particularly with VAdm. Richmond Kelly Turner. Naval commanders were always placed in charge of an expeditionary force. The key question in tactical terms in the Navy-Marine Corps debate was, When does command responsibility devolve upon the ground force commander? Turner insisted that he should retain that responsibility and authority after the Marines had made a lodgement on an island. H. M. Smith argued that a Naval commander on board his flagship many miles offshore could not effectively exercise such command. This conflict between the two commanders was not settled until the Saipan operation when Admiral Spruance, commander of the Fifth Fleet, made the decision in favor of the Marine point of view. Perhaps this difference of opinion would not have been so intense had it not been for the personalities of Turner and Smith. Each was combative, intolerant, and reluctant to admit that he had made a mistake.[24] Only the diplomatic handling of each of these men by Spruance and Nimitz made possible their cooperation in the amphibious assaults on the Gilberts, Marshalls, and Marianas.

Personalities also played a role at command levels below that of the most senior commanders and on Saipan resulted in a major breach of relations between the Army and Marine units involved. However, there was a minimum of friction between all command elements chosen for the invasion of Guam. Although technically Admiral Turner and General Smith, two very abrasive personalities, were in overall charge of the Guam landings, these were for all practical purposes completely separate from the invasion of Saipan. After the plans of III Amphibious Corps had been approved, Turner and Smith had little direct input into the Guam operation. They remained tied to the surprisingly difficult reduction of Saipan and limited their inspection tours of Guam to a minimum. Even at that, General Smith's visits could hardly have been welcome since his observations were normally negative, and because of his lack of complete knowledge of the situation were unduly and unfairly critical of General Geiger's handling of the operation, reflecting his opinion of the performance of the 3rd Marine Division. There were few examples of a lack of harmony between units on Guam and most of them could be traced directly to the attitude of Gen. H. M. Smith, the overall commander of the Marianas' operation.[25]

Since personalities play such a large part in the success or failure of any campaign, a brief look at the five men most directly responsible for the Guam operation is revealing. The first of these and the man in overall charge of invasion forces was 52-year-old RAdm. Richard Conolly. By this time he was recognized as one of the Navy's most experienced amphibious commanders. He had initially served as a destroyer commander, screening Admiral Halsey's carriers early in the war. He subsequently served on Admiral King's planning staff whence he was transferred to Europe to command one of the transport groups involved in the Sicilian invasion. In late 1943 he was once again in the Pacific, this time as commander of the third group of the V Amphibious Force, and later commanded the ships and troops which reduced Roi and Namur in February 1944. By the time he became involved in the Marianas campaign he was already being called "Close In" Conolly for his belief in close naval support of the troops actually involved in the landing. This fact in itself would have endeared him to Marine commanders.

Admiral Conolly saw his primary duty as supporting the assault forces and therefore he took great pains to listen to what the Marine planners had to say. He did not attempt to force his preset conclusions upon them. As already mentioned, he brought his staff to Guadalcanal, pitched his tent with the Marines, and there jointly worked out the important details of the Guam invasion. His later performance in directing fire support for them only embellished his reputation. Indicative of most Marine officers' opinion of Conolly is that of Gen. Robert Hogaboom who in 1944 was a member of Gen. H. M. Smith's staff. He wrote:

> Admiral Conolly was at Roi-Namur. I had met Conolly when he first came to the Amphibious forces. I would like to say just parenthetically that I was greatly impressed with Admiral Conolly. He was one of the great amphibious commanders that I have met. I think he had all the great features of Kelly Turner and none of his faults. He was a very splendid,

strong, able man who would listen. He would send for Marines and listen to them talk about amphibious operations. He would send for me and sit at a table and talk with me by the hour, questioning me and then he would put on his field boots and go ashore and follow the Marines all through the operations. He studied and mastered the Marines' problems as well as the Naval problems.[26]

The commander of III Amphibious Corps, General Geiger, in many ways conformed to the picture just drawn of his superior, Admiral Conolly. He, too, was a compromiser, and although there was never a doubt among his subordinates of who commanded, he was not a shouter nor did he assume that anyone who disagreed with him was an enemy of the Corps. In this he was a contrast to the Expeditionary Force commander, Gen. H. M. Smith. While the relationship between "Howlin Mad" and "Terrible" Turner was stormy before and during the Saipan operation, that of Geiger and Conolly was one of mutual support.

Roy Geiger, at age 59, could look back on a career unusual even for an eclectic organization such as the Marine Corps. He had been a teacher and lawyer before becoming an enlisted Marine in 1907. Commissioned two years later, he then served six more years in routine assignments on board ship and in Nicaragua before being selected for pilot training, becoming one of fewer than a dozen commissioned officers in Marine aviation. He spent the next quarter of a century flying and commanding flyers. He then served under General Vandegrift on Guadalcanal as the chief of aviation on that beleaguered island. Geiger moved from there to the United States where he became Director of Marine Corps aviation in charge of sixty squadrons and 60,000 men. He would undoubtedly have been happy to continue in this position for the rest of the war, but fate intervened to cast him in even a larger role. Major General Charles Barrett, commander of I Amphibious Corps, was involved in a tragic freak accident and died on Bougainville. General Vandegrift, then on an inspection tour of the South Pacific theater personally chose Geiger to replace Barrett as Corps Commander of, by then, the newly renamed III Amphibious Corps.[27] Geiger would justify the commandant's faith in his leadership ability at Guam and later at Peleliu and Okinawa.

The Guam operation was also fortunate in the divisional and brigade commanders. MajGen. Allen Turnage, commanding the 3rd Marine Division, had a long career dating from 1913 before assuming command of the division just prior to the Bougainville operation. He had distinguished himself during World War I and later in Haiti and China. He had also served as director of the Corps Basic School, commandant of the training center at New River, North Carolina, and finally in the fall of 1943 was appointed Assistant Divisional Commander, a post he held until General Barrett was selected to be the corps commander. Turnage, soft spoken, self-effacing, and competent, could be depended upon to carry out his assigned tasks with efficiency, causing his superiors a minimum of worry.[28]

BrigGen. Lemuel Shepherd, who had inherited the unenviable task of putting together the Provisional Brigade from a number of disparate and in some cases hostile units had by this time an enviable record of command in the Pacific. He had been in charge of the 9th Marines for a crucial nine months when the 3rd Division was completing its training in the United States and New Zealand. Later he served with distinction as the Assistant Division Commander of the 1st Marine Division during the difficult Cape Gloucester campaign. Given the command in April 1944 of the 1st Provisional Brigade, Shepherd had faced almost impossible organizational problems while at the same time planning for the Guam operation. Later he wrote that "the limited staff provided the 1st Brigade and lack of an adequate Headquarters organization placed a heavy load on the Brigade Commander and his Chief of Staff." Minimizing the many difficulties, he noted: "With customary Marine sagacity, however, plans were completed and units readied for embarkation on schedule."[29]

Perhaps even more important than the leadership qualities and personalities of the Marine commanders was that of their Army counterpart, MajGen. Andrew Bruce, a veteran of the First World War, pre-war service in Panama, and only recently in command of the Army's tank destroyer school. He was an intelligent, cooperative, and aggressive commander. There would be no hint

of the jealousy and rancor that so marred the interservice cooperation on Saipan, and his 77th Division, untested before Guam,
was later considered one of the premier Army divisions in the
Pacific. The Marines after Guam meant it as a compliment when
some referred to the Army division as the 77th MAR DIV.[30]
Parenthetically each of these commanders' services would later
be recognized by promotion to the highest echelons of command
within their branches. All would receive the coveted fourth star,
and General Shepherd would eventually become Commandant
of the Marine Corps.

The plans that evolved during April and May for STEVEDORE
were deceptively simple and daring. The best place for a landing
on Guam was Tumon Bay north of Agana. The reef was not
too wide at that point and could be crossed by all landing vehicles
without too much difficulty. The fine sand beach at Tumon Bay
was a broad arc approximately two miles long. Behind this the
land sloped gradually upward toward the high ground inland.
However, the planners suspected that the Japanese expected any
invasion to strike that area first. They were correct in this surmise.
The Japanese had mined the bay, the beaches, and approach
roads; had strung barbed and accordion wire in the water; and
covered the inland approaches with machine guns and 20mm
all-purpose guns. The planners at III Amphibious Corps decided
not to risk a direct assault through Tumon Bay, but rather they
gambled that they could land below Agana in the most difficult
area of the west coast. Here the assault troops would have to
contend with wide reefs and shallow water which might hold up
the landing craft, forcing the troops to wade ashore. The beaches
in this region are narrow and fronted by cliffs and hills located
only a few yards inland. The Japanese could be expected to defend
the high ground with their usual tenacity for from these positions
they could literally look down the throat of any invader.

The initial plan then called for the 3rd Marine Division to
land on four beach areas between Asan Point and Adelup Point.
The 3rd Marines would land on the northern beaches, code named
Red 1 and Red 2; the 21st Marines in the center would hit Green
Beach; and the 9th Marines in the south would assault Blue Beach.
Once ashore, units of the 3rd Marines would secure Adelup Point

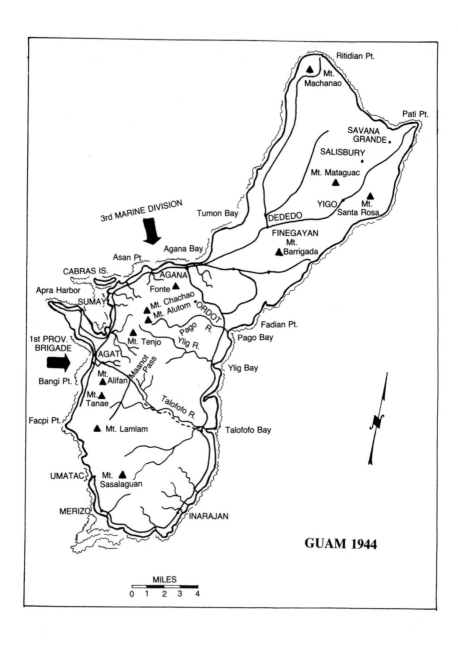

Ritidian Pt.

Mt. Machanao

Pati Pt.

SAVANA GRANDE

SALISBURY

Mt. Mataguac

YIGO   Mt. Santa Rosa

3rd MARINE DIVISION   Tumon Bay   DEDEDO

FINEGAYAN

Agana Bay   Mt. Barrigada

Asan Pt.

CABRAS IS.   AGANA

Apra Harbor   Fonte

SUMAY   Mt. Chachao   ORDOT

Mt. Alutom

Pago R.   Fadian Pt.

Mt. Tenjo   Ylig R.   Pago Bay

1st PROV. BRIGADE   AGAT

Mt. Alifan   Maanot Pass   Ylig Bay

Bangi Pt.

Mt. Tanae   Talofofo R.

Facpi Pt.

Mt. Lamlam   Talofofo Bay

UMATAC   Mt. Sasalaguan

MERIZO   INARAJAN

GUAM 1944

MILES
0 1 2 3 4

while another battalion would strike straight inland toward the Mt. Tenjo Road and the Fonte Plateau. The 21st Marines also were to drive inland roughly paralleling the banks of the two branches of the Asan River. The 9th Marines were to seize Asan Point and push southeastward along the coast road in order to secure a juncture with the 1st Marine Provisional Brigade as soon as possible.

The Marine Brigade, over 9,000 strong, divided into two regiments, the 4th and 22nd, was to land on the Agat beaches between Apaca Point and Bangi Point at the same time as the 3rd Marine Division was assaulting the areas north of the Orote Peninsula. The 22nd was assigned the two northern Agat beaches, codenamed Yellow 1 and Yellow 2, while the 4th Marines would come ashore on the southern landing areas called White 1 and White 2. Once the beachhead was secured, one battalion of the 4th was to drive inland toward Maanot Pass while another cleared Hill 40 to the south, a rise which could give the Japanese an opportunity for enfilading fire. In the meanwhile, the 22nd Marines would exercise a turning movement and drive toward the north, securing the town of Agat and the main road junction of the Agat-Sumay and Old Agat roads. Despite the dangers of exposing the regiment's right flank to counterattack, this turning was absolutely necessary if the brigade's primary objective, sealing off of the Orote Peninsula and its defenders, was to be achieved.[31]

Although the postponement of W day necessitated some minor changes in plans for both units, the tactical plans as outlined above remained basically unchanged. The idea was to consolidate secure beach positions then choke off the Orote Peninsula, capturing as quickly as possible the serviceable airfield there. Once a linkup between the Marine units operating to the north and south of the Orote Peninsula had been achieved, there would be a drive eastward across the island in order to establish a stable front line before the final conquest of the island. The direction of this last offensive would largely depend upon the Japanese. However, the capture on Saipan of the basic Japanese defense plans confirmed to General Geiger and his Corps staff that Takashina intended to make his last stand in the northern part of the island.[32]

The various rehearsals for the landings were completed by

the last week of May. Admiral Conolly aboard his flagship, the *Appalachian,* arrived at Lungi Point in the Solomons and took on the Landing Force Commander, General Geiger, and his staff and proceeded on 4 June to follow the slower moving LST group northward, rendezvousing at Kwajalein four days later. All appeared in order. The V Amphibious Corps made its assault on time, landing the 2nd and 4th Marine Divisions on Saipan on D day, 15 June. With Phase 1 of the Marianas operation underway, Admiral Spruance sent a dispatch to Conolly on the evening of D day confirming that STEVEDORE should be launched on schedule.[33] W day was still to be 18 June. No one suspected at that time that the invasion of Guam would be postponed for more than a month.

CHAPTER IV
Softening Up the Defenses

Concentration of ships and supplies for the Guam operation had begun while the tactical planning was in its early phase. Most of the ships that would make up Task Force 53 had been assigned earlier to the Southwest Pacific theater and were involved in General MacArthur's attack on Hollandia. Although scheduled for action in the Marianas, most had not reached the Solomon's staging area by 1 May, but within two weeks they had arrived and were sent to various locations for servicing. By mid-May the various types of transports were in the vicinity of Guadalcanal and Tulagi where loading was begun.

Although there were enough ships to carry the combat troops, there was not sufficient cargo space for all the organic equipment and transport. There was always a shortage of shipping space in the Pacific theater since Europe had first call for the various types of ships and landing craft. This European bias was even more pronounced in the early months of 1944 since the invasion of Europe had been projected for either May or June. Even for the proposed action in the Marianas, the Guam operation was of secondary importance. The major emphasis was placed on Saipan. Therefore, due to the restricted cargo space available, the logistical planners had to continually revise their loading plans right up to the date that the task force sailed. This paring down process meant that a significant number of the vehicles organic to the 3rd Marine Division and the 1st Provisional Brigade were left behind.[1]

Not cut back however, even with the restricted cargo space, were the amphibious vehicles. The reefs surrounding Guam had to be crossed and the more amphibious vehicles available, the quicker the Marines and their very necessary supplies could get in to the beaches. The 3rd Amphibious Tractor Battalion with 180 LVTs was assigned to the 3rd Marine Division while its counterpart, the 4th, with 178 LVTs, would carry the men of General Shepherd's brigade. After the first assault waves were on shore, the LVTs would be supplemented by amphibious trucks (DUKWs). There were 100 of these available. The division had 60 assigned to it and the rest were to carry equipment for the brigade.[2] First priority for the DUKWs was to bring in the 105mm howitzers of the artillery battalions. The loading of artillery on board DUKWs had first been tried by the Army's 7th Division at Kwajalein and had been so successful that in all subsequent invasions the medium artillery was transported early into action. As soon as possible the DUKWs and LVTs would bring in other large items such as the extra radio equipment for the major headquarters, antitank guns, and of course ammunition of all calibers. Some DUKWs were also to be used as mobile command posts.

The problem of transporting large quantities of supplies of all types over the reefs to the beachheads with a limited number of amphibious vehicles was partially solved by planning to use self-propelled pontoon barges. Four of these were scheduled to be brought in to the northern beaches, while a like number were assigned to the 1st Provisional Brigade sector. These huge barges and piers were side-carried by LSTs. Twelve pontoon causeways each in two sections measuring 14 feet × 100 feet were also loaded on an LST carrier. Eight of these were to be put in place in the northern sector while four would be eventually set up for the Agat beaches. Once established, these would be used as floating docks, storage points, and refueling stations. In addition, each LST of the attack force carried three reinforced wire mats to be laid down over the coral to provide better traction for the wheeled vehicles being offloaded.[3]

In order to eliminate as much confusion as possible, a special staff was created by grouping officers and men of the Corps engineer and quartermaster staffs under the direct command of LtCol. Francis McAlister. This staff was to be responsible for all incoming supplies and would oversee the establishment of depots, transport facilities, and medical operations. As soon as possible all brigade and division pioneer units as well as the Navy's construction battalions would also come under this unified command. In addition McAlister would be in charge of operating the port to be established at Apra and the airfields, until relieved by General Larsen's garrison command. Later the relatively smooth functioning of these vital support operations and facilities justified the creation of a single command structure for the Guam invasion.[4]

The special amphibious training for the Marine units, many of which were composed of troops which had not yet seen action, did not begin until the first week in May. One of the reasons was that some of the troops of the 4th and 22nd Marines were at Emirau and Kwajalein and did not arrive at Guadalcanal until late April. Training for the 22nd was further hampered by the need to replace the 1,800 men who had contracted filariasis while in Samoa. Most of the replacements came from the 3rd Marine Division which had more men assigned than authorized. The tasks of preparing the brigade were more difficult than that facing General Turnage and his staff of the 3rd Marine Division. Newly formed, the brigade had hardly worked out the organizational problems before having to begin training for the invasion. A further difficulty was the restricted area available for maneuvers and training at Tassafaronga where the brigade was located.

The first phase of training for all units concentrated upon toughening up exercises although some, such as the artillery, practiced more specialized tasks such as loading and unloading their 105s from the DUKWs. The final part of this first phase concerned practicing unloading troops and their supporting equipment from the LVTs. The final pre-rehearsal training began on 12 May near Cape Esperance. Six days were devoted to ship-to-shore exercises followed by two days of air support operations in conjunction with regimental landings. The troops maneuvered ashore according to their tactical plans, supported by a token amount of their heavier equipment. Two more days were then devoted to air and naval gunfire activities to test out the naval support for the assault troops.

Finally on 22 May there began a five-day period of landings under as near combat conditions as possible. Both the 3rd Marine Division and the 1st Provisional Brigade practiced landings, attempting to simulate the conditions each would encounter on Guam. Task Group 53.1 moved the division to prearranged locations in the Cape Esperance area and offloaded the assault troops and their supporting equipment. Once ashore the units began operating according to the preset plans. After two days of practice the troops were reembarked to Tetre where shore party units practiced unloading reserve equipment. While this was going on, the brigade was duplicating the division's landing training at Cape Esperance. Its shore party units later practiced unloading supplies and setting up dumps at Tassafaronga. The one major difficulty in these final rehearsals was that no reef was present and the units had to play at unloading and transfers under combat conditions. There could be no practice in surmounting the difficulties that would confront them during the actual landings. In this final phase of training, naval, air, and surface units participated with the exception of a cruiser division then at Majuro and Carrier Division 24 still undergoing repairs and fitting at Espiritu Santo.[5]

After concluding the training exercises, the support groups were dispersed throughout the Solomons to prepare for the final move to the Marianas. On 1 June the LSTs carrying the tractor battalions were all loaded and left Guadalcanal for Kwajalein. The rest of the convoy and support ships which could travel faster did not leave until three days later. By 8 June all transports had rendezvoused at Kwajalein. There the task force took on what the commanders believed to be final supplies. After last-minute meetings at all levels, Task Force 53 with the LSTs leading, cleared Kwajalein anchorage by 11 June. It proceeded to a predetermined assembly area east of Saipan. At this time Admiral Spruance reconfirmed the invasion date for 18 June.[6] Given the presuppositions concerning Guam, the Marines were as well prepared for the assault as was possible. The transit from Guadalcanal to the assembly point had been tedious, particularly for the Marines on the transports who had limited space in which to move around. But they could easily shake these feelings once they were in position to go over the side. They could not have imagined that the conditions under which they had lived for over two weeks would be continued for yet another month. The high-level planners of the Marianas operations had made some very basic miscalculations and these would result in the postponement of the assault on Guam.

Two factors that should have been seriously considered before planning the joint operations against Saipan and Guam made necessary a major change in the date of W day. The first factor was the fierce resistance met by the 2nd and 4th Marine divisions on Saipan; the second was the long-delayed commitment of the Japanese combined fleet to the battle for the Marianas. Gen. H. M. Smith later noted that he considered the conquest of Saipan the key land engagement of the Pacific war.[7] If he believed this at the time, it is difficult to understand why it was not conceived that the Japanese also would conclude that it was important enough to hold at all costs. Located only 1,200 miles from the Japanese homeland, its continued possession was obviously vital to an ultimate Japanese victory. Although the capture of Kwajalein and Eniwetok had been relatively easy, there was still enough evidence of the tenacious nature of Japanese defenses to suspect that they would not concede Saipan without making the attackers pay for every inch of ground. A close inspection of the terrain of Saipan should have indicated how those interior highlands east of Mt. Tapochau could have been defended even against an enemy which controlled the air and sea. Despite such evidence, the naval and Marine planners had designated only two divisions for the capture of Saipan. The reserve force, the Army's 27th Division, had also been directed to make plans for an almost simultaneous invasion of neighboring Tinian or perhaps even support the Southern Attack Force at Guam.

None of these overly optimistic plans proved feasible. The two Marine divisions, from the minute they hit the beach on 15 June, began to take very heavy casualties and it was obvious that the 27th Division would have to be committed very soon. The decision by Japanese Imperial Headquarters to order Admiral

Ozawa to utilize his still powerful fleet units to bring the American Fifth Fleet into a showdown battle only speeded up the landing of the 27th Division. American submarines reported sightings of this large fleet heading out from its long-time Philippine base at Tawi Tawi. It was clear to Admiral Spruance that a major fleet confrontation was in the offing. He conferred with Admiral Turner on 17 June and the two arrived at important alterations in the carefully drawn plans. Spruance would take Task Force 58 out to confront the Japanese. Admirals Turner and Hill, until the issue had been resolved, would abandon covering the Saipan coastline and retire to safer positions far from the island. That meant that the 27th Division floating in reserve would have to be committed. Within hours of Spruance's final decision, the 165th RCT of the 27th was, despite all its careful planning, unceremoniously dumped on shore and immediately swung into line. The other two regiments followed the next morning. This is not to suggest panic among the senior commanders, but because the Army division was so hastily sent in much of its vital equipment was kept on board ship for over a week. These actions partially explain the subsequent bad feelings that arose between Gen. Holland M. Smith and the Army over the performance of the 27th Division.[8]

The commitment of the 27th Division and the departure of the Navy left the Marines on Saipan in a potentially very dangerous situation. Against stiffening Japanese resistance, they had no planned reserve to commit. This is the major reason why Admiral Spruance at 1100 hours on 16 June sent a dispatch to Admiral Conolly postponing the Guam invasion. Conolly's task force, already steaming toward its final approach for the invasion, halted and returned to its previous station. The Marines of III Amphibious Corps thus became the floating reserve to be used on Saipan if necessary. Until the danger from the Japanese fleet was ended Conolly's task force was held in limbo.[9]

The subsequent Battle of the Philippine Sea proved a great victory for the Fifth Fleet. The "Marianas Turkey Shoot" was the last time that normal air operations from the Japanese navy threatened American operations. Back on station after the engagement, Admiral Spruance conferred with Turner and decided on

25 June that III Amphibious Corps would probably no longer be needed to support the Saipan offensive. The bulk of Conolly's attack group which had been maneuvering for over a week in a long ellipse from 150 to 300 miles east of Saipan was released and ordered back to Eniwetok to await further orders. Transports carrying the 1st Marine Provisional Brigade were to remain in the Saipan area just in case it was needed on Saipan. Then on 30 June, it too was ordered to Eniwetok.[10]

The commanding general of the Marianas operation, Gen. H. M. Smith, in his remembrances of the Pacific War devotes only nine pages to the entire Guam campaign and says nothing about the long interlude between the original W day and the actual date of the invasion.[11] General Silverthorn, Chief of Staff of III Amphibious Corps, later noted that the Marines had been on board the APAs or LSTs for fifty-two days, but claimed that they suffered no debilitating effects from such long captivity.[12] Such a claim defies credibility. Much more to the point is the comment of one official Marine historian who wrote about the APAs:

> The tropical sun beating down on the steel decks turned the troop compartments into infernos. Sleeping proved difficult if not impossible, and a much sought after privilege was bedding "topside" under the night sky. Heat rash prevailed but the opportunity to eat good food, including fresh meat offset the discomfort caused by the skin irritation.[13]

Although it is doubtful that even the best steak could make one forget heat rash, this is still a valid glimpse of the discomfort suffered by the Marines. An Army writer who was with the 77th during its shorter two-week transit commented about:

> . . . the monotony of the trip, the sweat, the endless chow lines where only debarkation drills, weapons inspections interfered with the card games, reading, letter writing and over the rail conversations.[14]

Men on the LSTs had it better than their counterparts on the APAs. However crowded, the Marines could move about more freely. Some captured space on the vehicles that were tied down while many pitched tents on the decks. Others simply found a place which had not already been claimed and made themselves as comfortable as possible given the high temperature, the humidity, and the seeming endless pitching of the LST. One solution devised by senior officers was to have briefings on the upcoming operation. By the time W day arrived, the officers and men were most thoroughly briefed on every phase of the operation and were also thoroughly sick of the briefings. In an attempt to keep the combat troops from going stale, rigorous calisthenics were required each day and a series of amphibious and land operations were planned. The major drawback to such plans was the size of the land area at Eniwetok. Only small unit land maneuvers could be scheduled. One Marine officer recalled the minimal time his unit had on shore:

> We pulled into that area, I don't recall how many days we were there, but they did allow one day for each vessel to disembark its human cargo and we were allowed to go to shore and our group got to participate in about a three hour softball game. Some of the others may have done other things, may have just jogged or hiked around the island.[15]

Although such actions might have in part alleviated the boredom, they also wreaked havoc with personal equipment, particularly shoes. Tramping around on the coral cut the soles of shoes and boots to pieces very quickly.[16]

Admiral Spruance's Fifth Fleet had ended the threat from the Japanese navy by 22 June. However, he showed no desire to begin the invasion of Guam immediately. Obviously the earlier unwarranted optimism had disappeared in the face of the fierce Japanese resistance on Saipan. Then, too, captured documents had shown that the original estimate of Japanese strength on Guam had been grievously wrong. There were twice as many Japanese soldiers there as had originally been estimated and the terrain of Guam offered even more opportunities for defense than did that of Saipan. Admiral Spruance later confirmed this in his Final Report on the operation when he wrote:

The character of enemy resistance being encountered in Saipan and the increase over the original estimates of enemy strength in Guam made the presence of the entire 77th Infantry Division necessary.[17]

This decision had been made after a series of conferences at the highest level which began on 29 June. Admiral Conolly, General Geiger, and General del Valle accompanied by a portion of their staffs flew to Saipan. There the key decisions were made on the use of the Army's 77th Division and the new date for the Guam assault.

The 77th Division had only arrived in the Hawaiian Islands in March 1944.[18] Although it had been activated two years before and had undergone extensive training in desert and amphibious warfare no part of the New York National Guard unit had seen combat. Located on Oahu, the division and part of XXIV Corps remained under the overall command of General Richardson until just before it was to embark when it was released to V Amphibious Corps for administrative details. The decision to use the 77th was not made until the end of June although the division had been undergoing rigorous training for the previous three months, including amphibious exercises, infantry-tank tactics, artillery support training, and jungle warfare practice. However, ship-to-shore exercises for most of the division's personnel were not conducted, due largely to the pressure of time. Gen. James Landrum, then a Lt. Col commanding a battalion in the 305th RCT, recalled the hurried nature of the regiment's preparation for Guam:

Needless to say the fact that we were going to participate in the retaking of Guam was a complete surprise to those of us at the battalion level. We had been given to understand and had done some preliminary work on it, that we were going into Palau. The news that we were going to be detached from the 77th Division and attached to the 1st Marine Provisional Brigade was a complete surprise. I didn't know all these details originally. We were told that we were going to load out and some of us were told why just a few days, I believe only one, before we started loading. . . . We had to be loaded and out within five days of when we really got started.[19]

General Bruce, the energetic commander of the 77th, notified General Geiger that all elements of the 77th could be present offshore of Guam by 18 July, four days earlier than had been expected. On that assurance Admiral Spruance set W day for 21 July.

The 77th Division had only two weeks to prepare for the invasion. General Bruce's staff prepared three alternative plans for submission to III Amphibious Corps. Long lists of supplies and equipment were made and much of the requisite materials were placed on pallets for transshipment onto the beach. This was a scheme for landing supplies pioneered by the Army which the Marine Corps had yet to adopt. Understandably things did not all flow smoothly. Many of the ships did not arrive in Hawaii until just before loading was scheduled. In most cases troops and supplies were being loaded at the same time. Ultimately the approximately 21,000 tons of supplies were loaded on the seven attack transports, four transports, three AKAs, two AKs, and three LSTs. In addition the division carried 53 DUKWs on the LSTs. No LVTs were included since the 77th was not to be one of the assault units.

General Landrum recalled some of the results of the way the 77th Division was notified of its mission:

> As a result of the hurried nature of this we had to leave a lot of our equipment behind and we had absolutely nothing for comfort when the fighting was over and so were left there with very little tentage; we didn't even have enough food after combat was over which was one of the main problems we had from an administrative and a convenience point of view.[20]

The 305th RCT was loaded first and departed Oahu on 1 July. The division's other two regiments did not leave Hawaii until a week later since they had to wait for the return of transports which had been involved in the Saipan operation.[21]

One of the alternative plans submitted by General Bruce to III Amphibious Corps headquarters on 14 July envisioned a diversionary landing by two of his regiments after the 305th had gone ashore to support directly the 1st Provisional Brigade. He wanted to use the 306th and 307th RCTs to land on the north-western coast between Uruno and Ritidian points from where he could then move southwest catching the Japanese along the coast near Tumon Bay between the anvil of the 3rd Marine Division and the hammer of the advancing Army units. General Geiger, after considering the proposal, believed it to be too risky to commit the entire reserve to open another beachhead, and besides it was too late to make such a radical change in the overall plan. Instead, he approved the plan to hold those two regiments in reserve and to land them directly into the area cleared by General Shepherd's unit as soon as practicable. General Bruce's proposal caused some concern at General Smith's headquarters since Howlin' Mad apparently believed that Bruce was appealing above Geiger's head for the adoption of his plan. This was not the case and fortunately Smith did not cause problems with regard to it.[22]

The long delay between the originally scheduled landing and W day, however great an irritation for the combat troops penned up in their transports, was in retrospect very fortunate. It enabled the Navy to provide the longest prolonged air and naval shelling of any of the landings in the Central Pacific theater and thereby undoubtedly saved thousands of American casualties. The first concerted bombardment of Guam began on 16 June, the precursor of only two days of planned shelling of the beach areas. A portion of Task Force 53—two battleships, the *Pennsylvania* and *Idaho,* the cruiser *Honolulu,* and several destroyers—pounded the landing sites and adjacent areas for almost two hours. This was accompanied by air strikes at targets along the west coast. The Japanese believed correctly that this was the beginning of the bombardment preliminary to the invasion. It was fortunate that circumstances postponed W day since this shelling and air attack did little damage and served to confirm the Japanese hypothesis about landing sites. After the decision to call off the landings planned for 18 June, there were only two minor strikes against the island during the rest of the month. One, a small detachment of cruisers and destroyers from Admiral Mitscher's fast carrier fleet, Task Force 58, hit Apra Harbor on 27 June sinking three small ships and causing minor damage to storage facilities on shore. On 30 June a destroyer division shelled the Japanese airfields on Orote Peninsula.[23]

The serious bombardment of Guam did not begin until 8 July when Task Group 53.18 commanded by RAdm. C. Turner Joy arrived off the west coast to begin thirteen days of continual bombardment. Admiral Joy had at his disposal four heavy cruisers, twelve destroyers, and two escort carriers. In addition, two task groups from Task Force 58 worked in conjunction with the surface ships. The plan was to divide the island in half; during one day one part was the responsibility of the naval gunners while the other half was being worked over by the air groups. The next day the roles were reversed. The primary targets were the coastal defense guns, anti-aircraft positions, the airfields, and the probable defensive fortifications on the high ground inland and on the Orote Peninsula. Troop concentrations, communications lines, warehouses, and command posts were chief among secondary targets. On 12 July, Combat Division 3 with the battleships *New Mexico, Idaho,* and *Pennsylvania,* arrived on station, and two days later Combat Division 4 arrived with Admiral Conolly aboard his command ship the *Appalachian* accompanied by the battleship *Colorado.* As the need for direct naval support lessened for the Marines on Saipan Admiral Spruance could direct more of his fleet to bombard Guam. By W day, Carrier Division 22 was added along with two cruiser divisions and Combat Division 2 with the battleships *Tennessee* and *California.* In all, the Navy expended 836 rounds of sixteen-inch, 5,422 rounds of fourteen-inch, 3,862 rounds of eight-inch, 2,430 rounds of six-inch, and 16,214 rounds of five-inch shells. By W day, planes from the various task forces had flown 3,332 sorties and dropped 1,245 tons of bombs on various targets, generally on the western side of Guam. On W day, naval pilots flew an additional 967 sorties and dropped 405 tons of bombs.[24]

To direct the delivery of such a weight of metal against Guam, Admiral Conolly departed from the usual fire control procedures.

Instead he created a six-man target board with representatives from intelligence, air, and gunnery sections. It became the responsibility of this board under the direct supervision of Conolly to assign primary and secondary targets to the various ships and air sections. Aerial photos were taken each morning to enable the board to determine the effectiveness of the previous day's bombardment and to plan for that day's air strikes and naval gunfire. The process was also undoubtedly aided by the presence of General Geiger on board the *Appalachian*.

The aerial strikes were not without cost. Some of the main targets were on the heavily fortified Orote Peninsula and adjacent areas. The Japanese air force which had been reasonably strong in early May had been systematically destroyed by the various air strikes, particularly those of Task Force 58 on 11–12 June which destroyed approximately 150 of their planes in the air and on the ground at Rota and Guam. Later, on 15 June, Admiral Mitscher's planes once more worked over Guam's facilities and, on 19 June, just before the "Turkey Shoot," another fifty Japanese planes were shot out of the sky in the vicinity of Guam.[25] Thereafter, the Japanese defenders of Guam were for all practical purposes without planes. However, the Japanese anti-aircraft gunners gave some protection to their installations. They brought down sixteen planes before W day. Some of these pilots were able to ditch at sea and were rescued, but woe betide any who were forced to crash land on Guam. One such unfortunate pilot in mid-June landed near Finaguayac where approximately three hundred Chamorros were clearing land for an agricultural project. The pilot was pulled from the cockpit by a number of the workers. The name tag on the flight jacket of the wounded American said "Henderson." One of the rescuers, Jose L. G. Cruz, recalled that before the pilot could be revived a patrol of Japanese soldiers arrived and carried him away to the local field office where he was immediately shot.[26]

To the observers on board the *Appalachian* on the eve of W day, it appeared that the concerted heavy bombardment coordinated with air strikes had knocked out all the fixed guns and coastal emplacements and the presumption was that the vital communications system on the island had been crippled. One could see that most of the major buildings in Agana including the government house complex had been destroyed as had all those warehouses and some of the docking facilities on the Orote Peninsula. The report on the effectiveness of the pre-invasion bombardment summed up the considered opinion of the members of Admiral Conolly's staff who noted, "Not one fixed gun was left in commission on the west coast that was of greater size than a machine gun."[27] The Marine commanders who had watched the devastating performance of naval and air strikes can be excused for believing that W day would see a comparatively easy establishment and widening of the beachhead.

Once again the over-optimism of the Marine and Navy commanders proved to be incorrect. They would meet considerable opposition on all beaches when they landed. Despite this fact, the physical and psychological devastation had indeed been immense and undoubtedly upset the well-laid plans of General Takashina. The best analysis of the actual effect of the prolonged bombardment came from LtCol. Hideyuki Takeda, a former staff officer on Guam who in 1952 replied to questions posed by BGen. J. C. McQueen, then Director of Marine Corps history. A synopsis of his report reveals:

1. All naval gun emplacements along the western shoreline completely demolished. One half of guns placed in caves remained operational until landings when counterbattery fire from naval vessels destroyed most of these.

2. Anti-aircraft artillery received only slight damage.

3. Communication lines were hardly damaged at all. Most harbor installations remained intact as did water and power supplies.

4. Temporary defensive positions along the beaches were destroyed as were most of the half-permanent positions. However, installations with concrete over a meter thick remained sound even though taking a direct hit. There was little effect on defensive positions in the valleys or in the jungle areas.[28]

Aside from the obvious damage done to the defensive positions within four miles of the western coastline, the Japanese combat units suffered very heavy casualties in the days before W day. This fact is confirmed by the reports of a number of Japanese prisoners who were interrogated within a few days after the landings. One man, Lance Cpl. Shohei Yokota, who with about half his regiment had survived the sinking of the *Sakito Maru*, estimated that of the estimated 500 men of his battalion located near Tepungur, only half survived the naval bombardment. The rest deserted their positions on 23 July and fled toward Mt. Chachao. Another Lance Corporal, Keisuke Yuhana, estimated that all but a few of his regiment's 2,500 men who were in position from Agat to Piti were destroyed by gunfire. He also reported that a number of senior officers of the regiment committed suicide before the landings. All the other interrogation reports extant reflect similar information.[29] There is no doubt that the continuous rain of bombs and shells not only killed a significant number of Japanese but also affected the will to fight of many of the defenders. But once again it would be wrong to assume that just because any sensible Japanese could see that the situation was hopeless this meant they were prepared to give up. Rather, the willingness of most to do their duty and die for their emperor remained the dominant feeling. One enlisted man expressed these feelings most eloquently when he confided to his diary:

I will not lose my courage, but now is the time to prepare to die! If one desires to live, hope for death. Be prepared to die! With this conviction one can never lose. . . . Look upon us! We have shortened our expectancy of 70 years of life to 25 in order to fight. What an honor it is to be born in this day and age.[30]

Despite such fatalism or perhaps bravado, the long interval of the preparatory bombing and shelling must have seemed an eternity to the Japanese defenders. The waiting was soon to come to an end to be replaced by direct assaults by the Marines. On 20 July, Admiral Conolly received the optimistic report that the weather would continue to be good. He confirmed that W day would be 21 July and H hour would be 0830. All his staff believed that everything that could have been done to make the landing a success had been done. It was now up to the Marines to accomplish what they had set out to achieve over fifty days before.

CHAPTER V
W Day

The way into the invasion beaches had been cleared by Navy Underwater Demolition Teams (UDTs) working within a few hundred yards of the Japanese defenses. Teams 3 and 4 had joined the invasion force at Guadalcanal and had shared the boredom and discomfort of waiting with the rest of the Marine and Naval force. UDT6 had been involved in the Saipan invasion and joined Task Force 53 at Eniwetok on 9 July. Under protective cover of the fleet, two teams made physical reconnaissance of the reefs and beach landing sites beginning on 14 July. Despite the danger of such operations only one member of the teams was killed during this phase. On 17 July the task of clearing barriers and blasting paths across the reefs began. Destroyers came in closer to shore to provide covering fire for the UDTs, aircraft strafed the beach lines, and smoke screens were laid down. The teams encountered very little barbed wire and only a few underwater mines, most of which were off Asan. Many of the barriers constructed off Agat were palm log cribs filled with coral and joined together by wire cable, while at Asan they were cubes of heavy wire filled with cement and coral.

For three days the teams placed demolition charges and blasted away almost a thousand such obstacles. The work of these unsung heroes was absolutely vital for the success of the invasion. Admiral Conolly in his Operations Report made this very clear when he wrote, "Landings could not have been made on either Agat or

Asan beaches nor any other suitable beaches without these elaborate but successfully prosecuted clearance operations."[1] Perhaps more important than the admiral's accolade was the fact that the frogmen gained an advantage in one-upmanship over the Marines. They left behind a large sign nailed to a tree. It read, "Welcome Marines! USO that way."[2]

On 15 July the long, vegetating wait ended for the Marines on board the LSTs. Escorted by destroyers and minesweepers, they left the anchorage at Eniwetok bound for Guam. Two days later, accompanied by a similar screen of naval combat vessels including escort carriers, the transports weighed anchor. The transports carrying the advance unit, the 305th RCT of the 77th Division, arrived at Eniwetok on the same day, and took on full and last-minute supplies before leaving in order to time their arrival off Guam on the early morning of W day. By the evening of W − 1, all other ships were in position to support the invasion. These included the fifteen carriers of Task Force 58 and the five attack carriers of TF53. Four battleships, three cruisers, and four destroyers would give close-in fire to the 3rd Marine Division's landing at Asan while two battleships, three cruisers, and three destroyers would support the 1st Marine Provisional Brigade at Agat.[3]

The conditions on the morning of 21 July were nearly perfect for a landing. It was clear with only a slight overcast; a light wind hardly disturbed the surface of the calm sea. Before the first wave of Marines went over the side, they listened to General Geiger's message which was relayed to all the transports. He said:

> The eyes of a nation watch you as you go into battle to liberate this former American bastion from the enemy. Make no mistake, it will be a tough, bitter fight against a wily, stubborn foe who will doggedly defend Guam against this invasion. May the glorious traditions of the Marine *esprit de corps* spur you to victory. You have been honored.[4]

After Geiger's speech, the Marine hymn was played as the first assault units began loading.

At 0530, the immediate pre-invasion bombardment began with

the support ships firing at prearranged targets along the western beaches and into the hills beyond. All the assault units were in position at 0600 and the LSTs disgorged the LVTs and DUKWs which moved closer into shore and began to circle, waiting for the signal to move to the reef. In the meantime the tempo of support fire increased. Planes from the carriers strafed and bombed the targeted coastline. At 0803 the Navy shifted to targets in the immediate beach areas. By this time the LVTs, packed with Marines of the first waves, had already headed for shore. Ten minutes before the scheduled landing the naval fire intensified. Some of the five-inch guns of the destroyers and cruisers were firing at ten rounds per minute. When the assault waves were a thousand yards from shore, the rocket-carrying LCIs opened up and the rockets struck the beach and hills with terrific impact. When the leading waves were about three hundred yards out, the naval fire was lifted to inland targets and those on the flanks.[5] The LVTs crawled across the reef with, at most places, only inches of water over the reeftop. A few were grounded and the Marines on board had to wade ashore.

For the first few days the fighting on Guam was not a single battle but resolved itself into two separate engagements. Not until the Marines on the two beachheads joined forces could it logically be considered a single battle. So the landings and subsequent fighting at the Asan and Agat beaches should be viewed separately; however, there were a few items of concern to both. One is the quickness with which heavy materials were brought in. By midmorning of the 21st, tanks were ashore on both beach areas and although the rice paddies and heavy undergrowth limited their usefulness for the first few days, their presence was important in a number of early engagements while the Marines tried to expand their beachheads. Bulldozers were also brought in early and were used to help build emplacements and cut roads from the beaches up to the hills, expediting the movement of ammunition and water to the riflemen. Another important factor in the success of the Marine units was the early presence of their own artillery. The pack 75mms had been brought in by LVTs while the 105mm howitzers had been offloaded from DUKWs which were equipped with special A frames. By 1215, the 1st battery of the 3rd Battalion, 12th Marines, had landed and was emplaced and firing support for the 3rd Marine Division. By 1700 all the integral artillery was ashore, every battery in place and firing. By nightfall even some of General del Valle's heavy Corps artillery howitzers were in place.[6]

General del Valle, one of the superb Marine commanders in the Pacific theater, appeared to have enjoyed himself during the Guam operation, an opinion not shared by most of the attacking force. Much later he recalled some of his experience on the southern beachhead:

> I tell you, I just relaxed on Guam. I just had a wonderful time. The first couple of nights were kind of sticky because we had a very shallow beachhead. The bastards would take pot shots at us from the old Marine barracks. I had stopped beside a very deep shell hole, and there were a couple of Japs down there that were dead as hell, and they were smelling to beat hell, and the first two nights were very uncomfortable. But after that, when we started moving and we got up to the former officers' club, and I found under the rubble the tile-paved front porch of the thing overlooking the sea, and I captured a Japanese glass, and they had a compass rose that the Japs had built there and I put this thing on, and I could see my 155s fire. . . .[7]

The main Marine attack was directed at 2,000 yards of landing beach between Asan Point and Adelup Point. Here the first assault wave arrived at the beach at 0829. The plan called for the 3rd Marines to land on Red Beach 1, the 21st to assault Green Beach in the center, while the 9th Marines struck inland from Blue Beach. South of the Orote Peninsula the 4th and 22nd Marines were to land on the beaches designated Yellow 1 and 2 and White 1 and 2. The Marine and Navy commanders had believed that there would be little resistance to the initial landings and had designated the D–1 lines along the crest of the hills inland from the beaches. However, the Japanese surprised them. Along the Asan front the Japanese retired behind the ridgelines and took shelter in caves and in prepared positions during the bombardment. When that was lifted they resumed their original positions and began to cover the beaches with mortar and machine-gun fire. This was supported by artillery fire from the interior. Especially vexing was the enfilade fire laid down from Adelup Point.

Japanese resistance to the landings was even more severe along Yellow and White beaches south of the Orote Peninsula. From the high ground leading up to Maanot Ridge and Mt. Alifan they poured a murderous fire on the Marines of the 1st Provisional Brigade. The memoir of Thomas R. O'Neil, a platoon leader in the 22nd Marines, illustrates as well as any can what was happening on all the western beaches during the few minutes after 0830 on 21 July. He later wrote:

We moved up to the LOD where we transferred to Amtrack's to take us over the reefs. The amphibious tractors could only carry 25 men, so Lt. Humphrey [the platoon leader], platoon headquarters and the 1st squad got into one, the second and third squad and I in the other. Overhead a squadron of Navy divebombers were making a run on the Orote Peninsula. Suddenly the Japs let loose an A.A. barrage. The lead plane took a direct hit blowing it to bits. It was the first show of fight the Japanese had shown until then. We reached LOD which was about 15 thousand yards from the beach. Here began our final dash for the beach. On both flanks Amtracks were strung out in a long line and were coming under heavy flanking fire from Bangi Point from the south and Gaan Point. The Jap anti-boat gunfire was quite heavy. I chanced to look and counted 6 Amtracks burning in the water. We had just reached the reefs when we took a hit. There was a sudden explosion. I lost all count of time although I couldn't have been out more than a second. The heat and acid smell of powder was still in the air. We had taken a hit on the port bow, the port track had been blown off and she had taken about a 20 percent list and the driver's compartment was on fire. We inflated our life belts and ordered everybody over the side. We were sitting ducks and there was every chance that the Jap gunners would lay another round in on us . . . About 3 feet of water covered the reefs. We had to wade 500 yards to the beach. Like the beaches in other operations we found all bedlam and confusion. The beaches were under fire. All hands were digging in or seeking cover of some sort. We had come ashore on the left flank of the 1st Battalion, 4th Marines. We found the rest of the platoon. They had landed without any mishap. There were others who weren't as fortunate. One Amtrack of the Battalion Headquarters Company had taken a direct hit, killing all hands including the Battalion Executive.[8]

Despite the beach casualties and the loss of thirty-six DUKWs during the immediate assault phase, the landings at Asan were as successful as General Geiger could have expected. The 9th Marines landed in a column of battalions on schedule at Blue Beach. Marines of the 3rd Battalion hit the beach first, followed by the 2nd, with the 1st as the regimental reserve. Men of the first waves following the maxim of getting off the beach, charged ahead to try to secure the high ground immediately to the front and to the right at Asan Point. K Company met little resistance and moved straight ahead across the dry rice paddies and reached the first ridgeline without difficulty. However, the right-hand companies of 3/9 were held up by fire from Asan Point as well as from the ridges in front. Little progress was made until some of the tanks that had landed at H + 40 minutes moved up to support the attackers. By 1345 the reserve battalion had landed and the regimental commander, Col. E. A. Craig, decided to commit all his units to the attack. The 1st and 2nd battalions were passed through the lines of the 3rd at 1700. The Marines had secured Asan Point except for scattered resistance from Japanese hidden in caves on the western edge. They advanced slowly past the D–1 line but began to encounter heavier fire from the ridge dead ahead. They decided to dig in for the night and tie into the 21st Marines on the left flank approximately one-quarter mile short of the D–2 line.

The casualties for the regiment during the day's action were 231 killed or wounded, a relatively light figure considering what the Japanese could have done if many of their heavy guns had not been silenced by the long naval and aerial bombardment.

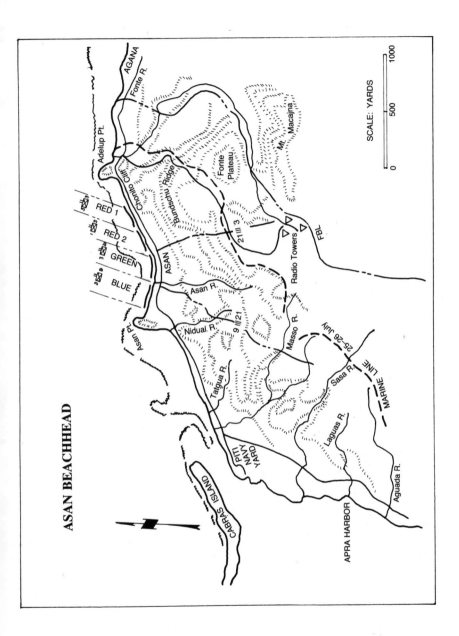

ASAN BEACHHEAD

The potential for this was recognized in the regiment's Unit Report which gave the combat efficiency at 1800 as 75 percent, with heavy officer casualties. It noted that the regiment needed replacements and that the enemy had not yet shown his full strength but was obviously well supplied with mortars and artillery and further that the "enemy is well supplied with new material. He still holds observation of most of our area."[9]

Meanwhile the 21st Marines had landed on Green Beach in a column of battalions on the left flank of the 9th. At first they encountered even less opposition than had the Marines of the 9th. The assault battalion, the 3rd, very quickly seized the rise immediately to the rear of the beach. Then the regiment was forced to halt because of the high, nearly vertical cliffs immediately to their front. The regiment's commander, Col. Arthur Butler, decided that a frontal attack would be suicidal. As soon as his reserve battalion was ashore, he ordered the 2nd Battalion forward to utilize a steep defile on the left of the cliff while men of the 3rd to the right advanced up the Asan River valley. Both units met heavy mortar and machine-gun fire as they moved up the steep defiles. By mid-day the temperature had risen into the nineties and this, combined with the physical exertion and nervous energy expended, began to take its toll of the Marines who had been confined so long on shipboard. Large numbers simply dropped from exhaustion. By mid-afternoon, however, the assault companies of the 2nd Battalion had reached the top of the cliff where their forward momentum was halted by concentrated machine-gun fire from another ridgeline directly ahead. A deep gully heavily overgrown with bushes prevented contact with the 3rd Marines on the left. The gap was covered by mortars and machine guns of the flank companies of the two regiments. Meanwhile, the 3rd Battalion encountered a Japanese strongpoint which blocked their way. In order to advance, they called in direct fire from the Navy, coordinated their attacks with fire from 1/9 on their right, and eventually overran the position. By late afternoon, despite the heat, lack of water, and Japanese harassing fire, the men of the 3rd Battalion had reached the top where they spread out, made contact with the 2nd Battalion on their left and 1/9 on their right, and dug in for the night.[10]

Although the fighting was severe and the advance slow in the center and right of the 3rd Division line, the worst situation developed on the left where the 3rd Marines landed on Red Beaches 1 and 2. Immediately to their front was a high ridgeline, noted on maps as Chonito Cliff, and to the left was Adelup Point. The coastal road intersected with that from the Fonte Plateau a few yards behind the point. Thus General Shigematsu, the Japanese commander of the Asan front, could move troops and equipment from other areas more quickly to the defenders of Chonito Cliff and Adelup Point. Although the big guns that had been emplaced on the point had been knocked out, much of the permanent defenses were still intact. One of these was a tunnel system 400 yards long which connected the point with Chonito Cliff. The Japanese from the high ground covered the beach road and could pour small arms and mortar fire directly and in enfilade into the Marines landing on the Red beaches. Despite heavy casualties from the long, thorough bombardment, many of the defenders were still alive and eager to destroy the Marines. These Japanese troops had retired to prepared positions on the backslope of the ridges and hills during the shelling and had returned to their original positions when the Marines began to land.

The 3rd Marines landed with two battalions abreast, the 1st on the right, the 3rd on the left; and the 2nd came in later in the morning and became the regimental reserve. The assault waves took heavy losses. On Red Beach 1, the Marines quickly regrouped and moved ahead, two companies abreast, in hopes of taking Chonito Cliff before the Japanese could recover from the shelling. They were not quick enough and were pinned down short of their goal by the Japanese on the cliffline and in caves. Sgt. Cyril O'Brien recalled the fight for the cliff and the bravery and tragedy of the men who assaulted it. He wrote:

Nearly half my old company lies dead on the barren slopes of Chonito Cliff. Four times they tried to reach the top. Four times they were thrown back. They had to break out of a twenty-yard beachhead to make way for later landing waves. They attacked up a 60–degree slope, protected only by sword grass, and were met by a storm of grenades and heavy rifle, machine-gun and mortar fire.

The physical act of forward motion required the use of both hands. As a consequence they were unable to return the enemy fire effectively. Most of the casualties were at the bottom of the slope. They had been hit as they left cover.[11]

Tanks from the 3rd Tank Battalion were eventually brought up to support the riflemen and a slow steady advance was made under their protective close-in fire. Flamethrowers were then used to clear the enemy from the caves. By noon, Chonito Cliff had been taken and the tanks turned their fire on the Japanese on Adelup Point who were delivering flanking fire on the Marines all down the beachline.

The worst situation in the 3rd Marines' area developed in front of the 1st Battalion which, after landing, advanced across the rice paddies toward a ridge which extended down toward the beach. This rise was later called Bundschu Ridge after Capt. Geary Bundschu, commanding officer of Company A. Machine-gun fire from the ridge struck Company A even before the men left the beach. Meanwhile the men of Company B cleared the woods of the enemy on the right of the battalion. They advanced quickly until they ran into very heavy undergrowth. Company A had made a direct frontal assault on the ridge with all three of its platoons, but rifle and machine-gun fire from two well-emplaced positions stopped the advance 100 yards short of the crest at about 1100. Captain Bundschu tried to flank the one machine-gun position but was unsuccessful. At 1400 he requested permission to disengage but was refused by the battalion commander, Maj. Henry Aplington. However, his right platoon, commanded by Lt. James Gallo had already fallen back to a safer location. A second direct attack was ordered by Colonel W. C. Hall, the regimental commander, after a heavy mortar barrage was laid down on the Japanese position. This barrage did little damage since the Japanese retired once again behind the crest only to come back to the original position once the barrage was lifted. Bundschu was killed during the second assault; his company was pinned down by machine-gun fire from the emplacement which had held them up all day. Ultimately under cover of fire from all available weapons, the Marines silenced the gun with grenades and reached the crest of the ridge. There were too few Marines left to defend the position during the night and what was left of the two platoons retired to their original jump-off lines. Here they were joined by the remnants of the 1st platoon under Lieutenant Gallo who also had found it expedient to retire from the woods on A Company's right. Gallo was the only officer of the company to survive W day's fighting for control of Bundschu Ridge.[12]

Although not as desperate as the fighting for Bundschu Ridge, the situation confronting the rest of the regiment in the afternoon was very difficult. Colonel Hall committed the 2nd Battalion, his reserve, to the central zone of action and at 1500 a general advance was coordinated with the attack of the 1st Battalion against Bundschu Ridge. The Japanese, however, were ready for this, having brought down reinforcements from the Tumon area and also from the Pago region and from Agana.[13] The 2nd Battalion was stopped after taking a low ridge in its sector where it sustained very heavy casualties. They dug in for the night short of the D–1 line. However, on the extreme left the 3rd Battalion supported by destroyers offshore, tanks, and LCI gunships managed to drive the Japanese off Adelup Point, thus cancelling the enfilade fire which had disturbed the Marines all during the day.

One factor seldom mentioned with regard to action in any Pacific island was the toll taken by heat and humidity. This was doubly so for men who had been cooped up on transports for almost two months and were therefore not at the peak of physical efficiency. *Time* correspondent Robert Martin noted one facet of the supply problem when he wrote:

Throughout Saturday while Jap mortars plastered the beach-head Marines struggled up hills so steep that supplies were brought to the front on ropes dangling over cliff faces. Water was scarce and the slack-jawed Marines cursed bitterly at their empty canteens and at sweating comrades struggling to carry precious five gallon cans up the ridge.[14]

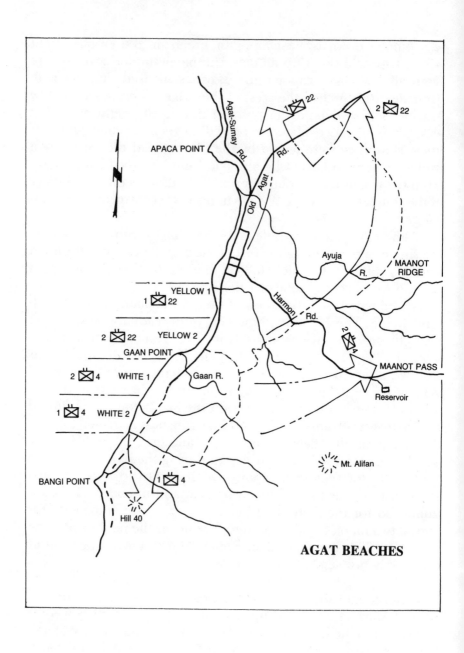

AGAT BEACHES

Adequate supplies of potable water continued to be a problem for both Marine and Army units until days after the breakout from the beachhead.

While the 3rd Marine Division was being hard pressed to establish a stable defensible beachline at Asan, the 1st Marine Provisional Brigade encountered even more intense enemy resistance in the south along the Agat beaches. This was partially because the reef guarding the beaches was much wider there and partially because the Japanese defenses anchored on Bangi Point and the high ground west of Mt. Alifan, despite the bombardment, remained relatively intact. Here, too, the Japanese had retired behind the hill during the most intense bombardment, relatively shielded from the low trajectory fire of the American naval guns. As General Shepherd later noted:

> They were strongly organized in from the beach in the vicinity of Agat town and across the neck of the Orote Peninsula in the Marine Barracks and rifle range area south of Sumi. A support position consisting of well defended caves connected by tunnels were found on the western slopes of Alifan Massif between Mt. Alifan and Mt. Tanae.[15]

The plan of Colonel Suenaga, commander of the Japanese 38th Infantry Regiment, was deceptively simple. LtCol. Hideyuki Takeda expressed it succinctly,

> The objective of the defense plan for the regiment's front was to attack and crush any enemy assault landing at the water's edge. If the enemy landed on the shoreline, counterattacks would be carried out in the direction of the ocean to crush and annihilate him while he had not yet secured a foothold.[16]

As the Marines approached the reefline, the Japanese attempted to carry out the first phase of the plan. From the high ground the Japanese of the 38th Regiment poured heavy fire on the White and Yellow Beaches. Some of the LVTs were hung up on the reef and made excellent targets for the Japanese mortars.

During the course of W day, the brigade lost 24 of these valuable craft.

The target of the 22nd Marines was the two beaches designated Yellow just north of Gaan Point; the 1st Battalion went in to Yellow 1 and the 2nd to Yellow 2. The plan called for a wide turning movement to the left after the beach had been secured, with the immediate objective of capturing Agat village and the western portion of Harmon Road and the ultimate objective of cutting off the Orote Peninsula and linking up with the 3rd Marine Division. At the same time the 4th Marines were to land on the White Beaches, with the 2nd Battalion assaulting White 1 and the 1st going to White 2. As soon as possible the 1st Battalion would wheel right through the dry rice paddies, secure the brigade flank, and drive toward Hill 40 inland from Bangi Point. Meanwhile the 2nd would move rapidly straight ahead toward the reservoir adjacent to Harmon Road just short of Maanot Pass. The Final Beach Line (FBL) had been drawn along the high ridgeline east of Mts. Tanae and Alifan. The hoped-for objective for the first day, the 0–1 line, ran from south of Bangi Point on the coast, inland including Mt. Alifan, and then bent back to the coastline just north of Agat village.

The landings went according to plan except that the losses, particularly in the zone of 2/22, were very heavy. Despite this, the Marines moved quickly inland although the 2nd Battalion was held up briefly by a Japanese strongpoint. Here, as in the 3rd Division area, the decision to bring in tanks on DUKWs early was vindicated. The fire of the Shermans cleared the Japanese from their strongpoint and by noon the 2nd had secured the high ground about three-quarters of a mile inland. The 1st Battalion, following the plan, wheeled left after landing and began to advance toward Agat village which had been destroyed by the naval bombardment. There was sporadic resistance from the Japanese on the southern outskirts of the village, but the battalion commander, LtCol. Walfried Fromhold, committed his reserve company and by noon the Marines reached and set up roadblocks on Harmon Road.[17]

LtCol. Shapley's 4th Marines landed on schedule, with the 1st Battalion on White 2 and the 2nd on White 1. Almost immediately the 2nd Battalion's advance was halted by concentrated fire from a small hill approximately twenty feet high located only 100 yards inland. This rise was not shown on any maps or photos of the beach area and the Japanese from this location were able to pin down the 2nd Battalion on the beach until the defenders were wiped out just before noon. Only then could the advance toward Mt. Alifan resume. The men of the 1st Battalion were more fortunate. They quickly overran the small pillboxes directly behind the shoreline and found a drainage ditch leading to the interior. Sheltered from the worst fire by this, they had moved over 1,000 yards inland by 1030. The reserve company was soon committed and swung right down the coast road toward Hill 40 and Bangi Point. They were halted briefly by fire from the hill but, as soon as tanks were brought up, the riflemen with their covering fire soon reduced all resistance there.

General Shepherd landed just before noon and assumed direct command of the assault. His command post was located just inland from Gaan Point. He found the situation critical. Had the enemy chosen at that time to launch coordinated counterattacks against the exhausted, decimated Marines, the invasion would have been in genuine difficulty. In addition to the condition of the combat troops, there was a shortage of supplies, particularly of ammunition of all types and water. The beach was also crowded with wounded whose evacuation was made difficult by the shortage of LVTs and DUKWs. The aid station on Yellow Beach had taken a direct mortar hit, all its personnel were killed or injured, and badly needed medical supplies were destroyed. There was no doctor present in the 22nd Marines area until the afternoon. Of the many problems facing Shepherd, perhaps potentially the worst was the communication problem. There was no contact with the regimental CPs until after noon. Thus 3/22, the regimental reserve, was not ordered in to the beach until it was too late to take part in the day's fighting.

Despite the problems, the attack eastward by both regiments was continued soon after noon. At 1245, 1/22 with tank support advanced through the rubble of Agat and soon the entire village was controlled by the Marines. East of there Company C ran into heavy fire coming from an emplaced machine gun on a small hill. The Marines took many casualties and despite reinforcements they could not take the hill. The troops then dug in for the night short of the hill. During this time 2/22 had reorganized along the cliffline and began its attack eastward in conjunction with the 1st Battalion. They were immediately pinned down by fire from the next ridgeline where the Japanese were operating a dual purpose anti-aircraft gun. An air strike against the ridge was called in but proved disastrous since the planes bombed and strafed Company F instead of the Japanese. After the confusion from this was over and the casualties removed it was too late to try to advance further and the men of 2/22 also dug in far short of the 0–1 line.

In the area of the 4th Marines, most of the afternoon's fighting occurred immediately on the flank of 2/22. Here elements of 3/4, the reserve battalion, as soon as they landed took over a part of the line of 1/4 and at 1345 attacked east toward the 0–1 line. Within three hours they reached Harmon Road and set up roadblocks. They could see the flank company of 2/22 to their left, but could not make physical contact because a deep ravine separated them. At this time they, too, prepared for the night, positive that the Japanese would counterattack heavily in the dark. The lines of the brigade were stretched thin and there were few reserves to oppose any concerted Japanese counteroffensives against the beachhead.[18]

With the riflemen available, General Shepherd tried to organize some defense in depth in order to contain any breakthrough. In the zone of the 22nd Marines he held back the 3rd Battalion to act as a stopper to handle deep infiltration and to counter any serious threat to the rear echelon and the service personnel who continued frantically to unload supplies during the night. In the sector of the 4th Marines, the regimental commander moved five tanks into a hollow just behind the furthermost position along Harmon Road. Company C of the 1st battalion was placed in reserve and sited near the regimental CP, and the Reconnaissance Platoon and an engineer detachment were sent forward to strengthen the line directly opposite the foothills of Mt. Alifan. Artillery had previously been registered in on likely approach areas and the Navy was alerted to provide illuminating fire on call. These preparations were the best that could be done under the circumstances. The Marines settled in to await the Japanese night attacks.

A careful look at the Japanese response to the relatively slight Marine gains during W day shows that the decisions made by General Takashina and his subordinates during the afternoon of W day determined the outcome of the battle for Guam. Although the Marines had established a lodgement at both Asan and Agat, their position was far from secure since each beachhead was very shallow. In general, the Marines held only the first line of ridges while the Japanese controlled most of the interior high ground from which they maintained a fairly continuous fire on the beach parties trying desperately to land supplies for the attackers. Granted the Japanese forces had suffered heavy casualties before and after the landings, and there were acute shortages of ammunition, they still had command of the situation on W day. The history of amphibious landings everywhere during World War II showed that the best chance a defender had was to destroy the enemy before a beachhead could be consolidated. This was presumably Takashina's objective. However, he seems not to have had any cogent plans for coordinated counterattacks against the Marine positions or to have heard of the *schwerpunk*, the concentration of forces in order to achieve a major breakthrough at one point. He and his subordinate commanders also seemed to prefer night attacks where presumably the Japanese talent for infiltration, combined with darkness would negate the Marines' naval support, and secure success. Night attacks, however, are very tricky operations, and to succeed need much planning and practice.

General Takashina did not even contemplate any massive counterattacks against the beachheads during the day and only reluctantly gave his approval to the night attacks launched against the Provisional Brigade's position at Agat. Colonel Suenaga asked permission to launch such an attack at 1730 and, after first refusing, Takashina gave his permission. There is every evidence that he did not really believe the attack could be successful. By his actions neither did Colonel Suenaga. He argued that it was pointless for any of his regiment to survive since they had lost most of their main weapons and to retreat would only postpone the inevitable since they would have given up their good positions. Once General Takashina had given his approval, Colonel Suenaga ordered that the regimental colors be burned before his proposed night attack began. This was a sure sign that he believed his command would be destroyed.[19]

Japanese commanders during World War II generally suffered from their warrior code. Bravery in the face of death was presumably preferable to a rational plan to destroy the enemy. This was Colonel Suenaga's problem. LtCol. Hideyuki Takeda, the senior survivor of the Japanese Guam garrison, described Suenaga's decisions and their aftermath when he later wrote:

> On the middle of the night of the day the chief of this garrison [Suenaga] attacked against the landing forces with three infantry battalions. He poured two of them into both franks [sic] of the enemy and with one of them he attached of himself on the front for the purpose of annihilating the landing forces toward seaside. But it could not be accomplished owing to the severe fire of the landing forces. Colonel T. Suenaga and most of his men were killed.[20]

Although this terse statement expresses adequately the failure of the Japanese on the night of 21–22 July, it does not explain in detail what was attempted and how it was thwarted.

At about 2330 the Japanese began probing attacks all along the line held by the brigade. Thirty minutes later a heavy mortar barrage began on the right flank of the 4th Marines. Platoon-size Japanese forces then struck the 3rd Battalion. Charging ahead throwing grenades and demolition charges, they caused a few casualties before being repulsed in close-in fighting. They next directed their attack against Hill 40 which was held by a platoon of Company K and, after heavy fighting, forced the platoon to withdraw at about 0100. The Marines regrouped, charged up the rise, and retook the hill only to be driven off once again. Finally, with reinforcements, the Marines once again captured the hill and this time held it. About 0330 another attempt was made by small units advancing from the Mt. Alifan area to broach the 3rd Battalion's lines but, despite a serious shortage of ammunition in some of the Marine units, there was no major breakthrough.[21] It was in this fighting that Colonel Suenaga, acting the part of the warrior, led his troops into action. First struck by a mortar fragment, he continued on until killed by a rifle bullet.[22]

A major threat developed at approximately 0230 in the Harmon Road region. There Company B of the 1st Battalion had to confront infantry supported by four tanks and a number of mobile guns. The tanks and guns were knocked out by a bazooka team and by the Sherman tanks hidden in the defile. Without the protection of tanks, what was left of the Japanese infantry retreated.[23]

The attacking Japanese illuminated by star shells generally made easy targets for the men of the 4th Marines. In some cases they seemed to want to call attention to themselves, doing things that convinced the Marines that they were either crazy or drunk. A commentator reported one such occurrence:

> Just before the opening of a Banzai attack this Nip jumped to the crest of a ridge above the Marines. "One, two, three, you can't catch me," he shouted. Two dozen .30 caliber bullets promptly proved him wrong.[24]

Similar strange and unnecessary heroics were noted some days later during the major *banzai* attack which was launched against the 3rd Marine Division. Even when there was no play-acting, Japanese officers appeared to court death by charging straight at the Marine lines waving their swords as if to terrify the Marines in their foxholes. The Japanese were much more successful when individuals or squads used the terrain and darkness to slip through the front lines. Some infiltrators reached the beach area before they were discovered and killed. One particular Japanese squad just before dawn almost reached a beach ammunition dump before being halted by men of a rear area ammunition company.

The 22nd Marines had a relatively easy night largely because one battalion of the Japanese 38th Regiment located near the Maanot Pass did not receive orders from Colonel Suenaga to attack when the other units struck the Marine lines. Therefore in only a few areas of the 22nd's front, such as a part of that held by the 2nd Battalion, was there heavy fighting. One enemy force of about company strength did break through and almost reached the regimental CP before being halted and driven off by headquarters personnel.

Despite the fact that the most serious threat to the 22nd Marines was from bands of infiltrators, there were also examples here of Japanese actions which were totally inexplicable to the Marines. One such was in front of Company C, 1/22, where twelve enemy soldiers suddenly topped the crest of a hill and started marching toward the Marine lines:

> The men of Nippon carried one light and three heavy machine guns and walked steadily toward the center of the position. If their mission was to die for the Emperor, the Marines helped them accomplish it. Machine gun fire riddled the oncoming Japanese who made no attempt to set up their weapons and defend themselves, and most of the group never reached the front lines.[25]

Subsequent discoveries of huge supplies of liquor of various types in warehouse caves on the island perhaps could explain some of these nonchalant activities. The Marines later became convinced that many of their enemy were drunk before they began their suicide attacks. However, Lt. Shigenori Yoshida, a surgeon of the 3rd Battalion who was ordered not to participate in the attack and thus was one of the few officers who survived the Guam battles, cast doubt on this as the sole explanation for the Japanese actions here. According to his account, the officers and men accepted the decision to attack calmly. They burned all their letters and pictures from home and prepared their personal belongings for the night attack. Capt. Heroshi Naganawa, commanding the 3rd Battalion, distributed *sake*. This was consumed by the troops who also had a last meal of salmon and rice. Yoshida reports that many men cried when informed of the plan for the suicide attack.[26]

General Takashina had been reluctant to approve the attack on the Agat beachhead and it did not seem to occur to him to attempt to press his advantage against the thinly held lines of the 3rd Marine Division at Asan. There were not even serious diversionary attacks during the night of the 21st–22nd in that area. From their secure positions on the ridges, the men of General Shigematsu's 29th Division were generally content with harassing the beach areas with mortar and artillery fire which eventually, at about 0230, became so heavy that the Marines and naval shore parties stopped unloading supplies. The only attempt made by the Japanese to launch a serious concerted attack against the Marine division came on the left in the 3rd Marine sector shortly after midnight. It was in this action that the first Marine to receive the Congressional Medal of Honor on Guam, Pfc. Luther Skaggs, although seriously wounded by grenade fragments, maintained his forward position keeping the Japanese attackers at bay during the long night.[27] Colonel Hall, reacting to the continual small-scale uncoordinated attacks, sent up all his reserve to reinforce the line and these attacks were easily contained. Elsewhere the Marines of the 3rd Division on line spent an uneventful, if sleepless, night.[28]

While the Marine units were fighting to hold their slight gains during W day, on the reef line and beaches another type of drama was unfolding which could have soured relations between the Marines and Army as had occurred a month earlier on Saipan. The scenarios for both operations were basically the same. On Saipan, despite the most meticulous planning, the Army 27th Division was literally thrown onto the beaches. Corps headquarters ordered the Army troops to disembark in the dark, communications with the Navy on moving them ashore were faulty, much of the Army regiment's equipment had to be left behind, and some units bobbed around offshore for hours. It was a near miracle that the 165th RCT could collect its units and be prepared for action the next morning. Although the reasons for bringing the Army units in to the beach so hurriedly were different on Saipan and Guam, it would seem at first glance that General Shepherd was following a script already written for Saipan.

The operation plan for Guam was to use the bulk of the 77th Division as floating reserve but to bring in one battalion of the 305th RCT early during the morning of W day so that it could be used by the brigade commander as a direct reserve in case of need. Col. Vincent Tanzola, the 305th commander, had selected his 2nd Battalion as this forward unit. Since the plan called for the battalion to be at the line of departure by 1030, LtCol. Robert Adair, its commander, had his men in the boats as soon as the Marine assault units had passed the line of departure. A liaison group from the regiment's supporting Field Artillery battalion also loaded onto the boats. Once they arrived at the control point things began to go wrong and for the rest of the day the Army units were plagued by foul-ups, none of which was caused by their actions.

Even though the fighting on Agat Beach at late morning was heavy, General Shepherd did not feel he needed the 2nd Battalion and did not want to be bothered by having them brought in under Japanese fire at that time. So Adair and his men on board the landing craft circled around waiting for orders to go in. The heat and humidity were high and this did not improve the feelings of the men who were involved in their first combat. The churning of the boats also made many of them seasick. Finally, shortly after 1400, they were ordered to land on White Beach 1 and assemble at a point approximately 400 yards inland from Gaan Point.

This order was far easier to issue than to achieve since the brigade could not spare any of its LVTs to transport the men of 2/305 across the reef and in to shore. They had to wade in for over 400 yards across coral heads, through potholes and shell craters, to a beach which was still under direct fire from an enemy who held the high ground. Generally, if one found good footing, the water was only waist deep but many an unlucky soldier stepped in a hole and found himself floundering in water over his head. Not only men but equipment, including that which would later be vital for communications, got thoroughly soaked. Because the men sought the easiest, not the most direct, way in, units became scrambled together and it took some time on White Beach to sort them out. Despite the foul-up, the men of the 2nd Battalion, following the most basic maxim, got clear of the beach in a hurry and made their way to their assigned area and began to dig in for the night.[29]

As if the problems with the 2nd Battalion were not enough

to give the officers and men of the 305th the impression that the senior officers most directly concerned were out of their minds, there followed even more inexcusable developments related to LtCol. James Landrum's 1st Battalion. Despite what was then happening to 2/305, General Shepherd at about 1430 ordered the rest of the regiment to land. Given the potential danger to his beachhead, this was a perfectly understandable order. He wanted to have as many men available as possible to counter the Japanese attack he knew was coming. Unfortunately, his order did not reach Colonel Tanzola until an hour later. There were not enough boats to take in both remaining battalions and Tanzola decided to disembark the 1st which, after a brief time, was loaded and taken to the Navy control boat for clearance to proceed to the beach. Apparently no one at brigade headquarters had alerted the Navy and since the officer in charge had received no instructions he would not allow the boats containing 1/305 to proceed. When he finally was given instructions to allow the 1st Battalion to land it was already 1730. The regimental commander, who had remained reasonably calm amidst the confusion, contacted Brigade Headquarters to register his concern about approaching darkness. He obviously had little faith that things would be better in the dark than during daylight. Therefore he sent the following message to General Shepherd:

> Order to 305th Infantry conflicting. Was ordered to land entire CT. Cannot complete unloading of team before dark. Instructions received by TD 38 differ. Suggest suspension of unloading. Request clear order be issued. Expedite reply.[30]

Back came the curt answer to land the combat team immediately. Tanzola probably did not expect sympathy, but he could have used some help from Brigade Headquarters.

The men of Landrum's 1st Battalion had an even more difficult time getting to the beach than those who had gone before. He recalled much later:

> Literally we were just dumped. . . . We at first waited intermittently to be told to go in the boats and then when we

finally got in the boats it was getting pretty late in the day and then we circled for awhile. We were supposed to be met by Amtracs at the edge of the reef. We were supposed to transfer to Amtracs. They just weren't there. It was our definite understanding that we would transfer to Amtracs at the edge of the reef and we would be put ashore that way. The chain of command seemingly just didn't work.[31]

By this time it was getting dark and the tide was coming in. This meant that the men had to wade or in some cases swim in to the beach. This was particularly difficult for the untested soldiers of the 305th who on their first operation carried a great deal of superfluous items. In contrast to the Marines, most soldiers were carrying over fifty pounds of varying types of equipment and ammunition. Many men received deep scrapes and all had their shoes cut up from the sharp coral underfoot. Many of the soldiers lost their way in the darkness and some narrowly escaped landing in enemy territory to the south. Colonel Landrum had hoped to land somewhere in the center of White Beach 1 where he could expedite gathering his battalion, but instead he found himself on the far left of the beach. This made it even more difficult to exercise control over his dispersed unit. Eventually most of the battalion either located the assembly area themselves or were led to it by guides. However, over one-third of the battalion could not get off the beach. Brigade Headquarters was expecting infiltration and direct attacks and did not want large numbers of men moving around on the beach. The military police halted further movement inland at approximately 2130 and thus many infantrymen spent the night on the beach. Landrum had to wait until after daylight on W + 1 before he could assemble his entire unit.[32]

What could have been a tragi-comedy for the 305th was not yet finished because Shepherd wanted the entire regiment ashore before morning. This meant that LtCol. Edward Chalgren's 3rd Battalion still had to be landed. They had to wait for the landing craft which had taken the 1st Battalion to the reef. This would have been enough to assure the Army troops a late, dark, rough walk and swim into the beach, but they were to be delayed even more. A false report of an enemy submarine near the transports was enough to send their transport out to sea where it stayed until the all clear was given at about 2120. Finally, 3/305 was loaded and started toward the reef a few minutes after midnight, but their problems were not yet over. Faulty boat compasses caused many to veer away from their target positions on the reef. It was hoped that with the tide running the boats could cross the reef, but this proved overly optimistic. Many of the boats of the first wave after reaching the reef at approximately 0200 nearly turned over trying to cross. Chalgren then ordered his men over the side and they made their way to the beach 400 to 600 yards away as best they could. Fortunately the Japanese were too busy with their attacks on the brigade's perimeter to pay much attention to the confusion on the beach and out toward the reefs. One of the few bright spots for the 3rd Battalion was the presence on the beach of guides provided by Colonel Tanzola, the regimental commander, who had preceded them some hours before by floating into the beach on a rubber raft he found drifting by near the reef. The guides met the men of the 3rd as they waded in water up to their chests and directed them to the beach assembly areas. Some elements of the 3rd did not reach these areas until 0600; all were wet and tired and many had become violently ill during their hours of bobbing around before crossing the reefline.[33]

Had the Japanese understood what was happening to the Army units during the long night they could have extracted heavy casualties. In addition to all the equipment and supplies stacked or strewn along the narrow beach and the men of the shore parties, there were now over one thousand men of the 305th in their assembly areas, the majority of them totally exposed to enemy fire. Much of the landing area was coral rock. Troops could not even dig the shallowest foxhole in such terrain. Fortunately, although there was severe fighting along the Marine lines only a few hundred yards away, there was only the occasional mortar round to contend with in most of the beach areas. At one place in the interior assembly area there was a brief but intense fire fight involving two companies of the 1st Battalion. As a part of the early morning attack against the 4th Marines, a group of Japanese infiltrated the Marine lines and attacked the Army perimeter. Seven soldiers were killed and ten wounded in the skirmish. Later twenty Japanese dead were found near the positions of Companies A and B.[34]

W day and the first night ashore passed and the Americans, in retrospect, were in much better condition than either Generals Turnage or Shepherd could have imagined at the time. What they could see then were two narrow shallow unconnected beachheads, with the enemy controlling the strategic interior high ground from whence they could bring down fire on almost any part of the beaches. The Marine casualties on W day were not such as to cause great concern, but they were significant. It was ascertained later that the 3rd Division had suffered 105 men killed, 536 wounded, and had 56 missing. General Shepherd reported that his brigade had suffered 350 casualties.[35] Other factors such as exhaustion, heat, and illness caused the commanders to rate their units at only 75 percent of their normal efficiency; the lines which they held were long; and almost all Marine reserves had been committed. However, other factors modified the gloomy picture. The island was still circled by the Navy's gun platforms and the Japanese were at the mercy of American planes. All Marine direct support artillery was ashore and functioning as well as the heavy guns of General del Valle's Corps artillery.

There were, on W + 1, three battalions of fresh Army troops, wet, tired, and disgusted, but nevertheless a reserve, ashore and ready to be used. The most encouraging factor, although unknown to General Shepherd at the time was that the piecemeal attacks by Colonel Suenaga's troops during the night had succeeded in doing only one thing: he had all but destroyed his 38th Infantry as a fighting force. When the Marines on W + 1 tried to break out of the southern beachhead, they found only sporadic resistance to their advance into the immediate interior. Time was also on the side of the Americans. The longer they held on, the more supplies and equipment could be unloaded, and there were still two regiments of the 77th Division on board the transports.

Copy of a photo of a Japanese general and colonel. (U.S. Army.)

The site of a former Marine barracks wrecked when American forces lost the island to the Japanese. (U.S. Army.)

Lt. Gen. Andrew D. Bruce.

Landing craft circle in rendezvous. (U.S. Army.)

Crowded troop transport. (U.S. Army.)

LST's on reef. (U.S. Army.)

U.S. troops of Company B, 305th Infantry Regiment, 77th Division, move up to the front lines. (U.S. Army.)

Tanks of the 77th Division get ready for an assault on Japanese. (U.S. Army.)

American alligators congest the beach. Note shell craters and damaged palm trees. (U.S. Army.)

Amphitractors lining part of the beach prior to bringing in supplies. (U.S. Marine Corps.)

Part of the Marine front line defending the Asan beachhead. (U.S. Marine Corps.)

Men crouch low as sniper fire whizzes overhead. Demolished Marine barracks in background. (U.S. Marine Corps.)

Arota airstrip being worked on by the CBs. (U.S. Army.)

Adelup Point.

Orote Field, three weeks after Americans began the operation. Marine crouches over body of a fanatical Japanese soldier killed by his own grenade. (U.S. Marine Corps.)

Remains of a Japanese 8-inch gun and gun emplacement on Bangi Point. (U.S. Marine Corps.)

Brig. Gen. Lemuel C. Shepherd, Jr., commanding officer of the First Prov. Brigade in the former radio shack (Japanese) on Ritidian Point. (U.S. Marine Corps.)

Mannot Ridge. Troops of the 2d Bn, 305th Regt., dug in along the sides of the valley surrounding the Regimental Command Post. (U.S. Army.)

A mopping-up patrol on the alert for hiding Japanese. Few surrendered; though starving, they preferred to fight it out and die. (U.S. Marine Corps.)

Major General Roy S. Geiger, Commanding General 3d Amphibious Corps; Admiral Spruance; Lt. Gen. Holland M. Smith; Adm. Chester W. Nimitz, and Lt. Gen. Alexander Vandegrift, in the field.

Gen. Vandegrift congratulating Maj. Gen. Allen Hal Turnage, commander of the 3d Marine Division for his part in the recapture of Guam. (U.S. Marine Corps.)

CHAPTER VI
Securing the Beachhead

General Geiger and Corps staff, although only partially aware of the strength of the Japanese defenses, had but one option. The Marines at both beachheads had to attack in order to expand the small lodgements and gain more maneuvering room. Thus on W day + 1, both the 3rd Division and the Provisional Brigade scheduled their attacks to begin at daylight. At the Asan beachhead the most crucial area was Bundschu Ridge and its adjacent highlands to the south. If the division was to break the deadlock, these heights had to be captured. General Shigematsu, the Japanese commander of the Asan front, aware of the importance of these positions if he hoped to keep the Marines tied down, had ordered his mortars and available artillery to bring the 3rd Marines' lines under fire just after first light. Japanese infiltrators had earlier penetrated the area between the 3rd and 21st Marines. Heavy mortar fire pinned down the largest portion of the 3rd Marines, and a direct hit was scored on the 3rd Division Message Center. LtCol. Chevey White, the D1, was killed and 20 Marines were wounded. It was not until 0830 that the infiltrators were eliminated and the general artillery and mortar fire had slackened enough to begin the assault of Bundschu Ridge. This unenviable task fell to 1/3 which soon found the ridge as heavily defended as it had been the day before.

The first direct attack on the ridge was immediately halted. Colonel Hall then changed his tactics. He ordered one company to move out through the rice paddies in an attempt to flank the Japanese on the ridge while the two other companies attacked directly ahead. In order to accomplish this, the left flank of the 21st Marines was moved in order to cover the area vacated by the 3rd. At the same time one company from 2/3 attempted to flank the Japanese on the right. At 1000, Company C 1/3 moved across the rice paddy on the right in their flanking attempt. They were almost immediately stopped by Japanese fire as many of the Marines got tangled in the undergrowth.

Meanwhile Companies A and E moved straight ahead against the ridge. They were supported by close-in massed fire from tanks, half-tracks, and mortars. By early afternoon this attack appeared to be successful since a few Marines reached the top of the ridge. It was during this action that Pfc. Leonard Mason of 2/3, on his own initiative, attacked two machine guns in a well-concealed location. Although mortally wounded he destroyed the position. Mason was the second of four Marines to win the Medal of Honor on Guam.[1]

Although the Marines had gained the ridge, they were too few to hold their gains against continuing mortar and machine-gun fire from adjacent areas. Thus W + 1 ended in frustration for the 3rd Marines who had taken a beating during their two days ashore. The regiment had suffered 615 total casualties; some companies were down to only 40 effectives. Hardest hit was Company A of the 1st Battalion which was no longer an effective unit with most of its officers and men either killed or wounded.[2]

By comparison, the 21st Marines in the center of the division's line had it comparatively easy during W + 1. They were mainly content to send out patrols to feel out enemy resistance along their front. Some Marines of the 2nd Battalion on an open ridge took a number of casualties from Japanese mortar fire, but in general the 21st was content to reorganize and shift the 1st Battalion into the lines instead of the 2nd. The 9th Marines on the right flank of the 21st were involved in considerably more action. Jumping off at 0715, they met only light resistance and by noon the 2nd Battalion had taken Piti Island Navy Yard. The 3rd Battalion was then ordered to take Cabras Island in a full amphibious operation. Loaded into LVTs in the early afternoon and under cover of heavy naval fire and aircraft strafing runs, 3/9 landed on the island's only good beach. Expecting the worst, the Marines were pleasantly surprised by the light resistance from only a few Japanese. However, their advance was slowed by the heavy undergrowth and the need to advance cautiously because a number of land mines had been found planted by the Japanese along the most obvious routes. The decision was made to halt the attack before dark after having advanced approximately 400 yards inland.[3]

General Takashina once again failed to take advantage of his position along the higher ridges and did not attempt a major counterstroke during the night of the 22nd–23rd. Instead the Japanese were content to lob a few mortar shells into the Marine positions. The one exception to this quiescence was in the 21st Marines' sector where shortly after midnight a number of Japanese charged straight at the Marine positions. This attack of indeterminate strength was doomed to failure since there was no prior preparation by mortars and artillery and there was no reserve to take advantage of a possible breakthrough. The Japanese unit of at least platoon strength simply attacked with bayonets and predictably they failed, leaving most of their men dead in front of the Marine positions. Once again the fatalistic warrior code had served to do nothing but reduce the number of men available to defend the ridges.[4]

General Turnage, following the course of the fighting of W + 1 and watching his casualties mount, was very worried about the position of his division. The enemy held the high ground, Turnage's available troops were tired, he had committed his reserves, and he was concerned that the Japanese would mount a major counterattack which even if uncoordinated like the one at Agat the night before could still do great damage to the beachhead. He therefore requested reinforcements from Corps. He was aware that there were two Army regiments still offshore on the transports and he wanted one of those to be attached as soon as possible. After considering it, General Geiger denied the request. He still wanted all the 77th Division available adjacent to the 1st Brigade if and when a breakout was achieved.[5]

Meanwhile, General Shepherd had changed his plans for the

attack at Agat on W + 1. He had initially planned to use the Army's 305th to relieve the 4th Marines and have it attack toward Mt. Alifan. However, the foul-ups of the previous day in landing the 305th had made it impossible for Colonel Tanzola to comply with Shepherd's plans. The best that could be done was to move 2/305 forward early in the morning to relieve 2/4 which then became Brigade reserve. Later in the afternoon the 1st and 3rd battalions moved into position. The 305th then launched its first attack in the direction of Maanot Pass in order to secure the high ground through which the main east-west route, Harmon Road, passed. Despite the terrain, the undergrowth, and difficulties of getting supplies, particularly water, forward, the Army units reached the 0–a line, their objective, by 1700 and the regiment with all battalions tied in settled down for the night.[6]

The objective of the 22nd Marines was to move from their positions north of Agat toward Old Agat Road, with the ultimate goal of isolating the Orote Peninsula. The 1st Battalion on the left attacked toward the junction of Old Agat and Sumay roads (RJ5) at 0830. The route of the attack was across rice paddies. Armor was supposed to support the attack but the Japanese had blown the bridge and the banks of the river were too steep for the tanks to climb. Thus the Marines of the 1st Battalion had to go ahead without direct support. Wading through the rice paddies and reducing the Japanese pillboxes one by one took time and resulted in heavy casualties. The 2nd Battalion to the right met less opposition and advanced north to Old Agat Road before noon where they halted because of the relative slowness of the 1st Battalion on their flank. Both battalions established good defensive positions for the night although these were still hundreds of yards short of their objective, the 0–2 line.

The 4th Marines at 0900 began their advance toward Mt. Alifan and immediately encountered rough terrain and heavy undergrowth. In addition the Japanese had established well-prepared defensive positions, particularly in the caves on the northern slope of the mountain. The day was hot and humid, the water supply chancy, and the advance very slow. The way forward was soon marked by the heavy packs and extraneous equipment discarded by the Marines. Demolition teams had to reduce the Japanese cave defenses one by one. As the advance squads neared the top of the mountain, the vegetation was thicker and the few trails were overgrown with high bushes and vines. Finally, Marines of 1/4 reached the summit but decided it would be too dangerous to stay there if the Japanese counterattacked so they withdrew to a more defensible position. Other units soon spread out southwest along the ridgelines toward Mt. Tanae. By nightfall the 4th Marines' lines were near the crest of the ridge almost to Mt. Tanae then bent back toward the west coast and Magpo Point.[7]

General Geiger decided during the evening of the 22nd to land the 306th RCT on the White Beaches beginning at noon the next day. The presumption that General Bruce and his staff had long entertained was that a portion of the functioning LVTs and DUKWs would be used to take the regiment across the reef. However, General Geiger did not believe he could spare his remaining LVTs and DUKWs from their task of unloading cargo. So the men of the 306th, like those of the 305th, were carried to the reefline and waded into shore. General Bruce had tried to land the unit at low tide; nevertheless most of the vehicles were drowned out and had to be pulled ashore later by bulldozers. One medium tank simply fell into a large pothole and disappeared from sight.[8] Needless to say, much of the communication equipment, even those radio sets which had been waterproofed, were ruined. The men, loaded down with much of what the officers later came to believe was unnecessary equipment, struggled more than one-quarter mile into shore. Fortunately the landing of most of the regiment was completed before dark and the Japanese were not in a position to take advantage of the daylight confusion.

First to land, 3/306 moved immediately into position south of Mt. Alifan and was involved in a brief skirmish action later that afternoon. The other two battalions, however, landed so late that it was decided to hold them in rear assembly areas for the night and move them in to relieve the other units of the 4th Marines the next day. Supplies and equipment for the 77th Division continued to be landed during the night of the 23rd–24th.

There existed a very real danger that the way the Army troops had been treated would lead to a clash between Generals Geiger and Bruce reminiscent of the Saipan affair of the previous month.

General Bruce could not have been any happier than his junior officers over the way the Army regiments had been landed, and later many of his subordinates were quite vocal in voicing their opinions about being "dumped on the beach." Although he might have believed that the operation could have been planned better, Bruce, a no-nonsense veteran of the First World War, said nothing at the time and later never publicly criticized the Marine commanders. He had held senior command before taking over the 77th Division and obviously realized the many problems confronting Geiger who had to make the decision with regard to the optimum use of the boats which could cross the reef.

Once the 306th had landed, control of the 305th which had been attached to the 1st Marine Brigade passed to Bruce and his staff who now had two-thirds of their division on line and had relieved most units of the 4th Marines. Bruce requested of Corps that the 307th be landed the next day beginning at 0530. He wanted the additional manpower to bolster the division's planned attack south and eastward which was designed to secure the Final Beach FBL as well as Facpi Point. Geiger denied the request to land the 307th so early since he was not sure that this RCT which was the last major reserve force would not be needed to support the thinning ranks of the 3rd Division at Asan. However, during the morning of 24 July, he decided that the situation on shore was such that he could dispense with his floating reserve and ordered the regiment to begin landing on White Beach 2 at 1300.[9]

The experiences of the 307th in landing duplicated the earlier efforts of the other two regiments with one additional complication—there had been a storm at sea which created very heavy ground swells. Just loading on to the LCVPs became a dangerous task. Two men were lost when they fell from the landing nets and could not be recovered. Then, once loaded, the boats circled for hours before making for the reef. This ensured that most of the men of the 307th were thoroughly seasick before they, too, had to make the long walk to shore. All the troops of the regiment were ashore by dark, however, and were in their assigned area near General Bruce's CP just to the rear of the 305th's lines. Although the 307th was still Corps reserve, Bruce finally had all his troops ashore. The division was plagued throughout the campaign by shortages of equipment, the most important being communications gear, which had been ruined during the transit to shore, and tentage. Even after the island was secure many aid stations and lower echelon headquarters were operating in the open instead of under canvas as in the Marine units. Most of the additional supplies which had been transported from Hawaii would be landed within the next two days.[10]

While the landings of the two Army RCTs was taking place, the rest of the 1st Provisional Brigade was moving rapidly to expand what had been a precarious hold on the beaches and adjacent high ground. On 23 July the 4th Marines held fast to their lines waiting to be relieved by the 306th RCT, but the 22nd Marines in the northern sector of the beachhead attacked toward the Ayuja River with the ultimate goal of sealing off the Orote Peninsula. The Marines met little opposition until early afternoon when they reached the rice paddies north of the river. Here the Marines could get little direct support from their armor and had to advance across swamplike land where they could sink into waist-high water and mud. A series of small hills west of the low rice paddies provided the Japanese with good cover from which to bring enfilading fire on the Marine units, who were also hit by mortar and artillery fire from the Orote Peninsula and from the high ground leading up to Mt. Tenjo. The Japanese positions in both areas were taken under fire by Division and Corps artillery as well as by the Navy. The battleship *Pennsylvania* stood in close to shore and pounded the Japanese positions with its fourteen-inch guns. This big gun support for the 22nd Marines continued throughout the night of 23–24 July. However, Shepherd had pulled the regiment back to a more defensible position south of the Old Agat Road and the Marines dug in there for the night.

During 23 July the 305th moved out in a northeasterly direction keeping flank contact with the 22nd Marines on their left. They met only scattered opposition north of Harmon Road from the one battalion of the Japanese 38th Regiment which had not destroyed itself during the abortive *banzai* attack. By evening they had reached the FBL and halted, with the 1st and 3rd battalions on line on the heights beyond and the 2nd Battalion straddling

Harmon Road. Meanwhile the 306th had relieved the 4th Marines and taken over the beach positions held by the brigade. This ensured that when General Shepherd began his assault on the Orote Peninsula he would have a rested Marine regiment in reserve.

General Shepherd's plan for finally isolating the Japanese forces on the Orote Peninsula was simple. On 24 July he would send two battalions of the 22nd Marines in column north along the Agat–Sumay Road with the objective of negating the Japanese strongpoints which controlled the approaches to the peninsula across the rice paddies. Once the units arrived at the junction of a minor north-south road with the Agat–Sumay Road, the 3rd Battalion would shift to the right and, roughly following this road, would reach Apra Harbor. Meanwhile the 1st Battalion would proceed along the major road, clearing out the mines and reducing any strongpoints which it encountered. While all this was happening, the 2nd Battalion would move from its right flank position approximately one-half mile to seize the heights controlling Atantano Village located near the eastern shore of Apra Harbor. If successful these maneuvers would seal off the Japanese garrison on Orote.

Despite a number of unforeseen problems, the plan as outlined by General Shepherd the night before the attack worked. After an hour and a half of preparatory naval barrages and air strikes, the advance began with a medium tank company in support. Progress was slow because the Japanese had mined the roadway. The mines had to be cleared and the covering pillboxes and log barricades reduced. The Japanese had also preregistered their mortars on the routes of advance. However, covering artillery and naval gunfire silenced most of the enemy guns and demolition teams took care of the barricades and also sealed up the few caves where the Japanese had placed machine guns. At one time the Japanese commander committed five tanks to the defense of the road. All were quickly destroyed by the accurate fire of the heavier Shermans. By nightfall the 1st Battalion had reached its objective but the 3rd which had the responsibility of clearing out the strongpoints north of the rice paddies was still 400 yards from the southern part of the beach at Apra Harbor.

Meanwhile the 2nd Battalion had reached its objective at Atantano despite being delayed in its attack by an unexpected Japanese counterattack. Once this had been defeated the Marines moved quickly to their objective against very light Japanese resistance. They were potentially in a dangerous position as they dug in for the night since they were relatively isolated, with the Japanese having free movement on three sides of the heights. In part to alleviate this problem, Company F of 2/4 was ordered to reinforce 2/22 while the rest of the battalion moved up to close the open space between the 2nd and 3rd battalions.[11]

The four days of hard fighting had been very costly to the brigade. It had suffered 1,003 casualties with 188 killed in action.[12] However, at the end of W + 3, the brigade at last had a firm foothold on the southern beachhead. The 77th Division which had yet to see any serious action had taken over the responsibility of the right flank, all Corps artillery was in place, supplies were moving into the beaches in a steady stream, the Orote Peninsula was sealed off, and although Shepherd did not know it, the earlier *banzai* charge had removed most of his opposition east of the peninsula.

The 3rd Marine Division at Asan on W + 2 had attempted to follow General Geiger's order to close up the flanks of the attacking regiments but found it extremely difficult to maintain contact because of the terrain. Action in the 9th Marine sector was relatively quiet all during the day; most of the activity there was devoted to patrolling and trying to link up with the 21st Marines. On Cabras Island, 3/9 completed its mission and turned the island over to the 14th Defense Battalion. In the center of the division's line the 21st Marines at 0900 attacked directly ahead in conjunction with the 3rd Marines' attempt to take the high ground on the left flank of the line. Despite the use of demolition squads and flamethrower teams, the attack was stopped by the Japanese from their dug-in positions along the ridgeline.

The heaviest fighting on 23 July was borne by the 3rd Marines who supported by naval gunfire, aircraft, Division and Corps' artillery, and close-in support from tanks and half-tracks, attacked the dug-in positions which had heretofore pinned them down to a very narrow foothold on the left flank. On the extreme left,

3/3 was hit by a counterattack which was contained only by the combined backup firepower and by the commitment of the last reserves. By mid-day the battalion had taken such severe losses that it could advance no further. Even before the attack had begun Colonel Hall had informed Division of the acute manpower situation and told them that he needed another battalion to carry out the day's mission successfully. At the close of the day's fighting, the situation was much worse, particularly in the 3rd Battalion area. Company A had fewer than forty men available, and Company E was down to half strength.[13]

Elsewhere in the 3rd Marine zone, the attack was more successful. Under cover of heavy support fire, the 2nd Battalion attempted to flank the Japanese positions on Bundschu Ridge. Hacking their way through the undergrowth, the Marines were surprised by the lack of hostile fire from what had been very good Japanese defenses along the ridge. Inexplicably, the Japanese had abandoned this excellent defensive position except for a few lightly held strongpoints in the cliffs. The Marines reached the crest by noon and spent the rest of the day cleaning out the few Japanese left behind.

At the close of the day's fighting on 23 July, General Turnage's division had reached the high ground in most areas. However, casualties had been so heavy that no continuous line could be established. The Marines held strongpoints, having to content themselves with hoping that the gaps between units could be covered by naval gunfire and the division's own artillery. The count of losses by the close of W + 2 for the division stood at 1,651, with 139 killed in action.[14]

The Marines resumed the attack the following morning with the key objectives of reaching the plateau and tying together the exposed flanks of the 21st and 3rd Marines. Elements of the 21st advanced up a ravine which marked the boundary between the two regiments and took heavy casualties from Japanese machine guns concealed in caves along the sides of the ravine. Nevertheless, by mid-afternoon of W + 3, aided by close-in air strikes, they had reached the top and tied in with a company from the 3rd Marines who had also fought their way to the plateau. Once more the scarcity of men and the nature of the terrain dictated the holding of strongpoints with gaps as large as 100 yards between units. The forward unit commanders hoped that these gaps could be adequately covered by supporting artillery.

During the morning of 24 July the 9th Marines attempted to link up with elements of the 1st Brigade. A patrol in strength moved south along the Piti–Sumay Road before being halted short of its objective by heavy fire from the high ground to its left. Although not successful in linking up with the 22nd Marines, the patrol did discover that the Japanese had retreated from the low ground leaving intact large dumps of ammunition, fuel, and general supplies. In their retreat they had not even attempted to blow the bridges, all of which were still standing. Elsewhere along the 9th Marine front there was little activity and only slight gains made as the exhausted Marines were generally content to hold the ground already won.[15]

Despite the heavy casualties and the slow advance inland, the position of the division at the close of W + 3 was generally very good. The Japanese seemed to be hurriedly abandoning even their strongest defensive positions. The Marine units had reached the plateau and although there were gaps in the line, these seemed to be adequately covered by the Navy and land-based artillery. At night the Navy moved destroyers in close to shore and used their powerful searchlights to illuminate these dangerous areas. All Corps and Division artillery was in place and working at a furious pace both day and night, limited only by the availability of shells. The engineers had extended the road net in the Marines' sector to all units. Supplies were moving in to shore in ever-increasing quantities. Some of the supply ships had been completely unloaded and the supplies from the others were rapidly being transferred to the reefline. The Seabees had placed five large cranes along the reef and these now assumed the formidable task of transferring the supplies to the LVTs and DUKWs. Shore parties were working around the clock to clear the once clogged beach.

The high temperature and humidity on Guam takes its toll on those involved in any strenuous exercise. The lot of all Marines, particularly those in the forward units, was made more difficult because of the shortage of water. This situation was partially corrected by the discovery on 24 July of good water at Asan Spring which made the transport of water in fifty-gallon drums from the ships offshore less critical.

At the same time, the situation on the southern beachhead was even more encouraging. Despite a more difficult reef to cross and the fact that cranes could not be mounted on the reefs to aid in unloading, a steady stream of supplies was reaching shore. All Brigade and Corps artillery had been landed. Most of the Japanese in this sector were now confined to the Orote Peninsula. The 77th Division had been landed, were well dug in, and had taken over the responsibility of defending the FBL. Defense on the shore area had also been assumed by Army troops and the Marines' own 9th Defense Battalion. General Shepherd could now complete his turning movement prior to the assault on the fixed defenses on the Orote Peninsula without having to reduce his attacking forces to guard exposed flanks.

Gen. H. M. Smith, in overall charge of the Marianas operation, had been deeply involved in closing down the Saipan and Tinian campaigns and therefore had little to do with the tactical details of the Guam assault. For this, General Geiger and his subordinates could be grateful. Despite the reputation that Gen. "Howlin' Mad" Smith built during the war, many of his decisions were questionable. Certainly those involving the Army's 27th Division on Saipan were not well considered, and later his intervention at Iwo Jima was criticized by even his contemporaries in the Marine Corps. Perhaps his worst faults were his almost blind faith in the heroism of Marines and their ability to overcome any obstacle. This, combined with his lack of knowledge of the geography of the areas under assault, made him minimize the difficulty of capturing outlined objectives.

The Japanese on Saipan had been more tenacious than expected and this had fortunately postponed the Guam attack. Otherwise the invasion might have proved disastrous. It was now Geiger's and Turnage's turn to be unjustly criticized by Smith who paid a visit to Guam on 24 July. In his memoirs written much later, Smith indicated the reasons for this belated visit. He was worried "that the Third and Seventy-seventh Divisions were not taking more aggressive action." After conferring with Admiral

Spruance and General Geiger on their command ships, he then went ashore where he was briefed by General Turnage and presumably visited a portion of the 3rd Division front. He noted, "I could see no evidence of Japanese in front of them" and "the situation did not please me."[16] Such statements combined with criticisms he levelled at Geiger's tactics four days later have been generally accepted as justified, and the 3rd Division has not been given the respect that its action on Guam deserved. If General Takashina had not been so obsessed with conforming to the model of a defeated hero, General Smith would have had much more to worry him. For like his subordinate, Colonel Suenaga, he would do as much to destroy his own army as did the Marines.

Despite what General Smith believed, the men of the 3rd Division had not been holding back. They had suffered heavy casualties and on the morning of W + 4 still had not secured the immediate high ground of the Fonte Plateau. General Turnage had put all available men including headquarters and service personnel on the line. Nevertheless, there were still gaps between units in his greatly extended lines, particularly at the dividing line between the 3rd and the 21st Marines. He had ordered the badly battered 1/3 into direct reserve. General Turnage shifted LtCol. Robert Cushman's relatively fresh 2/9 from the division's extreme right and attached it to the 3rd Marines. This unit was to spearhead the major thrust of the division on 25 July. At 0930, 2/9 having passed through the lines of 1/3 began the attack on the Japanese defenders of the Fonte Plateau. Within an hour, against sporadic resistance the Marines had secured the lower portion of the Mt. Tenjo Road. This allowed a more rapid movement of men and equipment, particularly tanks, from the rear areas to the front. Most of the battalion halted and regrouped while some platoons were detailed to sweep the areas through which the Marines had passed in order to clean out pockets of resistance, a task that would occupy some Marines for days.

The forward movement was resumed at 1530 after the entire front, particularly the Fonte Plateau, had been worked over by naval and Marine artillery. Even here the Marines were unlucky since some of the rounds fell short on one assault company, causing fourteen casualties. Cushman had also requested tank support, but the four Shermans detailed for this operation arrived too late to give any assistance. He later placed them in a draw to cover one of the relatively open night approaches through his lines. The Japanese, although obviously shaken by the bombardment, put up a determined resistance and denied the Marines access to the main part of the plateau. Only in the center of their sector did men of 2/9 gain a lodgement on the plateau where Company F held on to a rocky outcrop considerably ahead of the flank companies.

Elsewhere the division had limited success in advancing toward the FBL. In the center, the 2nd and 3rd Battalions of the 21st Marines moved directly ahead, bypassing a deep ravine in which the Japanese had strong defenses. Air and artillery destroyed these and a later body count showed the number of Japanese in the ravine to have been in excess of 250 men. In the center the 1st Battalion encountered a low-lying hill which the Japanese were determined to hold. They had fixed machine guns and mortar positions dug in and some of their remaining artillery had zeroed in on the possible approaches to the hill. The hill could not be bypassed nor, despite heroic efforts of the Marine riflemen supported by tanks, could it be captured. After taking heavy losses all day, 1/21 moved back to more defensible positions along the Mt. Tenjo Road for the night.

The 9th Marines were the most successful of all the regiments engaged that day largely because the Japanese had pulled back many of their troops from their sector. By mid-afternoon the Marines had taken the high ground north of the Aguada River and captured a number of supply dumps intact. Hampered by lack of manpower, General Turnage became very concerned over the length of his lines, which by this time were over 9,000 yards long. In order to shorten his lines, he stopped the advance of the 9th Marines and ordered the assault units to fall back almost a mile to a good defensive position for the night. This order obviously disappointed many Marines for reasons totally unconnected with the fighting. Among the supplies in the dumps were great quantities of soft drinks and beer. Only a few of the parched Marines had had a chance to sample these spoils of war. Difficult as it is to believe, at least some men of the 9th Marines seemed fated to be denied liberated liquid refreshments. A company commander, Wilcie O'Bannon, recalled one situation of belated deprivation when Colonel Cushman noticed long bottles protruding from the packs of some Marines. Although he knew what was in the bottles, he asked one of his staff for confirmation. When told "I believe that is Japanese Sake," he gave the order for the bottles to be confiscated and broken up. One suspects that in this case as well as other instances, the bottles were empty by the time they were smashed. Presumably in all such situations on Guam, there were some really happy troops, at least for a brief time.[17]

General Geiger's plan for the southern beachhead for W + 4 had originally called for the 77th Division to hold fast to the FBL line in the east while the two regiments of the brigade mounted a concerted attack against the first Japanese defenses on the Orote Peninsula. For the reduction of this strongest Japanese redoubt he had ordered all artillery of both the 77th and 3rd divisions to give priority to fire missions on the peninsula. General del Valle had also visited Shepherd's headquarters and taken him to task for not using Corps big guns to support his attacks.[18] Geiger's plans for the day were modified, however, when General Shepherd requested that the general assault on the Japanese on Orote be postponed for a day. Contributing to this request for a delay were the casualties that the brigade had suffered as well as the general fatigue of the assault troops. The most telling reason and the one which obviously convinced the Corps commander to grant his request concerned the difficulty that Shepherd had in moving the 4th Marines into position on the left flank of his line. Some elements of the regiment had been relieved in their previous positions by Army troops only in the late afternoon of the 24th. Although theoretically W + 4 was meant to be a day of rest and reorganization, some units were involved in heavy fighting and sustained considerable casualties. This was because Shepherd wanted to improve the brigade's position at the neck of the peninsula in preparation for the major offensive of the next day. In so doing, some units of the 22nd Marines were up against the Japanese first line of fortifications, pillboxes, and machine guns.

This was the Marines' first encounter with the best prepared positions on the island. The Japanese with tank support counter-attacked a number of times against the 22nd's front. Once again the Japanese tanks were not equal to the task. By the end of the day bazooka teams and the larger, heavier armed Shermans had destroyed eight of these poorly designed and antiquated vehicles. During the late afternoon of W + 4 the brigade extended its control over the base of the peninsula from Agat to Apra Harbor with the 4th Marines on line on the left and the 22nd on the right. This effectively isolated approximately 2,500 Japanese troops from contact with their main forces on the mainland. As darkness closed in, General Shepherd could feel optimistic despite the fact that some of his units had less than 50 percent effectives. The brigade had made contact with the 9th Marines to the north and were tied in to elements of the 77th Division to the east.[19]

During the fighting on W + 4, the brigade had encountered well-trained naval troops from the 54th Keibitai commanded by Cdr. Asaichi Tamai who had succeeded to the command of the Orote Peninsula after Colonel Suenaga's death during the *banzai* attack on the first night of fighting. In addition to the naval force, Tamai had remnants of the 38th Regiment, a collection of men from various anti-aircraft and aircraft units, and also some laborers who were pressed into service.[20] Despite the strength of Orote's defenses and the fatalistic bravery of his men, Tamai must have known that his position was hopeless. The peninsula was ringed with American warships which continued their fire at his fixed positions with everything from five-inch to sixteen-inch guns, and he had almost no defense against attacking aircraft. In addition there was the Marine brigade's own artillery, backed if necessary by the guns of the two other American divisions as well as the heavier caliber Corps artillery.

Tamai had only two choices if he was to save any part of his command and link up with General Takashina's main force. First, he could use the seaworthy barges at Sumay, load in as many troops as possible, and hope to run the gauntlet to land them north of the 3rd Marine Division positions on the mainland. This he tried. Beginning at mid-afternoon he loaded a large number of men on the barges at Sumay. However, they were immediately detected and naval and aircraft gunfire from the American ships offshore soon dispersed and destroyed the barges. There were few survivors. Some Japanese even tried to swim to the mainland in futile attempts to escape. Most of these were quickly shot in the water. Tamai knew that this minidisaster left him with only one other choice. He would try to break through the Marine positions that night in a series of frontal assaults which he would coordinate with the planned attack by General Takashina's main force against the 3rd Marine Division.

It is difficult at any juncture to probe the mind of another, but it is almost impossible to imagine what a leader such as General Takashina, raised with the military cult of *bushido,* was thinking when he planned his main counterattack. He had let the best moment for destroying the Marines pass and had suffered very heavy losses in men and material during the first four days of fighting. He was not yet beaten since he still had the tactical advantage of occupying the Fonte Plateau and the interior hilly, forested regions. He still had over ten thousand men at his disposal. If he had wanted to extract the heaviest price from the Marines as a gift for his Emperor, logic dictated a continuation of the defensive tactics which had bled some of the Marine units nearly to death. The attackers would then have had to take every hillock, draw, and cave. Instead, Takashina, like his subordinate Colonel Suenaga on W day, decided that his defensive positions were untenable and that he and his command should sacrifice themselves as a last act of obedience. It is only barely possible that he believed, despite evidence to the contrary, that a *banzai* type attack could gain him ultimate victory. In any case, on 23 July he had decided upon a general attack on the 3rd Division coordinated with Commander Tamai's attempt to break through the Marine lines on the Orote Peninsula. Although aware of how impossible it would be for reinforcements to reach them, many of the officers at Takashina's headquarters were obviously heartened by a message received on the 24th from Imperial Japanese Headquarters. It read, "Defend Guam to the death. We believe good news will be forthcoming."[21]

General Takashina pulled in reserve troops from Tumon, Pago, and Agana to strengthen his main attack. Unlike most *banzai* charges, this one, although desperate, was carefully planned. The general sent detailed instructions to his subordinates, complete with overlays, showing their main objectives and routes of advance. He still had direct communications with Tamai until the evening of 25 July and the commander was made privy to the details of the assault on the 3rd Division. Although Japanese from other units would participate, the main elements of the Japanese force commanded by General Shigematsu were the 18th Regiment and the 48th Brigade, a total of more than seven battalions. The plan called for the 48th Brigade to move against the lodgement in the 3rd Marine sector gained by Cushman's battalion on the edge of the Fonte Plateau. After achieving a breakthrough there they were to head for Red Beach 2 in order to destroy the Marine ammunition and supply dumps located adjacent to Chonito Cliff. Meanwhile, two battalions of the 18th would assault the 21st Marines while another struck the left wing of the 9th Marines. These units would attempt to use the shallow Asan and Nidual river valleys, trying to take advantage of the 800–yard gap between the two Marine regiments. Their objective was to reach the high ground southwest of Asan town. Further to the east, elements of the 10th Individual Mixed Brigade were to move toward the Tatgua River in the 9th Marine sector. Other small specialized demolition squads would individually create as much havoc along the beaches as possible.

The weather seemed to conspire with the Japanese. Rain had become a fact of life for the Marines on Guam, but beginning on the afternoon of the 25th, the intensity of the rain had increased and by midnight most Marine and Army positions were surrounded by seas of mud. The exhausted riflemen had to tuck their ponchos around them and try to keep out some of the water and prevent complete flooding of their holes. Lieutenant Colonel Coolidge commanding 1/307 located east of the areas designated by the Japanese for the main attack remembered the heavy rain and his comment could be echoed by every soldier and Marine huddled in the rain on 25 July:

> I remember one night. My orderly had dug me a foxhole and I was on a rise, the rest of the section was down below

me. I thought, "I have an ideal position here" and I got into my foxhole and put the poncho over it. Then it began to rain. It just poured and the rain just came down in sheets into my foxhole. I was just floating there and I decided to hell with it, that I'm going to have to get out of this even though there was a danger that my own troops would shoot at me. I rolled out of my foxhole—no one shot me and I stayed on the surface and waited until daylight. I couldn't get back in, the water was just being held there like a pond.[22]

The rainfall made it difficult to bring up badly needed ammunition to the front and hampered observation. This allowed the Japanese to concentrate their forces without being noticed. The Japanese attacks, although they had been expected for some time by higher headquarters, surprised most of the Marines in the 3rd Division sector when they were finally launched.

Commander Tamai's breakout attempt was certainly expected by the men of the 1st Brigade in the early evening of 25 July. This does not mean that General Shepherd and his staff were any more sagacious than his counterparts at Division or Corps, it was simply that the Japanese on Orote were noisier than elsewhere. They obviously were imbibing more than the traditional drink of *sake* normally indulged in before a *banzai* attack. Most of the soldiers were fortifying themselves with as much alcohol as possible before beginning their suicidal attacks. The front-line Marines knew that something was going to happen. One historian of the Marine Corps has recorded "the indescribable clamor" which erupted directly ahead of the 1st Brigade:

The Japanese were screaming, surging, laughing, capering—they were smashing empty bottles against the big mangroves and clanging bayonets against rifle barrels.

Hoarse voices cried, "The Emperor draws much blood tonight." Others rose in fits of cackling presumed to be terrifying. Some tossed grenades yelling, "Corpsman! Corpsman!" or "K Company withdraw!"[23]

The Navy had been warned and the besieging ships were ready with illuminating shells, and land-based artillery units with calibers up to six inches were on the alert. Further, in contrast to the extended lines held by the 3rd Marine Division, there were two regiments of the 1st Brigade packed into the neck of the peninsula holding positions extending less than a mile in length.

At approximately midnight, the attack by one battalion of the Japanese 18th Regiment began, with the main objective the center of the line of the 22nd Marines south of the triple road junction between Sumay and Agat.[24] Although most of the Japanese carried rifles and were led by officers brandishing swords, there were many who carried only the most primitive weapons. Like the attack earlier in the month at Tanapag on Saipan, some of the attackers carried knives, pitchforks, and sticks with bayonets tied to them. Before most of these desperate, drunken, would-be suicides reached the Marines in their holes they were caught in the open by Brigade and 77th Division artillery supplemented by Corps' 155s. This devastating rain of fire was complemented by the regiment's 37mm antitank guns, mortars, and machine guns. Most of the Japanese were simply blown to pieces. The survivors fled back into what they believed was the safety of the mangrove swamps from whence they came. But there was no escape. The entire area of their hoped-for sanctuary was saturated by heavy artillery fire for the next two hours.

Despite the failure of their first attack, the Japanese commanders ordered a second one aimed against the 22nd Marines. One historian of Marine actions in the Pacific described the mad scene which unfolded during this assault:

Over to the right, a second Japanese attack did succeed in reaching our lines. At its height, flares revealed an out-of-this-world picture of Nipponese drunks reeling about in our forward positions, falling into foxholes, tossing aimless grenades here and there, yelling such English phrases as they had managed to pick up, and laughing crazily, to be exterminated in savage close-in fighting. Succeeding waves were caught in a deadly crossfire. Not until dawn did this attack finally dwindle out, at which time more than four hundred bodies were counted in front of the position.[25]

A platoon from Company A of 1/4 which was acting as a stopper in the area between the 4th and 22nd Marines was at this same time involved in its own special type of war. The Japanese at their front were not only drunk, but confused and seemingly lacked any type of leadership. The Marine riflemen picked off the would-be warriors, as in their own version of the "Marianas Turkey Shoot." A count later in the morning showed 256 Japanese dead in front of their positions. The platoon had not lost a man in this engagement.[26] Another Marine rifleman described the indelible impression of the carnage left behind by the unsuccessful attack. He recalled:

> . . . The dead laid everywhere and many of the wounded yet to be evacuated. The enemy dead laid two and three deep in front of our lines. (Three days later we were informed by the engineers detail who bury the dead that over 500 Japs were killed along the front. Over 200 of these were killed in our Platoon sector alone.) There were many instances of Jap and Marine laying side by side. The ground was slick with blood. Water in the fox holes from the rain was reddish muddy liquid. . . .[27]

Takashina's main assault against the 3rd Marine Division had been preceded by a series of probing attacks illuminated by flares all along the thinly held Marine lines. The attack against the division that evening was not a complete surprise. On an afternoon reconnaissance Maj. Fraser West commanding G Company met Capt. Louis Wilson of F Company on a like mission. Together they stumbled upon one of the main Japanese staging grounds and managed to get back to their own lines by a combination of bravado and luck. The probing attacks when they began after dark varied in size and intensity, but in retrospect were probably meant by Takashina to find and exploit weak points. However, generally these attacks did nothing but dissipate his strength since the main outlines of his plans had already been formulated. The small-scale feeling-out attacks began at about midnight and continued intermittently for the next three hours. With only minimal casualties, the Marines killed all but a few of the Japanese who in many cases, disdaining cover, made direct frontal assaults against fixed positions.

The success of the Marines in warding off such tactics masked the very real weaknesses of the Marine division. The bad weather made supply difficult. At one time during the morning, Cushman's men were reduced to only two clips of ammunition per man. The most dangerous situation, however, concerned the length of the front. For example, in the crucial center of the Marine line, 1/21 had only 250 men holding a front of more than 2,000 yards. That length of line would normally be defended by about 600 men.[28] To compensate for the lack of a sufficient reserve General Turnage ordered the Engineers, the 19th Marines, and the separate 2nd Engineer Battalion to assemble and be prepared to reinforce the men on the line. Later Headquarters, Service, and Motor Transport personnel were placed on alert. Artillery units had already set up their own perimeter defenses to counter any Japanese special demolition teams that might infiltrate through the lines.

Shortly after 0300 on 26 July, a signal flare alerted the Japanese commanders to launch their main attack. One of the worst hit was the center of the 21st Marines where the Japanese 2nd Battalion, 18th Regiment, led by Maj. Chusa Maruyama struck a soft spot held by a weakened company of the 1st Battalion. The Japanese assault on both flanks was contained. By the light of flares the Japanese attackers were mowed down by rifle and machine-gun fire augmented by the very accurate fire from the howitzers of the 12th Marines who that evening added new meaning to close support. In the center the Japanese concentrated on a draw leading down to the beach area. To cover this potentially exposed position the battalion commander had parked a number of Sherman tanks. Despite the murderous Marine fire, a number of Japanese broke through to the tank area. An observer of this wrote:

At first the Japs attacked the tanks, firing rifles into the metal sides and then clambering up and over them in a vain attempt to get to the crews inside. They cursed and screamed and pounded drunkenly on the turrets, but failed to damage a single tank. Finally like a stream, many of them flowed past the tanks, down the draw toward the beach.

The rest, cringing before the tank fire, moved to the left, hoping to break through the Marine lines hoping to get to the draw further down the ridge, behind the tanks. The front they now charged was that of B Company. Here, against 75 men, the full force of the Japanese attack suddenly broke.[29]

Despite the volume of support fire, the 21st Marine line on the crest had by this time disintegrated into clumps of men fighting with the fury of those possessed with but one main objective—trying to stay alive. As the fanatical charges continued, the Japanese attackers became piled like cordwood in front of the main Marine strongpoints. Some Japanese carrying demolition charges blew themselves to bits in futile attempts to capture Marine machine-gun and mortar positions. The fighting in the forward positions soon became struggles between individual Marines and the Japanese. Marine correspondent Alvin Josephy has captured as well as possible the fury of the fighting that morning as he detailed the experiences of 2nd Lt. Edward Mulcahy and his understrength platoons of B Company, 1/21. In the forward positions of the company lines were Cpl. Carrol Hertzberg manning a heavy machine gun and Pfc. Edward Killian armed with a Browning automatic rifle. Josephy reported:

The same instant a wave of Japs appeared from nowhere and swept over Hertzberg and a wounded man. Killian saw a Jap plunge his bayonet into Hertzberg's back and fall over him as though in a struggle. At the same moment a mass of Japs came toward Killian. He emptied his automatic rifle into their faces and they turned and ran.

Changing his ammunition magazine quickly, the Marine looked up again just in time to see a single Jap slithering toward him with a saber raised slightly in the air. Killian backed up, and the Jap slashed at him hitting at the barrel of the Marine's BAR and glancing off his arm. The force of his own blow twisted the Jap off balance and he slid into the foxhole on his face as Killian let go a burst at him. The wounded Jap, bleeding from the head, pushed himself up and took another savage swipe at the Marine, nicking him above the right eye. Half blinded Killian threw his leg over the Jap's shoulder and pounded the stock of his BAR into his head. Dopp who had been busy with Japs in the other direction turned suddenly and seeing what was happening, drove his bayonet into the intruder's body. It was still not enough to kill him. The wounded man sprang to his feet and with a wild yell plunged down the hill in the direction of the beach. Lieutenant Mulcahy saw him coming and finally finished him with a shot from Wimmer's pistol.[30]

The second element of General Takashina's assault was the 3rd Battalion of the 18th Regiment led by Maj. Setsuo Yukioka. These Japanese captured two machine-gun positions before being stopped by Marine counterattacks. This repulse was only temporary since they found the nearly half-mile gap between the 21st and 9th Marines. Despite a roadblock established by Colonel Duplantis, the Japanese poured through the gap and Yukioka set up a line of men on the high ground behind the battalion from which he could continue to assault the Marines on line and still use some of his men to drive toward the regimental CP and the beach. As Colonel Duplantis prepared to destroy his cipher device, men of the Engineering Company and three platoons of the Weapons Company augmented by cooks, bakers, clerks, and other casual noncombat personnel beat back the Japanese. Aided by artillery and mortar fire, they counterattacked and by daylight had cleared their area of all but a few stragglers.

Another large group of Japanese from Yukioka's command stumbled into the divisional headquarters area. There they encountered a hastily organized defense force put together by LtCol. Ernest Fry, the regimental executive officer. This *ad hoc* group was composed of men of Headquarters and Service Company, members of the 3rd Motor Transport Battalion, artillery men of the 12th Marines, and any other noncombat Marines who could be rounded up. Despite its success in providing a defense of the headquarters area, it could not prevent numerous Japanese, some

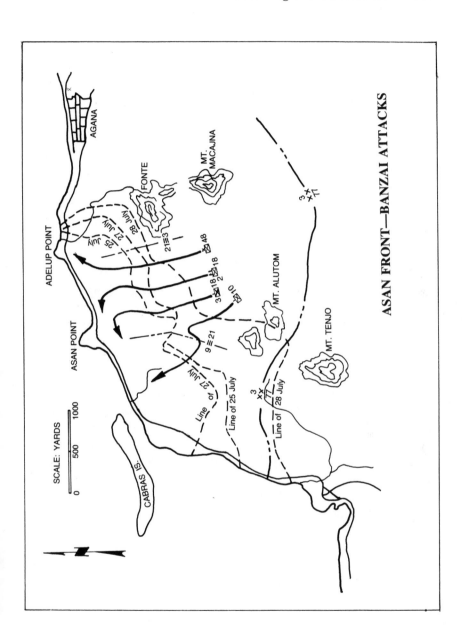

ASAN FRONT—BANZAI ATTACKS

drawn from demolition units, from breaking into the division's hospital area at about 0630. The doctors had already ordered the badly wounded evacuated to the beach. Doctors, corpsmen, and the less seriously wounded armed themselves with whatever weapons were available and beat back the Japanese attacks until they were relieved by two companies of pioneers commanded by LtCol. George Van Orden. They mopped up the area and pursued the remaining Japanese up the Nidual River Valley. They were aided in part by the Japanese who began to commit suicide in a way not observed before by the Marines. Soldiers would take off their helmets, place a primed grenade on top of their head, replace the helmet, and wait stoically for the inevitable.[31] The Marines were halted by a small force of Japanese who with machine guns raked the flanks of the 9th and 21st Marines and threatened the 21st's CP. This Japanese strongpoint was not captured until early afternoon of the 26th by a company of 1/9 led by Maj. Harold Boehm. This action cleared the danger to the CP and forced the few Japanese still alive into the firing area of 3/21.[32]

The CP and batteries of the 105mm howitzers of the 12th Marines, the division's artillery, were located in the vicinity of the Asan River. There were a large number of caves in the cliffs bordering the river directly ahead of the Marine artillery units. On the night of 24–25 July, Japanese, many with twenty pounds of TNT strapped to them with ready detonators, had crept down the valley and taken shelter in these caves. At dusk on the 25th, hours before the general attack further east, these soldiers began to fire randomly at the Marines, probably to cover the movement toward the beach of most of the demolition carriers who had lain hidden for almost 24 hours. A grenade duel followed, but the main attack against the artillery defensive perimeter did not materialize until daybreak of the 26th when a concerted attack against the CP and all three battalions was launched. The Japanese drove the Marines back, captured one machine gun, and got within ten yards of the Fire Direction Center. A counterattack pushed the Japanese back, recaptured the gun, and killed seventeen of the attackers along the river. Patrols later that day killed over fifty more Japanese in the vicinity and drove the survivors away from the artillery areas into the positions of the 3rd Marines where most were killed.[33]

One of the most bizarre incidents on Guam occurred to a young artilleryman of the 12th Marines during this portion of the Japanese attack. One reporter related the event:

> He had crawled into a cave to take cover from the Japanese shells. He had gone to sleep. He had awakened to find some-one sitting on him. He felt for his carbine. Someone was sitting on that. There were perhaps a half-dozen of these intruders. He could hear the clinking of their canteens and smell the sour reek of *saki*, could hear the soft jabbering of their voices, could feel on the man astride him the hard round shape of a magnetic mine.
>
> A squad of Japanese infiltrators had crept into his cave and were sitting there awaiting the daylight—when they would depart to attack the Marine guns.[34]

When the Japanese finally left the cave the Marine scrambled out to rejoin his unit, but the strain of spending the night with his unwelcomed guests had proved too much. He was evacuated that day as a mental patient.[35]

Some of the fiercest fighting during the *banzai* attack had occurred on the extreme left of the Marines' beachhead. The Japanese 48th Brigade made seven separate attacks against the positions of the 3rd Marines. The most vulnerable position belonged to Colonel Cushman's 2/9 which had been sent to reinforce the weakened 3rd Marines. Most of these men had already had an exhausting day and were dangerously low on ammunition. Tanks had been sent forward with ammunition but, hampered by the terrain and bad weather, these had not arrived until after the main attack had begun. Word finally arrived at the forward CPs that ammunition had arrived. After the second of the seven *banzai* attacks Maj. Fraser West of Company G took a number of men to the rear areas and they struggled back with boxes of grenades and ammunition which were distributed just before the Japanese launched a further assault. West recalled another reason for the Marines' successful defense of their position:

When I went down to get the ammunition from the tanks I called for naval gunfire support. Some commander on some ship wanted to know who I was and I told him. "You're breaking security," he said. I yelled back, "Security hell, you S.O.B., I'm up here and I need support. I want to get through to my battalion commander. His name is Robert Cushman." He said, "But you're giving away your position." To which I replied, "The hell I am, they know exactly where we are!"

I couldn't get through on any other circuit and the Japs had infiltrated and cut our land lines and our own radios, the batteries had run down as usual. But I brought in naval fire as close as probably any of that type of support that was done during the war and the star shells illuminated our whole front.[36]

To the right of West's company was that of Capt. Louis Wilson, a future Commandant who had already received three minor wounds during the fighting of the previous day. Returning to the action, he led the fierce hand-to-hand fighting that raged in front of his company for the rest of the night. At one time he ran through a hail of enemy fire to rescue a wounded Marine. Later in the morning he led a counterattack which wrested strategic high ground from a numerically superior Japanese force. For these actions Wilson was later awarded the Medal of Honor.[37] Although perhaps not as conspicuous as Captain Wilson's exploits, every Marine caught by the Japanese attacks in the 3rd Marine sector fought ferociously, and the 48th Japanese Brigade not only failed to break through, they left behind over 950 dead by the time the fighting subsided early in the morning of 26 July.

Daybreak partially revealed the carnage left from the previous night's savage fighting. The remnants of Takashina's attacking force were either behind the Marine lines wandering aimlessly around or they were in full retreat across the Fonte Plateau or had reached the safety of the dug-in positions on the Orote Peninsula. Takashina had committed all the troops available to him and had lost most of them. The exact number of killed would never be known, but the Marines placed the Japanese losses for the few hours fighting at over 3,500. Those Japanese who had successfully penetrated the Marine positions and were still there early in the morning were pathetic groups. Leaderless, they appeared not to know what to do. Their plight was captured by a commentator who wrote:

> A fine example of the utter futility of the whole business is furnished by the force which had captured nearly all the mortars of the 21st Marines. They did not turn these mortars against us, although plenty of ammunition was ready at hand. Evidently it never entered their heads to destroy the weapons to prevent their recapture. They simply dug in where they were. A few more temperamental characters practiced that odd ritual, the fine points of which Americans have never been able fully to appreciate: saving their faces by blowing out their intestines. Crouching in their foxholes, the rest awaited abjectly in the cheerless dawn the death they had sought so eagerly in the flaming hours of darkness. They were obliged presently by a detachment from Headquarters Company, made up of cooks, clerks, MPs and combat correspondents.[38]

While General Takashina was moving his headquarters from the Fonte area and trying to regroup what was left of his forces, General Geiger and his staff were afraid that the Japanese commander would launch still more follow-up attacks. Although General Turnage was elated by the night's victory, he too expected a continuation of the Japanese offensive. He established an emergency reserve force commanded by Colonel Van Orden composed of service troops which were to occupy a secondary line of defense in case of further breakthroughs. The casualty figures for the division during the period 25–27 July were 166 killed and 645 wounded, most of those occurring during the *banzai* charge.[39] Some Marine units, however, had taken the brunt of the attack. Sergeant Josephy in his account of the attack on the 21st Marines noted:

> As the units reformed their lines it was found that B Company [1/21] had almost been wiped out during the night. Captain

Beck, who had a bad time himself a little to the right of Lt. Mulcahy, discovered that he only had 18 men left out of an initial landing strength of 217.[40]

General Geiger who had moved Corps CP ashore at 1300 on 26 July decided to proceed cautiously and wait to see what the Japanese were planning. While the mopping up of Japanese stragglers was going on, the higher command was preparing for a watch-and-wait policy for the 3rd Marine Division. The division tightened its perimeter by pulling back almost a mile in the 9th Marines' area. Another battalion in Corps reserve was ordered to the Piti Naval Yard to be ready to check any possible break-through in that vicinity. Barbed wire was used where possible to improve defensive positions. From these actions it is obvious that the American senior commanders did not know the extent of damage that the Japanese had done to themselves.

The position of the Japanese on 26 July was summed up later by LtCol. Hideyuki Takeda, a member of Takashina's staff who survived the battle for Guam. He recalled that the conclusion drawn by Takashina on the morning of 26 July was that it was no longer possible to expel the American forces from the island and therefore the sole purpose of the coming struggle should be to inflict as much damage as possible on them as they moved into the interior. The chief reasons for this estimate were:

1. The loss of commanders in the counterattack of 25 July, when up to 95 percent of the officers (commissioned officers) of the sector defense forces died, had weakened the units.

2. The personnel of each counterattacking unit were greatly decreased, and companies were reduced to several men.

3. The large casualties caused a great drop in the morale of the survivors.

4. Over 90 percent of the weapons were destroyed and combat ability greatly decreased.[41]

The fighting on Guam would continue and both sides would take casualties for months, but from a strategic viewpoint, the outcome had been decided. The loss of nearly four thousand men during the abortive night attack had so weakened the Japanese that they could not take full advantage of the defensive possibilities of the interior regions of the island. Takashina had only made the ultimate American victory easier.

CHAPTER VII
The Breakout

In contrast to certain of the earlier phases of the Guam operation, the next forward moves against the enemy were carefully calculated. General Geiger resisted the temptation to begin an immediate major offensive to secure the waist of the island, as had been suggested by his superior, Gen. H. M. Smith. He and his staff were partially aware of the great damage done to the Japanese during their two *banzai* attacks, but he also knew that his opponent, General Takashina, still held strategically important areas from which to threaten the two beachheads. Weighing this and the losses sustained by the Marines, he decided not to commit most of the units of the 77th Division until the Orote Peninsula had been captured, the Fonte Plateau taken, and a definite linkage made between all units along the FBL.

The most important immediate task confronting Geiger was the destruction of the Japanese defenses on the Orote Peninsula. By this time the 77th Division had taken over the eastern facing positions of the Marine brigade, thus allowing General Shepherd to use both of his regiments against the Japanese fixed defenses. After reorganizing his units, Shepherd was prepared to attack at 0700 on 26 July with the 22nd Marines on the right and the 4th on the left. Geiger had ordered all artillery units to give precedence to fire missions on Orote and this the Marines received. Fifteen minutes before jump-off time, the Army's 902nd Artillery began firing the first of over 1,000 rounds in deep support. They were later joined by Marine and Army artillery, firing close support. By the last day of the offensive, guns of two Marine pack howitzer battalions, six batteries of Army 105mm howitzers, three Army 155mm batteries, and two 155mm batteries from Corps, as well as naval guns, were firing into designated targets and targets of opportunity in every part of the peninsula.[1]

Col. Merlin Schneider's 22nd Marines, despite the help received from the continuous artillery and mortar support, found it very difficult to advance because most of their front was a wide mangrove swamp inland from Apra Harbor. Their advance was thus channelled mainly along the Agat-Sumay Road where the Japanese could zero in their own mortars and artillery. Thus although the left flank units of the 22nd reached a major road junction (RJ15) by nightfall, most of the regiment was still east of the swamp. By contrast, the 4th Marines had met very light resistance and could advance rapidly, held back only by the necessity of keeping flank contact with the 22nd. Despite this concern, a gap did open between the regiments and LtCol. Shapley, commanding the 4th, requested that his unit shift to the right and take over part of the line assigned to the 22nd. General Shepherd agreed and the 4th's front then was extended as far as the Agat-Sumay Road.

In many ways the fighting on 27 July was a repetition of the previous day as Marines of the 22nd continued to struggle forward. Sgt. Thomas O'Neil remembered that day:

> Rain greeted us at dawn. We had left our foxholes because they were filling with water. Sitting around for orders to move out when I suddenly heard this shell coming in. There was a loud shudder. We hit the deck out of reflex, with shrapnel as thick as rain, we went for our holes, water or no water. We finally got under way. The site of yesterday's action was passed without any trouble, the area was flat with dense undergrowth. We of the first were on the right flank next to the swamps. The resistance was picking up. The area was full of pillboxes and bunkers, arranged in depth. It was a yard by yard fight.[2]

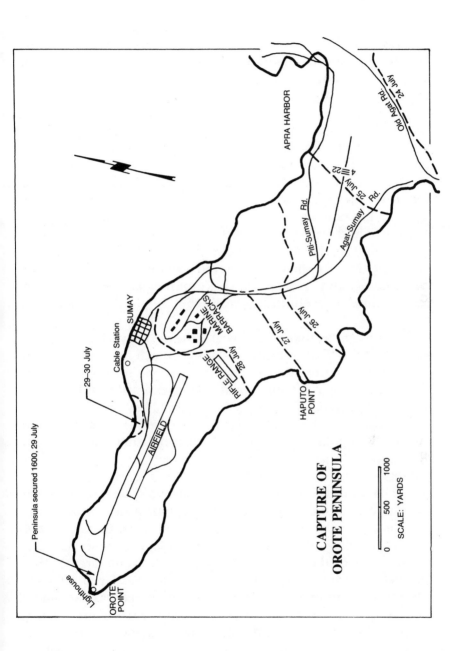

APRA HARBOR

Old Agat Rd.
24 July

25 July

Piti-Sumay Rd.

Agat-Sumay Rd.

22

26 July

SUMAY

Cable Station

MARINE
BARRACKS

27 July

29-30 July

RIFLE RANGE

28 July

HAPUTO
POINT

AIRFIELD

Peninsula secured 1600, 29 July

Lighthouse

OROTE
POINT

CAPTURE OF
OROTE PENINSULA

0   500   1000

SCALE: YARDS

At times the fire from the Japanese mortars and machine guns became so heavy that the riflemen were forced to withdraw, bring up tanks, and rake the contested area with 75mm and .50–caliber fire. Then the Marines would attempt to advance again. Slowly the Japanese were pushed back and by mid-afternoon the 22nd had broken out into the open. However, they confronted a new defense line of pillboxes and dugouts on a ridge just east of their goal, the old Marine barrack area.

The 4th Marines during the day had relatively easy going, but keyed their advance to that of the 22nd. By nightfall the forward position of the 22nd Marines was approximately one-quarter mile short of the barracks. There had been signs during the fighting of the late afternoon of a breakdown in Japanese discipline. Marines had encountered a number of individual suicide attacks and just before dark a group of Japanese broke and ran, an unusual event in the deadly fighting in the Pacific up to that time.

These signs were confirmed early the next day when resistance in front of the 22nd Marines collapsed, which led to the capture of the barracks ground by noon. They pressed on to the outskirts of Sumay. The riflemen halted there while demolition teams searched the ruins of the town for mines. They found and detonated many aerial bombs fused as mines as well as regular pressure mines. By nightfall of the 28th, the Marines controlled the town of Sumay. All that would be needed in this area was to rout out pockets of Japanese who had been bypassed as well as some who were holed up in caves in cliffs along the road west of the town.

The 4th Marines, whose forward movement earlier had hardly been contested by the Japanese, now found, on the 28th, their way impeded by dense undergrowth. The Japanese had constructed one of the strongest defensive lines in the area of their advance, comprising a number of dugouts and large pillboxes. After taking a number of casualties, Colonel Shapley asked General Shepherd, who was on an inspection tour of the front, for tank support. Two platoons of Marine mediums were ordered to back up the two assault battalions and Shepherd requested General Bruce to send some of his Shermans. Unfortunately, at this time the Army had landed only its light tanks. However, five of these and later two Shermans which had just landed from the 706th were detached to aid the Marine attack. The tank-infantry teams began the systematic destruction of the Japanese strongpoints at 1530 and forced the by-now dispirited defenders back to a ridge east of the airfield just before dark.

General Shepherd sensed that the end was near for the Japanese on Orote and he brought to bear at dawn of the 29th the heaviest bombardment in his brigade zone since W day. Air strikes began the show, followed by bombardment by attached and supporting land artillery, augmented by the fire of eight naval vessels standing just offshore. When the Marines attacked at 0800 they were supported directly by all the tanks that had been available the previous day plus a number of the Army's M–10 tank destroyers. The airfield was captured shortly after noon and the 4th Marines pressed on to the end of the peninsula. Many of the surviving Japanese soldiers began to commit suicide, some using hand grenades while some slashed their throats. A few attempted to save their lives by swimming to the ruins of old Fort Santa Cruz located on the coral reef in the middle of Apra Harbor. They were mercilessly killed by men on board LVT(A)s patrolling the water adjacent to the peninsula. On the following day, 1/22 and 2/22 were ordered into Corps reserve southeast of Agat while the remaining battalion cleared the last resistance on the peninsula—the caves west of Sumay.

The reduction of the Orote Peninsula had taken four days of hard fighting and had cost the brigade 115 killed, 721 wounded, and 38 missing.[3] No accurate account of Japanese losses during this period could be made, but it is certain that most of Commander Tamai's force of over 2,500 men died either in the abortive *banzai* attack or in the defensive battles that followed.

The conquest of Orote was celebrated on the afternoon of 29 July when Admiral Spruance and Generals H. M. Smith, Geiger, Larsen, Shepherd, and an honor guard of 2/22 witnessed the raising of the flag on the grounds of the old Marine compound. Addressing his men who had paid dearly for the victory, General Shepherd said:

On this hallowed ground, your officers and men of the First
Marine Brigade have avenged the loss of our comrades who
were overcome by a numerically superior enemy three days
after Pearl Harbor. Under our flag this island again stands
ready to fulfill its destiny as an American fortress in the
Pacific.[4]

During his inspection trip of 28–29 July, General Smith once
more pressed Geiger to begin his general offensive to bring the
fighting to a quick conclusion. He had been even more critical
four days earlier when the 3rd Division had only a precarious
hold on its beachhead, and Smith had sent a despatch to Geiger
after returning to Tinian urging more offensive action. Ignoring
the fact that the 3rd Division had been heavily engaged for two
days, had taken the Fonte Plateau, and finally reached the FBL,
Smith "thought that the time had come for a general movement
to capture the remainder of the island."[5] He stopped short of
more direct interference in Geiger's plans, perhaps realizing that
those called for a forward movement as soon as the gains of the
past few days had been consolidated. In later years Smith, ignoring
the facts of the situation after W day, criticized the 3rd Division
and by implication Generals Geiger and Turnage for the slowness
of their advance. Perhaps understanding that he had done an
injustice to his old friend, he specifically requested that all his
criticisms of Geiger be omitted in the official history of the Marianas
campaign.[6]

Any criticism of the performance of the 3rd Division during
that period after the *banzai* attack could only be made by someone
completely unfamiliar with what had been accomplished and
against what odds. It was absolutely necessary to reorganize the
front-line units and give the riflemen some rest after the desperate
fighting during the early morning hours of 26 July. Geiger and
Turnage also believed that the Japanese would launch further
attacks, particularly during the night of 27 July, and all units
were ordered to prepare for a possible repetition of the previous
night. These did not materialize; there were only a few minor
incidents of infiltration and these were dealt with quickly and
efficiently. Bolstered by the relative lack of Japanese offensive

operations, General Turnage and his staff planned a major assault against the Japanese defense line stretching from Fonte in the north to Mt. Tenjo in the south. The assault was to begin at 0900 on 27 July.

The plan called for the 9th Marines to hold their positions in the south while the major attack was carried out by the 21st Marines in the center and the 3rd Marines reinforced with Cushman's attached 2/9 who would attempt to capture the Fonte Plateau. The 21st supported by tanks began their attack promptly with three battalions abreast and the immediate objective of the high ground on which the radio towers and main north-south power line was located. The 2nd Battalion on the left was held up by a large swampy area and then Japanese machine-gun fire pinned down the unit 200 yards short of the towers. The supporting tanks moved around the swampy region and continued to pump round after round into the area of greatest resistance. By late afternoon, the 2nd was able to move up to a defensive position just short of the power lines.

The 1st Battalion had even a more difficult day. They were halted by concentrated fire from the Japanese who had dug in along the slopes of a small hill. These tenacious defenders could not be dislodged from their vantage point by the combined weight of air attacks, artillery, and tank fire. On the regiment's right flank the 3rd Battalion moved rapidly forward against very little resistance but was held up because of the need to keep flank contact on their left. Thus in the central sector of the 3rd Division front very little had been accomplished during the 27th, and the 21st Marines were still a considerable distance away from the FBL.

Much the same could be said of the main attack against the Japanese defending the Fonte Plateau. Only moderate resistance was met by 2/3 as it bypassed a number of enemy strongpoints which were left to be neutralized by later units. Although they very probably could have advanced further, they were ordered at mid-afternoon to hold up at the power line because of the trouble Cushman's 2/9 was having advancing to the plateau. That unit, which had the most difficult assignment for the day, began the attack at 0930 and was immediately hit by friendly fire from both artillery and air strikes. The Marines, forced back to cover, took over an hour to reorganize, but by noon they had taken all the ground they had given up voluntarily the day before. All companies were committed and by mid-afternoon they, too, had reached the objective of the power lines, having beaten off an ill-considered small *banzai* attack. By nightfall, although little territory had been taken during the day, the two regiments involved in the assault reached the last-phase line before the crest of the ridge.

General Geiger targeted not only the capture of the Fonte Plateau as the objective for 28 July, but also to have the other units advance all along the 3rd Division line to the FBL. This was achieved with little difficulty in all areas except in that part of the front facing the 9th Marines and on the far left in the 3rd Marine sector. The 9th Marines, now fully up to strength with the Army's 3/307th replacing Cushman's battalion, had to attack the Mt. Chachao–Mt. Alutom line. Here there was some heavy fighting, but by mid-afternoon they had reached their initial objectives and 3/9 began the assault on Mt. Chachao. The debilitating effects of the earlier *banzai* charges on Japanese resistance was clearly shown in this operation. The defenders possessed a set of potentially strong defensive positions on the mountain. In addition to controlling the high ground, which forced the Marines to advance directly uphill through rough brush-covered terrain, they had constructed a concrete emplacement on the summit. This was supported by foxholes and covered by machine-gun positions dug into the cliff. Despite all this, the men of Maj. Donald Hubbard's 3rd Battalion under the protective blanket of artillery fire and supported by tanks took the crest with very little difficulty.

On the extreme left of the division, 2/3 and 2/9 continued their advance toward the high ground of the Fonte Plateau. In contrast to the previous day's fighting, most units met little resistance and advanced to their initial objective lines overlooking the Fonte River. However, in front of 2/9 was a large depression which the Marines named "the pit." It was roughly circular with very steep sides in which the Japanese had dug caves. The pit proved very difficult to take since even small patrols trying to work their way down the declivity came under fire from many directions. The two flanking companies of 2/9 had little difficulty in their advance, but Company G which was directly in front of the pit was stopped cold. This company had already sustained very heavy casualties, particularly among the officers, having lost three company commanders since the landings; the fourth, Capt. Francis Fagan, was the only officer left in the entire company. The men of G Company found that they could not move forward, and in the early afternoon had to beat off a strong counterattack which almost broke through the right flank. Although this threat was contained, it was obvious that the Japanese in the pit had to be blasted out before there could be any thought of further forward movement for G Company. General Turnage approved Colonel Cushman's request for a delay in the attack and the remainder of the day was devoted to bringing up the necessary firepower to neutralize the Japanese defenders. Heavy demolition charges were prepared and extra flamethrowers and rocket launchers were shifted to the pit area. Zones of fire were established for the inside of the pit and tanks were moved up. Thus prepared, the men of 2/9 waited for the next day, confident that with all that firepower they would soon be able to overrun the pit.

At daybreak of 29 July, all the weapons Cushman had brought up the day before opened up a massive volume of criss-crossing fire directed at the Japanese in the pit. Assault teams then moved systematically to kill any Japanese left alive in the caves. Surprisingly, this operation was carried out without a Marine casualty. A later body count showed that the advance of G Company had been held up by over 50 Japanese.[7] Once the pit had been cleared it was a simple matter for all units in the 3rd Marine sector to move up to the FBL. The cost of breaking out of the narrow beachhead had been high, particularly for 2/9. Two of its rifle companies had taken 75 percent casualties and the remaining company had lost over 50 percent.[8]

General Takashina had belatedly recognized the importance of holding the Fonte Plateau and had resisted the Marine attacks ferociously. He had committed two battalions of his rapidly shrinking force in support of those troops already there. He had launched a total of eleven separate counterattacks, none of which seriously threatened the Marine positions. In this battle of attrition the Japanese had lost men who could not be replaced. In total, Takashina's dwindling force had been reduced by approximately 800 men in the defense of the Fonte highlands.[9] The 21st and 9th Marines resumed their advance on 29 July and encountered only sporadic Japanese fire before reaching the FBL. Most of the rest of that day was given over to consolidating these newly won positions and mopping up the few Japanese who had been bypassed by the forward movement.

The Army's 77th Division had seen little action after their landing. General Bruce in a letter to his wife pinpointed the most annoying factors for him up to this point when he wrote:

> We are living "dug in" in the side of a muddy hill where tropical rains make everything "gushy goo-goo." We wake up in the morning covered with mud but thankful to be alive with the promiscuous sniping that goes on by infiltrating Japs. I say "we" advisedly—I am referring to front line troops more than to my own CP. . . .[10]

Despite the weather conditions, the 77th and its commander were anxious to be moving and were in excellent condition. They had taken few casualties and had been able to bring in many of their most needed supplies. Bruce had the 305th and 306th on line by 26 July and in the next two days he cautiously extended the 306th's front almost a mile past RJ370, while the 305th moved farther south on the division's right flank. The 3rd Battalion of his reserve 307th had been sent by General Geiger to the 9th Marines zone to replace Cushman's 2/9 which had been shifted to the Fonte sector. Other elements of the Army division had also been moved to support the Marine attacks on the Orote Peninsula. This included some light and medium tanks and two battalions, 306th and 902nd, of field artillery. Most of the division simply waited in their dug-in muddy positions for the signal to attack across the waist of the island. Bruce already knew that in the final phase of the operation the 77th would hold the right flank in the drive to the north. The 3rd Marine Division would be on their left while the 1st Marine Provisional Brigade would have the relatively easy task of cleaning up any surviving Japanese in the southern part of the island.

Before Geiger would commit his two divisions to a northern advance he wished to determine whether Takashina had left a significant number of defenders in the south. General Bruce suggested that he be allowed to send a number of patrols south to see just how well that hilly, overgrown part of the island was defended. Geiger approved the plan and naval and air units were ordered to cease fire in the sectors where the 77th's patrols would be operating. On 28 July, five patrols each comprising five men and a Guamanian guide moved into the questionable areas east and south of the bridgehead lines. Able and Baker patrols left RJ370 to explore the eastern coastline, while Charlie, Dog, and Easy left the Mt. Alifan region. Charlie's objective was the area toward Mt. Lamlam; Dog's was the area between, and the coastline below Facpi Point; and Easy was to work along the coast toward Umatac. Members of Able patrol had to turn back because of illness which had affected most of the men, but all the others carried out their orders and reported that they had seen evidence of very few Japanese, and the Chamorros whom they encountered told them that all Japanese main units had moved north. This information was further confirmed by two more patrols sent out on 30 and 31 July, each covering areas not observed by the earlier sweeps. General Geiger and his staff had suspected as much, but they could now breathe easier knowing that their coming offensive would not be threatened from the south. Elements of the Provisional Brigade were given the task of taking care of the few Japanese left in southern Guam.[11]

While the 3rd Marine Division was struggling up the slopes to the Fonte Plateau, the Army's 305th was sending patrols out in the direction of Mt. Tenjo. They reported that there did not appear to be much Japanese activity near or on the mountain. General Bruce believed that the Japanese had all but evacuated this key defensive position and therefore asked and received permission to scout the mountain further and at his discretion to occupy its crest if that could be done without heavy loss. Acting on this, Company A of 3/305 reached the top of Mt. Tenjo at 0830 on 28 July without opposition. Later in the day, 2/307 took over the defenses in this sector, and by mid-afternoon tied into the 3rd Marine Division on their left. Thus by nightfall Marine and Army troops all along the line had reached the FBL.[12]

Phase One of the Guam operation was now complete. The second stage, the occupation of the north, was ready to begin, but the cost of the week's fighting had been heavy. Casualties by 1800 of 28 July totaled 5,733, with 513 killed in action. The Marine units had suffered almost all the losses. The Periodic Report of III Amphibious Corps reflected this when it reported the combat efficiency of the Provisional Brigade at 75 percent, the 3rd Marine Division at 80 percent, and the 77th Division as excellent. Although it was impossible to confirm the actual Japanese losses, the known enemy dead were 4,192.[13] Surprisingly, by this time over fifty prisoners had been taken, a number that would not rapidly increase as the fighting continued. Although more Japanese recognized the hopelessness of their situation, they preferred to die rather than surrender.

The story of the taking of one Japanese prisoner at the close of the fighting on Orote indicates clearly the Japanese soldier's devotion to orders from a superior. This prisoner was a "forlorn scrimp of a man dressed in tattered blouse and breeches much too large for him." But he seemed at ease and not unhappy at being taken. He had not attempted suicide nor asked for a weapon to commit *hara-kiri*. A Marine interpreter quizzed him and the following conversation ensued.

"Why did you surrender?"

"My commanding officer told us to fight to the last man."

The Marine's eyebrows rose.

"Well?"

The Japanese soldier's eyebrows also rose—in wounded innocence—and he exclaimed:

"I am the last man."[14]

In the final phases of the battle for Guam the Japanese had to operate with only a small fraction of their officer personnel. Most had been lost leading the futile *banzai* attacks against the Marine lines along the northern and southern beachheads. This included all the senior officers. Colonel Suenaga, commander of the 38th Regiment, had been killed on the night of 21 July leading an attack on the Agat beachhead. Colonel Ohashi had personally led one of the counterattacks against the 3rd Marine Division during the night of 25–26 July. Colonel Ogata was killed defending the Orote Peninsula, and his successor, Commander Tamai, was lost during the futile attempt to break out through the Marine brigade lines. The commander of the Japanese forces in front of the 3rd Marine Division and second in command to Takashina, MajGen. Shigematsu, was also killed along with his staff at his command post in the aftermath of the great *banzai* attack on 26 July. Takashina himself commanded the defense of the Fonte Plateau and when that position was lost, he ordered the bulk of the survivors to assemble north of the Agana River preliminary to withdrawal to the Ordot area. He was in the process of joining them in the early afternoon of 28 July when he was hit by Marine machine-gun fire and died immediately. This meant that only one senior Japanese officer was left and that was General Obata, the overall commander of the defenses of the Marianas, who had been stranded on Guam when Saipan was invaded. He would now direct the final stand of the Japanese on Guam.[15]

From his command post near Yigo, General Obata ordered a general withdrawal in the direction of Mt. Santa Rosa and planned to establish two strong blocking positions, one near Finegayan and the other near Barrigada Village. He would not seriously contest the ground between the expanded beachhead and this area where he planned to make his last stand. Obata's main force was composed primarily of remnants of the 29th Division, but contained many shattered units, a total number estimated by III Corps at the time to be 8,500 troops.[16] As events would later show, he still had a considerable number of tanks as well as small-caliber artillery. However, with his communications system almost completely destroyed, with most of his officers dead, and his units scattered throughout the central and northern sectors, there was no way he could utilize most of these men to conduct an orderly coordinated defense. The reality of Obata's defense was that the Army and Marines' advance would be impeded only by the terrain, the jungle-like growth, and by desperate individuals in a series of small unit delaying actions.

General Geiger could not know the true state of the Japanese defenses although the slackening of opposition and the body counts indicated that the Japanese had been seriously hurt. He and his divisional commanders had decided to advance cautiously in order to be prepared for any serious threats. Thus two days were spent reorganizing and resupplying the badly depleted 3rd Division units. Cushman's 2/9 which had sustained the most crippling losses was pulled out of the line entirely and went into division reserve. The 1st Marine Brigade moved to take over the southern sector of the 77th's position, while all Army units would ultimately be aligned to the east of the 3rd Marine Division for the main effort. It was planned that in the first period of the breakout the axis of the attack would be realigned from east to northeast. The 3rd Division had only to shift slightly to accomplish this, but the 77th had to first drive entirely across the waist of the island toward Pago Bay and then realign its regiments in order to take up its position for the move to the north. Ultimately the boundary between the two divisions ran almost down the center of the island. Tiyan airfield and Finegayan would be in the Marines' zone while Barrigada and Mt. Santa Rosa were to be the main Army objectives.

The Japanese continued to perform what to the attackers were acts which in most cases were not only unexpected, but irrational. Some of these, as in the earlier displays of bravado before and during the *banzai* attacks, could be attributed to too much liquor. But others demanded organization and presumably a sober mind to plan the event. Perhaps most bizarre during this lull in the fighting was the formal dress parade conducted in the ruins of Agana in view of the Marines' positions on the high ground overlooking what was left of the town. Dressed in full combat uniform with bayonets and swords polished, the Japanese without haste executed their review. By the time the Marines noticed this strange show and called down an artillery concentration, the parade had broken up and the men had dispersed.[17]

All during the night of 30–31 July the Navy, Corps, and Division artillery fired continuously, aiming for road junctions and possible concentration points. Then at 0630 the Marines began their advance. The 3rd Marines on the left who moved along and parallel to the main road met only sporadic fire from isolated Japanese. Most of the casualties they suffered were from mines the Japanese had planted in the roadway and along the line of advance. Within four hours they entered Agana and by noon the entire town was under Marine control. The Japanese had abandoned the town, leaving behind only a few wounded in the rubble of what had once been the major town of Guam where over half the pre-war population had lived. The Church of San Antonio, the Cathedral, Parochial Hall, the Bishop's Palace, and all the magnificent government buildings had been destroyed, most by the pre-invasion bombardment. Robert Martin, a newspaper correspondent, recorded his first impressions of Guam's capital on 7 August. He reported:

The cathedral and churches were gutted by shells and fires. It was not wanton destruction but incidental to the overall necessity of neutralizing Agana, which the Japs had made into one of their chief supply bivouac areas.

Power lines were stripped, but the steel poles reached gauntly toward the sky. Virtually every building was a shambles, most of them beyond recognition. The coconut trees which once shaded the streets had broken like snapped twigs withered by fires, while debris littered every foot of the once beautiful Plaza Espagna in the city's heart.[18]

Agana was merely the model for the rest of the island where 80 percent of all the buildings were destroyed. The majority of those which escaped destruction were in the southern part of the island which was spared most of the fighting.

The 21st Marines in the center of the sector moved rapidly ahead during the morning, with the 2nd and 3rd battalions in the assault. There was only one brief firefight on the left when a few Japanese from a concrete pillbox held up the advance briefly. By 1400 the regiment reached its initial objective line. On the right of the 3rd Division line, the 9th Marines also advanced with little opposition. That regiment's forward movement was slowed only because of the worsening terrain and increasingly heavy undergrowth. A few Japanese who had been left behind to defend some supply dumps near Ordot caused a problem: they occasioned a brief battle and later a counterattack led by two tanks, until they were knocked out by a bazooka-man. By mid-afternoon the 9th also reached its objective line and was tied in with the Army's 307th on the right. However, the dense undergrowth prevented similar contact with the 21st. A further advance was approved by General Turnage later in the afternoon and two motorized patrols from the Reconnaissance Company were sent ahead of the 3rd Marines preparatory to the next day's action. In all, the 3rd Division moved ahead almost three miles during the day.[19]

Meanwhile, the 77th Division had begun its drive across the waist of the island. The 306th remained anchored to the FBL in the division's southern sector while the 305th and 307th struck out eastward in a column of battalions toward Pago Bay. No enemy resistance was encountered until late in the afternoon when Company I, 3/305 was fired upon by a few Japanese who made a desultory defense of a supply dump near Yona. The speed of the Army's advance was slowed only by the terrain as the infantrymen had to traverse very rough country covered with underbrush which forced them to climb over hills, scale cliffs, and descend into narrow valleys. Much of this area was perfect for at least a temporary defense, but it was obvious that the Japanese had no troops to spare for any such holding actions. The division historian recalled the experiences of one infantryman on that day who later wrote:

> The distance across the island is not far, as the crow flies, but unluckily we can't fly. The nearest I came to flying was while descending the slippery side of a mountain in a sitting position. . . . After advancing a few yards you find that the [bolt] handle of the machine gun on your shoulder, your pack and shovel, canteens, knife, and machete all stick out

at right angles and are as tenacious in their grip on the surrounding underbrush as a dozen grappling hooks. . . . The flies and mosquitos have discovered your route of march and have called up all the reinforcements including the underfed and undernourished who regard us as nothing but walking blood banks. We continue to push on. . . .[20]

By early afternoon the terrain had become so difficult that not even jeeps could follow the infantry.

General Landrum, then a battalion commander, confirmed the difficulty of movement and also recalled a number of other noncombat problems which plagued the troops not only that day, but in the ensuing drive to the north. There were wild rats and a special variety of large frogs, one of which woke Landrum by jumping up and down on his head as he attempted to sleep in a foxhole. The climate on Guam was excellent for frogs since it rained almost every day. When the weather cleared, it soon became hot and humid. Mosquitos were also a major problem. In places they attacked in droves. A large number of men eventually contracted dengue fever despite taking measures against insects such as oiling their exposed skin and using the ever-present mud to cover face and hands. Perhaps the most pressing problem had to do with the difficulty of bringing up supplies to the advancing units. Water, particularly, was in short supply. Water points with 500–gallon tanks were established as far forward as possible, but the reality was that the majority of the men had to ration the water in their canteens very carefully. Landrum recalled:

I can remember it was damned hot and we never had enough water at first. We were taking water out of seeps in the hillsides and putting halazone tablets in it. We were short of water— our logistics failed us. Cutting across the island we didn't get water for 2½ days. After we turned up the east coast after crossing the island and cleared the transverse road which crossed the island then we got water from that vicinity.[21]

Despite the problems of terrain, the 77th had almost reached Pago Bay by nightfall of 31 July. The next day two battalions of the 306th moved forward to the east coast and the other two regiments realigned the axis of their advance parallel to the coast. The 307th was in the interior adjacent to the dividing line with the Marines, while the 305th occupied the territory to the east. By noon the 307th reached and secured the all important Agana–Pago Bay Road. General Bruce asked and received permission from Corps to begin using that part of the road to the west in the 3rd Marine Division sector in order to bring up badly needed supplies, particularly ammunition and water. From then on both divisions used this vital, although crowded, supply link. Despite the traffic jams on the road, trucks and artillery continued to move up during the night in order to better support the Army's attack on Barrigada. Especially important were the bulldozers which would be used to widen existing trails and cut new ones behind the advancing troops.

General Bruce was rightfully proud of the way his division had performed as he made clear in a letter composed for his wife later. He wrote:

You have probably read in the paper about our relatively rapid advance over very difficult mountain terrain, with heavy jungle growth in the river valley. Our division succeeded in crossing the island in one day, cutting it in two. . . . Have about got most of the division over the mountain by now except the rear elements that I intend to leave behind. It has been a battle not only against the enemy, whose resistance was relatively light, but a terrific battle against mud.[22]

All the advancing units had met Guamanians before. Some of these had hidden during the bombardments and fighting and others had volunteered to guide patrols into the densely overgrown southern areas. However, the first really large contingent of Guamanians encountered was during the late afternoon of 31 July when a patrol from Company L, 3/307, reached a large concentration camp near the village of Asinan. The Japanese civilian guards were only too happy to surrender and the infantrymen thus liberated an estimated 2,000 prisoners. They immediately began sharing their rations with the half-starved Guamanians. As soon as practicable, these men, women, and children were marched away to the refugee camp which had been set up under island command near Agat. As the fighting moved further north other smaller bands of Guamanians straggled back through the lines. Col. Coolidge recalled one group his battalion encountered:

Getting close to Barrigada village we ran into a large line of people and I understand they had come out of caves. They looked pretty bad and were eating food given them by American troops. A sadder lot I have never seen. Must have been a hundred of them. They passed by and were directed off to our left. They were dirty, they were hungry, and their clothes were filthy and wet as if they had come out of a damp crevice.[23]

By the evening of 2 August, General Geiger had both his assault divisions in position for the final offensive against Obata's hastily built up defenses in northern Guam. Despite the difficult terrain, the two regiments of the 77th had moved to the east coast more rapidly than was expected. This fact and the regiment's later performance earned the grudging respect of the Marines, some of whom would refer to it as the 77th MarDiv, an uncommon compliment for Army troops. Later an even more fulsome accolade was accorded the division by the irascible commander of the Marianas operation, Gen. H. M. Smith, who wrote that it showed a "combat efficiency to a degree one would expect only of veteran troops."[24] This was high praise from the commander who was still involved in controversy over his questionable dealings with the Army's 27th Division on Saipan. However, this time Smith was correct. The 77th, although not meeting the concerted resistance encountered earlier by the 3rd Marine Division, had shown that it could operate effectively as an equal partner with the Marine units.

Although one-third of the island was yet to be conquered and there were between eight and ten thousand Japanese defenders left, the outcome of the campaign was clear after the 77th

Division reached the east coast. It was only a matter of time before the entire island was under American control. Even the fighting tapered off in intensity as the near impossible terrain of northern Guam proved for most of the attackers to be the most difficult obstacle to surmount.

CHAPTER VIII
Conquest of the North

The final subjugation of northern Guam was in direct contrast to the earlier fighting and was not typical of most Marine operations in the Pacific. It was in fact a slow, cautious advance against only sporadic enemy opposition. In part these tactics were dictated by the terrain, but obviously General Geiger was aware of the numbers of men still available to his Japanese counterpart and was taking few chances. The Marine units had already taken very heavy losses; the island was, for all practical purposes, conquered. There was no reason to speed up the final phase; nothing could be gained by hurrying and it was possible that even major units could blunder into an ambush and lose not only time, but men.

The 3rd Marine Division was in a more favorable position than was the Army's 77th Division. Although the terrain was hilly and overgrown, the vegetation was not as thick as in the Army's zone of operations. Colonel Coolidge then commanding 1/307 recalled what it was like for the Army during the first few days of the northern operation:

We looked over a very flat valley and then we moved to the east side of the island and then we met some very dense growth. . . . We just got lost, we couldn't see where we were going. We had our compasses and that's the only thing that led us along, but to maintain contact on either side was impossible and I know the Marines were having the same trouble on my left. We really had no contact for almost 24 hours; we had voice contact between individuals but it was very hard to maintain even this between squads. We also had problems with our radios; we had very little use from them when we needed them badly.[1]

Coolidge's counterpart, Col. Landrum, commander of 1/305, had even more to say about the many difficulties presented by the geography. He also recalled the dense undergrowth, "towering trees up to a hundred feet tall," how there was little contact between units, and how they "never knew really where we were." He remembered the difficulty of preparing each night's defenses during the advance:

In some of those plateaus there was a few inches of topsoil over the underlying coral so that at night when you would dig in you were so damned tired you would throw up what dirt there was so that you would have something like a few inches deep slit trench. When we had our big counterattack of Japanese tanks, people went down into coral faster than you would think people could dig into coral that way.[2]

He also noted that the area was not totally covered by jungle, but was intersected by fairly large clearings. He recalled:

Our principal problem was that in these open spaces the Japanese could dig in to slow our advance. You couldn't see them. So we had tank destroyers break down the trails on both sides and had their guns traversed to the rear and this kept down the possibility of a real ambush.[3]

Despite these physical problems and the ever-present danger of individual Japanese, the advance of both divisions was never seriously checked. Certainly the Army and Marine troops confronted by the heat, mosquitos, rain, and the jungle-like terrain could not be expected to understand that these problems were even worse for the Japanese officers trying to establish some type of coordinated defense. LtCol. Takeda later stressed how much all these factors bothered them. He reported of the Japanese soldiers:

They were obliged to fight in the jungle where it was very hard to cooperate and communicate with each other. Therefore they could not fight satisfactorily to show their whole strength. And as American armored troops drove along the highways and trails in jungle to cut off the front line into several pockets, our troops were forced to be isolated.[4]

Before the drive to the north began, Admiral Conolly sent one battleship, two cruisers, and five destroyers to the eastern coastal waters to support the 77th Division and to prevent the Japanese insofar as possible from building up their defenses around Mt. Santa Rosa. An exact counterpart to this task group was retained along the west coast to support the 3rd Marine Division's drive to Finegayan. These ships joined Corps and Divisional artillery, particularly at night, in pounding areas near road junctions or other suspected concentration areas. One Japanese officer who survived the Guam operation recalled how effective was the artillery and air support given to the American infantrymen. He noted in an understated way:

The enemy airforce seeking our units during the daylight hours in the forest, bombed and strafed even a single soldier. During the night, the enemy naval units attempting to cut our communications were shelling our positions from all points of the perimeter of the island, thus impeding our operation activities to a great extent.[5]

Despite knowing the problems of the terrain, General Bruce sent his two regiments forward on 2 August with considerable optimism. In part this was due to the reports of a reconnaissance team of the 706th Tank Battalion which had gone through Barrigada Village and scouted as far ahead as the slopes of the mountain without meeting opposition. However, the gains made during the day did not meet Bruce's expectations: 3/307 ran headlong into a well-prepared Japanese machine-gun position near Barragida Well and was halted. A coordinated artillery, tank, and infantry attack at 1330 failed to dislodge the defenders. Elsewhere there was confusion as companies from the other two battalions of the 307th were mixed together. The 305th simply tried to keep contact between its units as they moved slowly through the underbrush on the right. At the close of the day, the 77th dug in short of all its objectives and counted 125 casualties for the short advances made.[6]

The next two days, however, were different. On 3 August the riflemen of the 307th, following a walking barrage, took the important Barrigada Well three hours after they began the attack. This important conquest all but ended the water problem for the division. The Japanese did not really contest the well or the village. Once again the undergrowth proved the major obstacle to any quick advance. Bothered only by snipers, 3/307 reached the top of Mt. Barrigada by mid-afternoon of 3 August. The following day was but a repetition of the slow methodical advance where the major problem continued to be the terrain, with a secondary one the need to maintain flank contact since all the commanders were worried that a Japanese counterattack would exploit any gaps in the line.

An unfortunate incident occurred on the division's left flank when a foul-up in signals between Marines of 2/9 and the 307th resulted in Army tankers mistaking the Marine positions for Japanese. Before the firing could be stopped the Marines had seven wounded from the friendly fire.[7] This was only one example of mistakes caused primarily by the heavy undergrowth which made it almost impossible at times to communicate with units more than a few feet away. Later, on 8 August, the Marines unknowingly reciprocated when their artillery firing in support of the 9th Marines ranged beyond the Marine limits so that the rounds fell on troops of 2/306 advancing along a trail near the boundary between the divisions. There were also a number of minor firefights generally at dusk or during the night between adjacent units who mistook each other for Japanese.[8]

It was obvious by this time that the Japanese had conceded most of the good defensive positions and withdrawn to their final bastion near Mt. Santa Rosa. The slow advance of the Army units

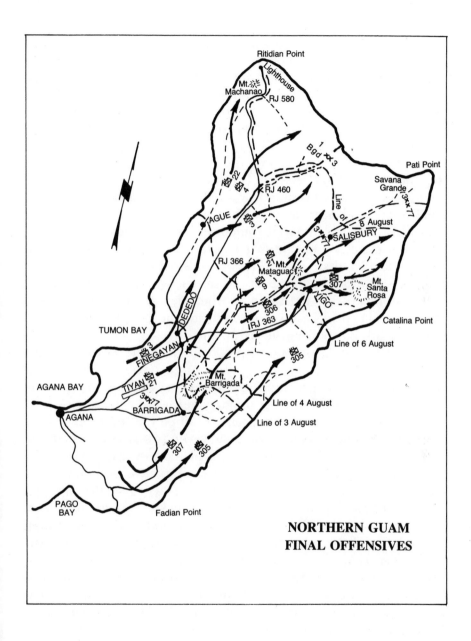

NORTHERN GUAM
FINAL OFFENSIVES

continued on 5 August over bad trails flanked by nearly impenetrable rain forest growth. The jungle in this area was the worst yet encountered on Guam. The various units of the 305th simply became lost following the winding trails made slippery by the rain which continued ceaselessly during the afternoon and evening. Many units had to resort to artillery to find their approximate location. They would set off flares and the artillery spotters would triangulate on them and radio the location to the infantry units. Regimental headquarters simply lost track of where their subordinate units were. By evening it was believed that advances of over 2,000 yards had been made with 2/305 in the center of the line and the other two battalions somewhere behind them, but higher headquarters could not be sure exactly where. In the advance of 5 August, all units of the 77th were also slowed by the fear of Japanese attacks and the reality of sniper fire. In all zones, tanks and tank destroyers led the way whenever possible. The 306th which had been in reserve pinched out the 307th and took up the left flank position in the Army line.

Troops of A Company of 1/305 holding the northern part of the perimeter on the night of 5 August paid the price for inadequate defense preparations. It was very difficult to dig deep foxholes in the coral so most infantrymen were content to scoop out only the few inches of topsoil and hope that there would be no Japanese attacks. This evening, however, two Japanese medium tanks supported by approximately a platoon of infantrymen attacked the company. The supporting Japanese infantry were quickly killed, but the tanks were impervious to small arms fire and the bazookamen failed to move quickly enough to knock them out. They broke through the perimeter, one tank cutting to the left and the other to the right. One stopped and took the immediate company area under fire while the other drove further on. Tanks of the Army's 706th Tank Battalion were paralyzed by fear of firing into the positions of A Company. After a few minutes of success, the Japanese tanks doubled back and fled the area, retiring relatively unscathed to the north. The Japanese sortie left behind a shambles in the area of 1/305. In all, forty-six men were wounded, thirty-three of whom had to be evacuated, and fifteen were killed.[9]

The following day, Company E, 2/305, encountered the same two tanks which had caused such damage the night before in defilade covering the only practicable jungle trail in the area, and there ensued a fierce firefight. The infantry had a difficult time at first locating the Japanese tanks because of a slight rise in the trail ahead and the dense undergrowth in which they were hidden. The Japanese fired into the trees along the trail adding wood fragments to the direct machine-gun fire pinning down the Army riflemen. Even the arrival of the heavy-gun Shermans, which had in this case been lumbering behind the infantry, did not dislodge the enemy. Finally a combination of heavy machine-gun fire, 75mm shells pumped from the supporting tanks, and 81mm mortars firing from the rear silenced the tanks. Infantry squads closing in on both sides discovered the two tanks abandoned, with only three Japanese dead left behind. The enemy tankmen had once again extracted a heavy toll, a reported sixteen more killed and thirty-two wounded.[10] In all probability the commander of this Japanese tank-infantry team had not planned either engagement but was trying to link up with other units in the area. When he made contact with units of the 305th, he simply decided to fight. One thing this episode illustrates clearly is what the Japanese could have done if only they had not thrown away their men and equipment earlier in the futile *banzai* attacks.

A further example of how unexpectedly dangerous was the methodical movement toward the town of Yigo was the presumably prosaic inspection of an area south of Ipapao by the 77th Division chief of staff, Col. Douglas McNair. Early in the afternoon of the 6th, he and his party in what was believed to be a safe area had just selected a site for the new divisional CP approximately 600 yards south of the village. By this time the trail in this vicinity was heavily traveled with infantrymen moving north. McNair's party noticed a hut approximately 200 yards off the trail and started to investigate. A sniper hidden in the building fired one round which struck McNair, killing him instantly. He was the highest ranking American officer lost during the campaign. Ironically his father, LtGen. Leslie McNair, commander of all American ground forces, had been killed in a freak bombing accident in Normandy only two weeks earlier.[11]

The reconnaissance party detected more Japanese activity in the region of the hut and General Bruce ordered 3/305 which had been in division reserve to sweep the area thoroughly. A large contingent, later estimated at over 150 men, was discovered only a third of a mile from the proposed site of the 77th's divisional CP. The Japanese were in well-prepared positions, many of them having dug foxholes between the roots of large ironwood trees, and these were almost impossible to destroy with only small-arms fire. Finally a platoon of medium tanks moved up to support the two assault companies and after a fierce six-hour firefight, the Japanese in this pocket were either killed or slipped away into the jungle.

The 77th Division was nearing the last Japanese redoubt in the sector—the Yigo–Mt. Santa Rosa defenses. Yigo was a small village located at road junction 415 on the Finegayan–Santa Rosa Road. The road itself was very narrow and except for a few openings was enclosed by dense undergrowth on either side. It is somewhat a misnomer to call Mt. Santa Rosa a mountain since its height was only about 800 feet. Located approximately two miles east of Yigo, its slopes were fairly open, covered with grass and coconut trees. The hill was also located only a mile from the sea which allowed the naval task force dispatched by Admiral Conolly to cover almost every part of the Japanese defense area with point-blank fire from battleships, cruisers, and destroyers. This they had done since 3 August. In addition, planes flying from Saipan had bombed the area intermittently. The terrain between Yigo and Mt. Santa Rosa was also such that Bruce could use his tanks en masse for the first time since landing.

On the morning of 5 August, General Geiger had issued orders for an all-out offensive to begin on 7 August with almost all III Corps units. Only one battalion from each division was to be held in reserve. Although the final drive would involve the Marine brigade on the extreme left and the 3rd Marine Division in the center, the main effort for the offensive would be made by the 77th which would break the Japanese defenses in the Yigo–Mt. Santa Rosa area. For the first time in the campaign General Geiger made it the responsibility of the Marine units to maintain flank contact with the 77th. General Bruce had already made plans for the reduction of the Japanese defenses and it was necessary to modify those plans slightly to be in conformity with the Corps directive. The plan as developed called for a turning movement, the division shifting the axis of its advance toward the east almost ninety degrees. This meant that the 306th would move along the division's left boundary supported by an attached company of medium tanks from the 706th Tank Battalion. As soon as it had passed Mt. Santa Rosa it was to turn eastward and seize the area north of the mountain from the village of Lulog to the sea. Adjacent to it initially was the 307th whose objective was Yigo. It was to advance up the Finegayan-Yigo Road, take the town, and then move northeastward to block the westward slopes of Mt. Santa Rosa. For this task it had most of the tanks of the 706th Tank Battalion and an attached company of Shermans in support. The 305th, minus the one battalion which was held out as divisional reserve, would be on the right and its task would be to support the 307th and also block off the southern slopes of the mountain.[12]

The three regiments moved out promptly at 0700 on 7 August in order to get into position for the turning movement and attack on Yigo. Because of a roadblock encountered by 3/307, the assault on Yigo was postponed until 1200. Before the infantry would move, Bruce planned for a concentrated artillery attack on the areas in front of the 306th and 307th by all three 105mm howitzer battalions as well as the regiment's mortars, beginning at 1140. After ten minutes of this barrage they would be joined by three battalions of Corps' 155mm guns. At noon the assault would begin, led by the light tanks of the 706th Tank Battalion. While this barrage was striking the areas adjacent to Yigo the Navy support vessels standing off the east coast would rake Mt. Santa Rosa with their big guns.

From all accounts the artillery preparation for the attack was devastating. Observers from a spotter plane reported dozens of Japanese fleeing the village which was being blown to pieces. According to Bruce's plan, the heavy concentration would lift at precisely 1200 at which time the tanks would be in position to lead the 307th in its attack on Yigo. However, the tank commander did not receive his orders on time and therefore they were twenty minutes late getting to the head of the infantry column. The light tanks swept ahead and quickly disposed of a number of Japanese machine-gun positions along the road before echeloning to the right in fairly open territory. Here they ran into a well-concealed ambush.

To the left of the road the Japanese had sited two light tanks, a 47mm antitank gun, two 20mm guns, and six light and two heavy machine guns. Catching the light tanks of the 706th climbing a slight rise, the Japanese gunners quickly knocked out two. The medium tanks which had been following close behind were then brought into action, but one of these was hit and was abandoned while another threw a track and another stalled. Most of the tanks then bypassed the roadblocks and entered Yigo by 1330. The infantrymen following approximately fifty yards behind the tanks also had difficulty pushing through the area which the tanks had passed through. Although some of the pillboxes had been blasted by the Shermans, there were enough Japanese left to pin down the men of the 307th with rifle- and machine-gun fire. Japanese resistance was finally broken by the action of LtCol. Gordon Kimbrell commanding the 3/306. Hearing the heavy firing to his right, he detached one platoon to move through the jungle-like terrain and try to take the defenders in the rear. The maneuver worked perfectly. The Japanese had been so intent upon halting movement to the north along the road that they had provided no cover for their flanks and rear. The strongpoint was quickly wiped out, as were other Japanese who had established positions along the road to the north.[13]

The action during the day produced fewer results than had been hoped. Nevertheless, by nightfall Yigo had been captured and the 1st and 3rd Battalions of the 307th had taken up positions 1,000 yards beyond the village. In the meantime, the 306th had moved rapidly up the Yigo Road using novel tank-infantry cooperation. The lead company of infantry was assigned a platoon of tanks. These took up positions on either side of the trail with one tank guarding the rear. The 3rd Battalion pushed through Yigo and dug in almost 1,000 yards beyond the village. The 1st Battalion met some resistance from Japanese machine guns late in the afternoon. By the time this was overcome and the units dug in they were just short of the boundary with the Marines. On the division's right, the 305th led by bulldozers to blaze the trail covered a mile during the day and by nightfall reached a position only a mile distant from Lumuna Point. All had gone almost as planned with only one potentially serious foul-up. Some Navy planes attacking Mt. Santa Rosa dropped a bomb on men of the 305th and strafed others of the 307th, causing a few casualties to the 305th.[14]

The Japanese began a series of infiltrating attacks against the 307th during the early evening. These were beaten off without the Japanese being able to penetrate the defenses. The last Japanese tank-infantry attack of the campaign was launched against men of the 3/306 in their exposed position along the road north of Yigo. Here Japanese infantry supported by three tanks tried to break through. The Japanese infantrymen kept the Army bazookamen pinned down while the tanks fired shells into the surrounding trees. Finally two machine gunners managed to fire their light machine gun into the forward opening of one tank which measured only six by ten inches, killing all inside. A rifle grenade finished off another. The third tank retreated having taken one damaged tank in tow. Despite the futility of the Japanese actions, they killed six and wounded sixteen at a cost to themselves of at least eighteen dead.[15]

On the morning of 8 August, the 306th moved rapidly along the trail to Lulog Village against weakening Japanese resistance. There was considerable evidence that many of them, believing that surrender would be a disgrace to their families yet knowing that resistance was foolhardy, committed suicide or waited meekly to be flushed out and shot. More than one hundred Japanese were killed as the 306th moved beyond Mt. Santa Rosa to within a few hundred yards of the ocean. Meanwhile LtCol. Thomas Manuel, commander of the 307th, was gloating over the view he had from the summit of Mt. Santa Rosa. His regiment had advanced rapidly toward the steep slopes early in the morning, killing thirty-five Japanese in that drive. However, no enemy were encountered as the infantry climbed the hill and gained the top by 1400.

By the evening of 8 August, the 77th Division had reached

the limits of its assigned sector in northern Guam. The two-day operation to secure Mt. Santa Rosa had not been as costly as expected. The division had suffered 30 killed and 104 wounded, and during the advance had counted 528 bodies of the enemy.[16] At the beginning of the action it was believed that the combined strength of Japanese army and navy personnel in the vicinity was almost three thousand men. Thus, despite having taken the last major strongpoints in eastern Guam, the Army had not sealed off the area totally; at least two thousand Japanese from the Mt. Santa Rosa region had escaped. This fact would make the tedious job of mopping up even more dangerous than expected.

While the 77th Division was making its slow and steady advance in the eastern part of the island, the 3rd Marine Division was equally methodical in advancing in its sector of operations. The problems encountered by the Army in the main were duplicated in western Guam. The terrain, undergrowth, insects, rain, and mud also presented problems which, although not as deadly as the Japanese snipers, were most immediately bothersome to the weary Marines. Flank contact continued to plague commanders at all levels and at times it was simply impossible to maintain, although all units from squad upward tried hard to keep in touch with adjacent units.

The Marine advance began at 0630 on 2 August with two regiments abreast, the 3rd Marines on the left and the 9th on the right next to the 77th Division. Gains were minimal because of the undergrowth, and the attempts to keep a relatively steady advance minimized gaps between battalions. By evening the Marines had gained only approximately one mile and General Turnage had committed 2/21 to fill the gap which had developed between the two regiments.

While the 3rd Marine Division and the Army's 77th were beginning the slow and at times frustrating campaign in northern Guam, the 1st Provisional Brigade had been resting in Corps reserve. Orote Peninsula and Cabras Island had been released to the control of General Larsen's garrison forces on 2 August and the 4th Marines had gone into bivouac near Toto Village. The eastern section of the island south of the Maanot-Talofofo Road was continually patrolled by the 4th Marines until 3 August. The 22nd Marines were also active, sending out patrols to eliminate Japanese resistance in the south. The largest and most ambitious of these was that of 1 August. Company A of 1/22 was given the task of proceeding along the west coast to Umatac, then to Port Morizo, Agafayan Bay, then up the opposite coast to Ylig Bay before returning to base through Maanot Pass. They were to be supplied by two DUKWs which would get the necessary food and equipment from an LCM. However, one DUKW was grounded south of Bangi Point and the LCM ran into rough seas and could not discharge its cargo. The patrol proceeded on its way, nevertheless, getting its supplies by airdrops. Another company of the 22nd was also sent to Umatac where it was to scout the immediate interior. Very few Japanese were encountered during the first few days of August, the largest number being a group of twelve who were holed up in a cave near Mt. Lamlam. Undoubtedly had these patrols continued they would have contacted more of the enemy who, relatively undisturbed after 3 August, proceeded to construct their hideouts, many of which served some of them for more than a decade.[17]

Patrolling in the deep interior of southern Guam ceased on 3 August when General Shepherd, responding to orders, moved the 22nd Marines north to join the 4th Marines near Toto. This was a preliminary move preparatory for the brigade to move to new positions directly in the rear of the 3rd Division by 5 August. General Geiger then planned to pass the brigade through the lines of the 3rd Division so that it could occupy the extreme left of the Corps line in the final drive against the last Japanese resistance in the north. Meanwhile Corps and Division artillery had displaced forward in order to give better supporting fire for the continuing offensive. Both continued to fire interdiction and harassing fire in front of the 3rd Division.[18]

On 3 August the attack in northwestern Guam continued, beginning at 0700 with the 3rd Marines on the left moving quickly ahead meeting only slight opposition and gaining over 3,000 yards before nightfall. The 9th, however, encountered heavy resistance, particularly in front of 1/9. Approximately two hours after the forward move began, this unit encountered a company-sized Japanese unit dug in on either side of the Finegayan–Santa Rosa

Road just below RJ177 west of Finegayan Village. Sgt. Alvin Josephy, the Marine correspondent accompanying the advance unit of the 1st Battalion, later recalled:

> Although the sounds of battle were all around us, we couldn't see anything. After some time we could reconstruct what had happened. It had been an enemy ambush. The Japs had had two road blocks in parallel lines across the road, about a hundred yards apart. There were mines in the roads, then antitank and heavier guns on both sides of the road, and, stretching inland, round spider pits dug into the ground to keep the tanks from going around the traps. The pits had been filled with Japs ordered to halt the tanks.
>
> Somehow the tanks got through, but the infantry didn't. The first row of Japs let most of our men through, then opened fire on their backs. At the same moment the second row of Japs opened fire on our men's faces. . . .[19]

Supported by two tanks and the company's weapons, Marines of B Company overcame the position by 1000. Later a count indicated 105 enemy dead at this location.

Five hundred yards up the road at RJ177, the regiment was held up by Japanese holding an even stronger position. Here the Japanese had sited machine guns in ravines and ditches, all well hidden by the dense undergrowth. It was at this location that Pfc. Frank Witek won the Congressional Medal of Honor by covering with his BAR the temporary withdrawal of his platoon. He killed eight of the defenders and then helped another wounded Marine to safety. Pinned down by continuing machine-gun fire, Witek decided on his own initiative to attack the position and destroyed the machine gun and an additional eight Japanese before being killed by a sniper.[20] With such heroic actions and the combined firepower of tanks and supporting arms, the Japanese defenses around RJ177 were cleared by early afternoon. Subsequently, Companies A and C advanced beyond the junction and dug in close to Finegayan Village.

General Turnage had alerted the Reconnaissance Company just before 0800 to stand by for a patrol northward toward Ritidian

Point. Later in the day, Company I of 3/21 in six trucks, a demolition squad, and Company A of the 3rd Tank Battalion also joined the company. LtCol. Hartnoll Withers of the tank battalion was placed in overall command and ordered to proceed with his mission at 1245. This *ad hoc* unit had been so quickly assembled that some of the vehicles did not have enough gasoline to make the entire journey to the point and return. Then the patrol was delayed by a firefight forward of RJ177 and Withers suggested that his mission be postponed until the next morning. This request was denied and he was ordered to proceed with the mission, but to return by 1800. The success of the mission was immediately compromised as the lead vehicle missed the turn to the left at the road junction which was the direction the patrol meant to take. Instead, it continued eastward passing through the forward lines of 1/9 and ran directly into enemy fire which immediately destroyed one truck and damaged another as well as a tank. The Japanese, reputedly of battalion strength, many of whom were Imperial Marines, had placed 75mm and 105mm field pieces to cover the road approaches. In addition they had machine guns and tanks in support. The reconnaissance patrol took cover and the Shermans of the 3rd Tank Battalion pumped dozens of rounds into the Japanese positions, ultimately destroying two 75mm guns, one tank, and several machine guns before the unit retired back to the regiment's main lines.

The Japanese during the evening continued their aggressive actions by opening up with mortars against the 3rd Marines and sending out patrols in the 9th Marines' area just before midnight. One patrol sent up flares to alert two medium tanks which began a dash down the road and these penetrated the Marine lines despite concerted fire from antitank weapons and machine guns. Fortunately these tanks caused little damage before withdrawing. At the same time, Japanese mortar rounds began dropping in the boundary area between the 3rd and 9th Marines and this was followed by an infantry attack of undetermined size. Marine small-arms fire and artillery support soon broke up the attack.[21]

Much of the morning of 4 August was taken up by a cautious reorganization of the Marine lines. Guam widened out in the area the Marines were now passing through. Therefore, General

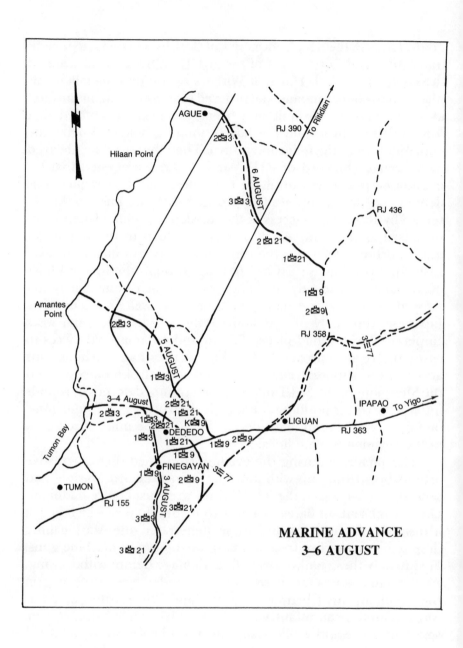

MARINE ADVANCE
3–6 AUGUST

Turnage ordered the 21st Marines to take over the center of the line which would then be composed of all three regiments. The gap between the Army and the 9th Marines on the right flank continued to grow and 2/9 and 3/21 were ordered to take over the extreme right of the line. It was Marines of 3/21 who were later fired on by Army units which mistook them for the enemy. Despite the delay occasioned by the reorganization, there were a few gains made during the day. Enemy resistance was almost non-existent, except in front of 1/9 where the Japanese still maintained their roadblock which had caused the reconnaissance patrol so much trouble the day before.

In many ways the fighting on 5 August was a repetition of the day before. The 3rd Marines met no organized resistance as they moved through the undergrowth and established themselves adjacent to Bija Point approximately 1,000 yards beyond the line of departure. In the center, the 21st Marines kept pace, meeting hardly any opposition from the Japanese. When pockets of resistance were encountered they were quickly eliminated without difficulty. However, the 9th Marines operating to clear the road eastward from Finegayan ran into problems almost immediately. LtCol. Randall's 1/9, with two platoons of tanks attached, engaged in a number of blind firefights with the enemy concealed in the brush along the route of advance. Little by little the Japanese were driven out or killed, and late in the afternoon the last 75mm gun manned by the defenders was knocked out by a tank destroyer. This opened the road in the area of the roadblock. Meanwhile, 2/9, the other assault battalion, had not been held up, and by evening had advanced almost to the village of Liguan.[22] No contact existed with the 77th Division, but by this time neither the Marine nor Army command was as worried about open flanks as they had been at the beginning of the offensive.

The defense of the Finegayan area was the last serious organized attempt to halt the Marine advance. Until the Mt. Santa Rosa region was cleared by the Army, the Japanese had fairly good observation for the few light artillery pieces they still had and these continued to harass the Marines at night, firing their concentrations at the road junctions. Unfortunately for the 9th Marines, RJ177 was one of their favorite targets. Corps and

Division artillery in reply fired constant counterbattery missions but were unable to silence the Japanese weapons.

General Turnage decided on 6 August to concentrate his advance along the roads and trails since it seemed apparent that the only organized Japanese resistance was to be along these. This decision simplified the final days' offensives since movement could be much more rapid if flank contact was not a major factor. Japanese who were bypassed could be left to be dealt with later. The tactical plan was to search and destroy the enemy found approximately 200 yards on either side of the roads and to search carefully all open areas. All forward movement was covered by tanks and tank destroyers. By the end of the day the last defenses around Finegayan were destroyed and the defenders pursued into the Army sector. This opened up the front to a general advance. By evening the Marines had moved forward almost three miles all along the front and had finally tied together their lines near RJ358.

General Shepherd's 1st Provisional Brigade had, in the meanwhile, moved into designated areas near the village of Dededo. He received orders from Corps during the late afternoon of 6 August to be prepared to take over the left flank of the Marine advance the next day. At 0730 on 7 August, the 4th Marines joined the fight in the north by passing through the area held by 1/3 and 2/3. Colonel Shapley's regiment encountered almost no opposition and by nightfall had reached RJ460 approximately four miles south of Ritidian Point, the northernmost part of Guam. Shepherd had alerted the 22nd Marines shortly after noon to move west and be prepared to pass through the extreme left units of the 4th Marines and advance along the coast trail toward the point. Later he decided to wait until the next morning before committing the 22nd.[23]

The 3rd Division meanwhile had advanced on a northeastern axis through the dense undergrowth without meeting any organized resistance. The total advance during the day in the division's sector had been more than three miles. Contact between all units had been maintained. By the close of the day the Army was preparing to attack Mt. Santa Rosa and the Marine division and brigade

were about to drive toward the end of the island. All senior commanders could sense the campaign was about finished.

The final three days of the official campaign witnessed increasing pressure by elements of all major units against only scattered
pockets of Japanese resistance. The jungle-like growth and rugged
terrain, however, continued to hamper movement, particularly
in the 3rd Division area. On 8 August the 2nd Battalion led the
advance northeastward in the 3rd Marine area but literally became
lost as they searched for a road northeast of the village of Salisbury.
The trail was shown clearly on the map, but it could not be found
until late afternoon. The maps were incorrect; it was merely a
trail which did not begin until some distance outside the village.
The Marines eventually hacked their way through the jungle until
they found the trail. Behind them came bulldozers which cut a
wider and better path. Further advance up the newfound trail
was briefly halted until a roadblock two miles north of Salisbury
was cleared of the nineteen Japanese defenders. The 9th Marines
in their sector had many of the same difficulties but by evening,
2/9 was located in Salisbury and the forward unit, 3/9, was 500
yards further along the trail to Savana Grande just short of Pati
Point. Although he was not aware of it, Colonel Craig's CP was
sited only 300 yards away from General Obata's final command
center.

Meanwhile, General Shepherd's brigade had moved out at
0730 in a coordinated two-regiment attack parallel to the west
coast. The 22nd Marines was assigned the left sector while the
4th was adjacent to the 3rd Division. Air strikes and artillery spread
a blanket of fire ahead of the Marine riflemen. Reports by airmen
of enemy activity in the Mt. Machanao area caused the brigade
to slow its advance until the area could be thoroughly worked
over by Naval and Corps artillery. Shepherd then sent a patrol
out to scout toward Ritidian Point, the northernmost part of the
island. Men of Company F of 2/22 thus had the honor of reaching
the northern coastline of Guam first. These advance units were
pulled back and established a roadblock on the trail and dug in
for the night. The 4th Marines also had reached their objectives
by the end of the day and went into defensive positions which

could block any enemy attacks from the Mt. Machanao region.[24]

During the day the 21st Marines in Corps reserve had patrolled aggressively in the bush area behind the lines. One patrol from 3/21 made a grisly discovery indicative of the savage treatment meted out by some of the Japanese to the native Guamanians. One of the Marine scouts, Pfc. Joe Young, related what they found:

> Suddenly we came to a clearing. There, spread out on the ground, were about forty bodies of young men. They had their legs drawn up against their chests and had their arms tied behind their backs. They lay in awkward positions—on their sides and their stomachs, and on their knees—like swollen, purple lumps. And none of them had heads, they had all been decapitated. The heads lay like bowling balls all over the place.
>
> There was a truck nearby with more bodies and lopped-off heads in it. It looked as if the Japs had been loading all the bodies and heads into the truck, but had been frightened away and had left everything behind.[25]

The following morning another patrol found twenty-one more beheaded men near the same village. All of the dead Chamorros were from a concentration camp near Yona and had been conscripted to work on Japanese defenses in the north.[26]

This was the worst single instance of Japanese brutality although there were many other examples of unnecessary savagery, as if some of the Japanese, realizing that their end was near, had every intention of taking as many innocent people with them as possible. Lt. Wilcie O'Bannon of 2/9 remembered his encounter with such practices. He recalled:

> After Fonte there was a situation where as Wilson's Exec I would follow a particular platoon and this time we found in a shell hole four bodies with their throats cut. It appeared that the Japanese had practiced their samurai sword action, just chopped across the body horizontally. We were told that a good swordsman could cut off a head and leave it still

attached to the body with a strip of flesh and it appeared that was what they had attempted to do. We also found in another shell hole further on another four bodies treated the same way.[27]

Such unreasoning brutality did little to alter the attitudes of the Americans toward taking prisoners. Even during the latter stages of the fighting very few Japanese surrendered or were permitted to. By 10 August in all sectors, the American forces had taken only eighty-seven prisoners.[28]

Although there were many Japanese who had been bypassed in the latter phases of the battle, the only really organized resistance was expected to come from those who had taken refuge in the northeastern part of the island. On the 9th and 10th, the pursuit of the elusive enemy continued. Particularly frustrating was the search for five enemy tanks which broke into the lines of 2/3 on the night of 8 August. They escaped completely and were probably abandoned in the deep bush near Savana Grande. On 9 August, the final push to the northeast was halted because of civilian reports that there were three thousand Japanese in the northern cliff area. The twelve 155mm guns of the 7th Gun Battalion joined the 3rd Division artillery and both units fired almost four thousand rounds into the suspected area in two and one-half hours. Later it was discovered that the intelligence reports were incorrect. But as one Corps artillery officer commented later, the artillery concentration "did provide a bang-up end to the campaign."[29] By the evening of 9 August, Marine and Army units had reached the extreme end of the island and even Tokyo radio admitted that most of the island was controlled by the Americans.

While the Marine units were pushing through the bush during the last phase of the battle for Guam a drama was unfolding in the 77th Division sector. On 8 August a patrol from the 9th Marines drew fire from Mt. Mataguac, actually a small hill, located in the Army's zone. Colonel Craig then notified Col. Aubrey Smith commanding the 306th of this fact. Later, Guamanian civilians informed the Army that the hill was the location of some type of command post. A unit of the 77th Division Reconnaissance Company investigated the area, but drew such heavy fire that it retired.

It was decided not to take immediate action against the Japanese there since the advance was not being hampered by their presence. Finally on 10 August, 1/306 moved into the area and discovered a brush-lined hollow approximately 100 yards long and 40 to 50 feet deep, the sides of which contained several caves. The approach to the slash was difficult and as the men maneuvered to get into position to use a flamethrower, the defenders from their concealment opened up with rifle and machine-gun fire. This fire killed eight and wounded an additional seventeen men before the unit could retreat to safety. Establishing themselves in a position to block any escape attempts, men of the 1st Battalion waited for the next day.

Earlier that morning General Obata wrote his last messages. One was to the Emperor expressing the general's appreciation for the favors bestowed on him during his career. He also expressed his sorrow and apologized for what he conceived was his fault in losing the Marianas to the Americans. He also wrote Imperial General Headquarters in candid terms. A portion of that message indicates clearly the fatalistic attitude of most of the Japanese on Guam. General Obata wrote:

We are continuing a desperate battle on Guam. Officers and men have been lost, weapons have been destroyed, and ammunition has been expended. We have only our bare hands to fight with. The holding of Guam has become hopeless. I will engage the enemy with the remaining strength at Mt. Mataguac tomorrow, the 11th. My only fear is that report of death with honor [annihilation] at Guam may shock the Japanese people at home. Our souls will defend the island to the very end; we pray for the security of the Empire.[30]

The death with honor mentioned by Obata had, by the end of the day, already come for most of the personnel at his headquarters. The next morning the infantrymen of 1/306 again attacked under cover of mortar and machine-gun fire. They tossed white phosphorus grenades into entrances to the caves and eventually used massive charges of TNT in order to seal their entrances. They had been surprised by the fierce resistance from the caves because no one knew at the time that this was General Obata's elaborate underground headquarters. Days later when demolition teams opened up the entrances, they found over sixty bodies including that of General Obata who, true to the code of *bushido,* had committed suicide some time during the morning of 11 August.[31]

At 1130 on 10 August, General Geiger declared that all organized resistance on Guam had ceased and the island was thus secure. This announcement, although Geiger did not plan it that way, was made just before the visit of Admirals Nimitz and Spruance and Generals Vandegrift and H. M. Smith who arrived later in the day for a conference with Geiger. Geiger's pronouncement, although welcomed, did not mean a halt to the military operations. By that date 10,984 Japanese bodies had been counted. Even considering that many dead had not yet been found in the deep bush and ravines, this meant that there were still over 7,000 Japanese on the island hiding out in the bush and they would eventually have to be killed or forced to surrender. This task would fall primarily to the men of the 3rd Marine Division which had already paid the highest price in casualties of all combat units. The cost of the conquest of Guam for the Army and Marines had been high. In the twenty days fighting, the American forces had suffered 7,714 casualties. The bulk of these were Marines, who counted 1,190 killed, 377 dead of wounds, and 5,308 wounded. The 77th Division during its drive to the north had 177 killed and 662 wounded.[32]

Despite the continuing dangerous situation from roving groups of Japanese in the interior, the island was secure and the senior commanders could begin the next task. This was nothing less than the transformation of the island into the major Central Pacific command post for the Navy and headquarters for the recently created Twentieth Air Force whose B–29 bombers would soon bring the Japanese home islands under attack.

CHAPTER IX
Aftermath

General Geiger's announcement of the end of organized resistance on Guam was the prelude to wholesale changes of command in the Marianas. Even before this, Admiral Nimitz had ordered Geiger and his staff to Guadalcanal as soon as possible to resume command of Operation STALEMATE, the projected two-pronged invasion of the Carolines. The Guam operation taking longer than planned had kept one part of his staff, code-named X RAY, working on the plans for that operation without Geiger's overall supervision. MajGen. Julian Smith, Deputy Commander of Fleet Marine Corps Pacific, had been placed in temporary command of the projected operation. Geiger left Guam on 12 August, the day after his pronouncement of the end of hostilities there.[1] On the same day LtGen. H. M. Smith, the overall commander of the Marianas operation, turned over V Amphibious Corps to MajGen. Harry Schmidt and assumed command of Fleet Marine Corps Pacific. All assault troops remaining in the Marianas were assigned to V Amphibious Corps, and the headquarters of III Amphibious Corps was reactivated on Guadalcanal. Admiral Conolly had already left Guam with most of the ships of Task Force 53. Control of the small naval force left in Guamanian waters, which had no ship larger than a destroyer, was assumed by Admiral Reifsnider. Most of the ships of Task Force 53 joined the 3rd Fleet whose commander, Admiral Halsey, replaced Admiral Spruance as commander of the Central Pacific areas.

The most important change of command for the Army, Marines, and Guamanians occurred when Marine MajGen. Henry Larsen assumed operational control on 15 August. His base commander's office had already taken over all communications responsibilities and those related to the unloading and disposition of supplies. However, after mid-August, with the assumption that the combat phase of the operation had been concluded, Larsen assumed the management of the manifold tasks of the mopping-up campaign, resettlement of the Guamanians, and all the construction projects necessary to house a permanent force of Navy and Marines as well as attempting to carry out the goals of making Guam the site of major naval and air base facilities.

Before leaving, General Geiger had ordered that one Marine regiment and one Army regiment be left in position in northern Guam to carry out continuing search and destroy missions to bring Japanese resistance to a final end. This responsibility fell to the 22nd Marines operating in the area north of Tumon Bay, and the 306th RCT based in the Yigo–Santa Rosa area. All other combat units were moved to semipermanent bases in the rear areas. The 1st Provisional Brigade did not spend much further time on the island since General Shepherd was ordered to prepare to move it to Guadalcanal. There the unit would receive replacements not only for those lost during the campaign but also enough men and equipment to bring the unit up to divisional size. Once this was done it would be redesignated the 6th Marine Division. The first units of the brigade left Guam on 21 August and within ten days all elements were on their way to the South Pacific.

The 77th Division, except for the 306th, was pulled back into camps sited in the hills east of Agat. By the end of August they were joined by the 306th at what was called Camp McNair after the division's chief of staff who had been killed on 6 August. The living conditions of the Army units were much worse than those of the Marines since much of their equipment, including most of their tentage, had been left behind on Oahu. Their rear detachment in charge of these supplies had been ordered to Guadalcanal where presumably the division was to be sent. While the men of the 77th suffered during the rainy season on Guam, their equipment was transferred from Guadalcanal to New Caledonia. It would eventually catch up only after the 77th landed in the Philippines. Meanwhile, the rainy season was on and the men in pup tents could not keep their bedding from getting soaked, and clothing and leather equipment mildewed. Harmon Road was the only supply route and it soon became a muddy morass dubbed by the men, Harmon Canal. Eventually the 132nd Engineer Battalion borrowed heavy equipment from the Seabees and laid down a deep carpet of crushed coral over the road. But until then all supplies had to be transported by *carabao* or carried by the men.[2]

During this time, the 77th was theoretically preparing for its next mission, although that was not clearly defined. At first it was to be a reserve for the XXIV Corps in the invasion of Yap and Ulithi. When this was cancelled the 305th remained at Orote, where it had shifted preparatory to embarkation, and the 307th moved to an area above Asan. Finally General Bruce was alerted that the division would be used as a reserve for the Leyte invasion. After the Philippine campaign had begun, the 77th was finally ordered from Guam to a staging ground on New Caledonia. All units left Guam on 3 November and while they were still at sea, they were diverted to Manus in the Admiralty Islands. After a brief stay there, the 77th was ordered to make a landing on the eastern side of central Leyte. The division further distinguished itself during that campaign.[3]

The 3rd Marine Division had thus, by November, become the only combat unit on Guam. It, too, had undergone considerable reorganization while still involved in the pacification of the interior areas. The 21st Marines located in the northwest had taken over the major mop-up role although patrols from the other two regiments continued to operate from the main base camps located along the east coast road between Pago and Ylig Bay. Replacement troops began arriving in late August and continued for over a month. The continuous patrols into the bush gave the lower echelon commanders an excellent opportunity to indoctrinate these new troops into the problems of combat in difficult terrain.

The 3rd Marine Division also received a complement of new officers, the most important being a new commanding general. General Turnage had earlier been ordered back to the United

States to assume the position of Director of Personnel. His place was taken in mid-October by MajGen. Graves Erskine who had been H. M. Smith's chief of staff during the Saipan operation. He brought with him Col. Robert Hogaboom as his chief of staff. Changes were also made not only at the divisional staff level but also throughout the regiments, including a new commander for the 9th Marines.

Much of the later criticism of the performance of the 3rd Marine Division is traceable to two sources. The first, already alluded to, is that of H. M. Smith's remembrances based upon his two brief visits to the island during the height of the fighting before the breakout from the Asan lodgement. The other is the assessment of the division given by Erskine. He later said:

> The division was not functioning as a division. It had been divided up into 3 combat teams with division support behind. An artillery battalion was assigned to each regiment, some amtracks. They did have a division hospital, but each one of the regiments was doing some hospitalization by having a company of the division hospital over there.
>
> I felt it was not a division from my viewpoint. . . . I felt even regarding the training—you would have three differ- ent ideas, you would have directives from division headquar- ters, but when it is broken down by three different people, it doesn't say the same thing. I immediately changed all that.[4]

Considering that the division had been involved in some of the worst fighting in the Pacific theater, much of it through almost impenetrable jungle-like growth, it is reasonable to assume that General Turnage and his temporary successor, Gen. Alfred Noble, had adopted this more flexible organizational structure. Fresh from a staff position taking over divisional command for the first time, Erskine should not have been surprised that the 3rd Division did not meet his arbitrary standards. If Erskine, known for his opinionated positions, could still hold to these ideas over twenty years later, there is no doubt that his concerns, added to those of H. M. Smith, contributed greatly to denigrating the efforts of the 3rd Division on Guam. Erskine's chief of staff was much kinder and much more accurate in his recollections of the division. He noted that the division and assistant divisional commander and many of the senior staff had been transferred out. It was the rainy season and all units were living in very poor conditions with water and mud in all the camps, and a large number of wounded were still waiting for transport off the island. The division appeared to him to be at a "very low ebb" and Erskine began to make changes which brought all units directly under his control, and when possible began new training procedures.[5] Perhaps as effective as anything done by the new commander was the passage of time. The division was gradually being reequipped and replacements had arrived almost every day beginning in September. Not the least of the factors involved in rehabilitation was that the deadly fighting was over and the combat veterans could settle into a more normal cycle of living for the remaining months before being shipped to an even more forbidding island, Iwo Jima, in February 1945.

The thousands of remaining Japanese on the island presented a constant hazard to the many Guamanians who were returning to their home areas as well as to the Marines and men of the construction battalions. Long before the arrival of General Erskine, patrols at first of Army and Marines pushed out into the bush seeking those Japanese still alive. After 26 August the Marines were left to comb the interior with their major zone of operations in the far north. Guamanians had played an important role as guides to Army and Marine units from the earliest period of fighting. They continued to help ferret out Japanese during the many patrol sweeps in the north and south during August and September. Supplied with arms and equipment, the Guamanian volunteers acted as regular members of the patrols. In August, Admiral Nimitz authorized the creation of the Local Security Patrol Force, a combination of Marines and Guamanians, many of whom had been members of the Insular Patrol Force which had existed before the war. The head of this organization was a Marine officer from the police detachment. In addition to their normal policing functions, members of the Patrol Force were involved during the remainder of the war in anti-Japanese patrols. How well these men performed in combat situations is shown by the awards given to them. One man received the Silver Star and twenty-eight others were awarded the Bronze Star.[6]

The conditions of the Japanese who refused to surrender were unbelievably difficult. In most cases a few Japanese banded together to search for food and give some type of organized resistance to the patrols, but often each man was on his own. Wet and cold, they concentrated on their main objective—finding food. The diary of a Japanese navy corpsman killed by a Marine patrol in November reveals in stark detail such problems. He wrote:

12 August—Fled into a palm grove feeling very hungry and thirsty. Drank milk from five coconuts and ate the meat of three.

15 August—Tried eating palm tree tips but suffered from severe vomiting in the evening.

23 August—Along my way I found some taro plants and ate them. All around me are enemies only. It takes a brave man, indeed, to go in search of food.

10 September—This morning I went out hunting. Found a dog and killed it. Compared with pork or beef it is not very good.

19 September—Our taro is running short and we can't afford to eat today.

2 October—These days I am eating only bread fruit. Went out in search of some today but it is very dangerous.

15 October—No food.[7]

As time passed the condition of the remaining Japanese worsened. They could survive only by eating coconuts and edible roots or by sneaking from their hiding places to try to steal supplies from the Marine or Navy dumps or from the Guamanians. A high percentage of Japanese killed during the latter weeks of 1944 were in the vicinity of these storage dumps. The only organized Japanese resistance was that undertaken by LtCol. Takeda operating in the north and Major Sato in the south. Both of them planned and carried out extensive nuisance raids. During the early fall of 1944 each commander had direct control over more than 100 men. But as Takeda later wrote, "Owing to the loss of men and weapons and shortage of food under successive subjugations accompanying [sic] with a skillful psychological warfare their men dropped gradually into the hands of the Americans."[8] Because the Marines had no love for their enemy and under the best of circumstances expected all kinds of treachery, the patrols, despite specific orders to bring in prisoners, at first took very few Japanese alive. Sgt. Alvin Josephy noted the Marines' normal attitude toward their enemy when he wrote:

In battle therefore we learned to live by the rule of kill or be killed. We refused to risk our own safety to test the good intentions of the Japs who indicated a wish to surrender. In face-to-face encounters we knew that the man who shot first won—he lived. That is not to say we never took prisoners. We captured many wounded Japs during the fighting on Guam—men too injured to put up resistance. And finally we were beginning to bring in sick and starving men who could hardly stand up without our help. Our people were finding them lying in cave entrances or in the jungle.[9]

During August, the Army and Marine patrols averaged 80 Japanese killed each day, and as late as February 1945 there were 141 killed by garrison patrols that month, while only 44 prisoners were taken.[10]

The largest and best organized attempt to destroy what remained of Japanese resistance was that set in motion by General Erskine in late October. He saw this as not only an opportunity to get rid of the Japanese, but also to provide further training for the division. He requested General Larsen's approval for a sweep through central and northern Guam by the entire division. Colonel Hogaboom was requested by General Larsen to provide an estimate on the number of the enemy still operating in the interior. Drawing a number out of the hat, Hogaboom stated that there were more than a thousand, a figure which as events later proved was very conservative.[11] Receiving the base commander's concurrence for the offensive, Erskine on 24 October moved the 3rd Marines to their right extending to the east coast. The 21st Marines, already operating in the Tumon Bay area, were reached on the second day and then that regiment formed the extreme left unit of the division. The two regiments moving slowly northward flushed out and killed over 100 of the enemy before reaching the north coast on 30 October.[12]

There was at the same time a concerted, well-organized effort to get the Japanese to surrender. Leaflets were dropped into areas where large numbers were believed to be hiding. In Japanese script, these called upon them to surrender, promising that they would not be harmed but would be given food, water, and medical treatment. Teams of Marines would take trucks and in some cases boats into the more inaccessible places and using bullhorns would try to induce the Japanese to give themselves up. Sgt. Alvin Josephy described in detail one such attempt by boat to get to a group of Japanese in an area below the sheer 600-foot-high coral cliffs along the north coast. This mission was very successful and a number of prisoners were rescued when a small boat was rowed into shore to bring them back to the larger ship anchored offshore. Josephy recalled:

They would be hoisted aboard, scared that we would kill them. We would make them undress and that only added to their terror. We then gave them soap and hosed them off with salt water and they knew they wouldn't die immediately. We gave them clean Navy skivvy shorts and shirts and our pharmacist mate looked them over and dressed their wounds and jungle sores.

They were all in bad physical condition. Some of them had been living on coconuts and bread fruit for weeks. Their bones showed through their skins and their stomachs were distended. Many had open wounds which they had been unable to clean or dress properly. A young soldier had a mortar fragment wound in his shoulder which was full of maggots. The prisoners were also filthy dirty from their days of living in the bushes. Their matted hair was full of lice. Their legs and feet were covered with running sores. We sprinkled them with everything from Sulfa powder to the new DDT which had just come out to the Pacific.[13]

Despite near starvation, physical debilities, and the ever-present danger from Marine patrols, large numbers of Japanese refused all offers to surrender. One reason was obviously fear that the terrible Marines would kill them. However, for many, the compelling reason was loyalty—either generalized to the Emperor and homeland or in some cases to a specific officer. Major Sato operating in southern Guam was one such officer who continued the struggle throughout the winter of 1944 and into the spring of the following year. Finally he, too, recognized the futility of further resistance and on 11 June 1945 he and thirty-four men surrendered. His counterpart in the north, Lt. Col. Takeda, how-ever, continued to hold out despite the presence of over two hundred thousand allied personnel on the island and repeated searches for him and his men. He was mute about his operations during this period in the replies to questions submitted to him long after the war by the Marine Historical Section. One can only speculate on the kind of loyalty which kept him in the bush where he could observe the huge B–29 bombers taking off to bomb the Japanese home islands. Only after the Emperor broad-cast his order to all his troops to lay down their arms did Takeda surrender. He and sixty-seven men laid down their arms on 4 September 1945. Later he was instrumental in persuading an additional forty-six to give up.[14] By this time over 1200 Japanese had surrendered.

Long after the war was over there remained a few Japanese who refused to surrender. They hid in caves or built underground tunnels and lived by eating roots, snails, or building traps for rats or shrimp. The harsh life eventually took its toll and most of the holdouts died in the bush. In 1960 two fugitives, Tadeshi Ito and Bunzo Minegawa, surrendered to authorities and were repatriated to Japan after being used to help scout southern Guam for any others who might have been in hiding. It was then assumed that these two were the last holdouts. They had survived for over fifteen years without detection. No one on Guam or in Japan was prepared for the improbable saga of Sgt. Shoichi Yokoi who with ten companions in August 1944 disappeared into the jungle-like terrain inland from Asan. Over the years his companions died until, in 1964, he was left alone. He had dug a tunnel in which he lived underground for most of his days and nights and had so cunningly concealed the entrance that it was impossible to detect. Yokoi fashioned clothes from the bark of the Pago tree, utensils from canteen cups, and constructed various traps which he used to catch rats. He also gathered shrimp from a tributary of the Talofofo River which was located near his hide-away. Yokoi had learned that the war was over in the early 1950s, but he had been so well indoctrinated in fear of the Americans that he was convinced he would be shot if he surrendered. The lonely vigil for the 58-year-old Japanese came to an end on 24 January 1972 when two Guamanian fishermen stumbled upon him as he was trying to set his shrimp traps. He was overpowered and turned over to the authorities. Overnight the simple sergeant from Nagoya became world famous. He was the last soldier of the Emperor to surrender twenty-eight years after organized resistance on Guam had been declared at an end.[15]

Long before General Geiger proclaimed the end of organized resistance, the island commander faced a problem of staggering proportions—how to provide adequately for the civilian population. The long pre-invasion bombardment and subsequent artillery and air strikes had destroyed most of the houses and buildings in the main towns. As the fighting moved into the interior, Guamanians in ever-increasing numbers came into the American lines. Later the Japanese concentration camps were captured. The main one near Yona had at one time housed over 15,000 prisoners, who lived in coconut thatched huts with few sanitation facilities and little food. Almost without exception the Guamanians who were liberated were in bad condition and needed more than the small amounts of food and candy sympathetic American troops could share with them. Two camps for the refugees were established before the Marine breakout occurred, each under the temporary authority of the Provost Marshal. One of these was located at Asan near the 3rd Division CP. A Marine correspondent recalled the indelible impression this early camp made on him:

The biggest problem seemed to be the babies, of whom there were many. Like the adults, most of them were suffering from malnutrition, and from dysentery and other illnesses, and were covered with jungle sores. At first we had no baby specialists with us, so our Navy corpsmen had to do what they could. As the corpsmen, in turn, were puzzled over where to find the supplies they needed, the problem created confusion around our Division CP. Day and night we heard babies crying as we went about the work of battle or lay in our foxholes listening for Japs.[16]

Eventually three large refugee camps were established—one near Agat, another near Yona, and the third at Anigua. All the camps were very soon placed under the control of Col. Charles Murray and his 185–man team of the Department of Civil Affairs. The task before Murray's group daily became more difficult as the numbers of refugees in each of the camps continued to mount. The largest of the centers was that near Agat which by 5 August had almost 7,000 refugees. Here, as elsewhere, the most pressing problems were food and shelter. Fortunately at first large caches of food had been found in the Japanese supply dumps. Later a steady flow of supplies was assured the refugees from American sources. Complicating all efforts to provide adequate services was the weather. The rains which made the lives of Marine and Army personnel miserable were even worse for the malnourished and oftentimes sick Guamanians. Civil Affairs personnel at each of the camps organized large-scale work parties which were set to work to improve the roads and dig drainage ditches, latrines, and sumps for the galleys. Tents, whenever available, were used at first, but in many cases crude shelters of pick-up materials had to be constructed. Finally, more permanent shelters such as the twenty by sixty-foot standard barracks at Anigua were built.[17]

Services provided the Guamanians improved, but the island commander wanted as soon as possible to phase out these camps which by mid August contained almost 18,000 people. As early as 3 August, General Larsen established the policy of returning Guamanians to any region which had been declared free from Japanese. They would be given rations to sustain them and could return for further supplies when these were exhausted. This policy soon became very difficult to carry out because the increasing demands of the military for camps, training areas, and air bases simply took away vast amounts of land which previously had been owned by Guamanians. Within a year there were over 200,000 service personnel on the island and this factor alone made it difficult to return many civilians to their homes. There was litigation over Guamanian land claims which continued for years after the war. Despite all the problems, the Civil Affairs Section managed within a few months to resettle most Guamanians if not on their own land, then in a number of new towns. Offshore fishing, disallowed by the Japanese, was encouraged by the Americans in hopes of making the Guamanians more self-sufficient. In the years that followed, considerable sums were expended to try to restore the copra trade, without much success. The war had irretrievably changed the island and most Guamanians earned their livelihood by becoming workers in the burgeoning military establishment or in one of the service industries.[18]

This revolution in Guamanian life had begun on 9 August 1944 when Admiral Nimitz announced his intention of making Guam the forward base for the Central Pacific Command preparatory to an assault on Formosa. This meant that the work of engineers and construction crews which had been so vital during the combat phase of the operations had to be greatly expanded. Initially, the main task of the 25th Naval Construction Battalion attached to the 3rd Division and the 53rd assigned to the 1st Brigade had been to work the beach areas and maintain the roads and trails into the interior. This was duplicated by the Army's 302nd Engineer Battalion. During the early stages of the operation there was a severe shortage of earth-moving equipment. The Army did not bring along any of its heavy equipment and the landing of the Seabees' equipment took secondary priority to more needed supplies during the first few days. For the first two days, Corps artillery's dozers with their angled blades were used by the Seabees until the 155s were landed. However, by the time of the breakout much of the heavy equipment was ashore and the engineers were involved in a twenty-four-hour work schedule to cut trails for the combat units and to maintain the roads. During the rainy season, this latter task proved to be a nearly insoluble problem because the heavy clay soils of central Guam simply acted as a sponge soaking up the water.

The method of constructing new roads did not follow the best construction procedures. Once a route was decided upon, a D–6 dozer simply dug out a two-lane path, shoving the excess dirt aside. If there was time, coral was moved in and compressed. Later, huge amounts of coral were hauled in for the major roads and for the airstrips. The 3rd Marines must have rejoiced as Chonito Cliff, where the Japanese had put up such a stubborn defense, was gradually levelled. Until the fighting was over, however, little could be done of a permanent nature for the roads. When the rains came they became muddy channels; the dozers would move in as soon as possible and scrape down to a firm base. In some cases deep holes and low places were filled in with logs.[19]

Later when Orote and Tiyan airfields had been captured, the Seabees began work immediately to repair the facilities and to lengthen the runways. So successful were they that six hours after the first engineering unit began work on the Orote strip, a Navy TBF touched down. By 30 July, Marine light observation planes were using the field, and on 7 August, VMF–225 flew the first combat missions from Orote. Tiyan airfield, taken on 2 August, was transformed within two weeks into an excellent fighter strip.[20] These were but preliminaries for the Navy and Army construction units which were soon involved in preparing facilities for Admiral Nimitz's forward base as well as working on three separate Very Heavy Bomber (VHB) fields.

With the end of the fighting and Nimitz's announced plans for Guam to become his headquarters, the various engineering units were brought under the control of Capt. William Hiltabiddle commanding the three regiments which by then made up the 5th Naval Construction Brigade. The admiral's decision confronted the island commander, General Larsen, and Captain Hiltabiddle with the need to establish construction priorities. Road building and improvements continued to be high on the list, but improvement of Piti Naval Yard, building service facilities at the two airports, living quarters for the expected influx of naval personnel, and the usual administrative centers were obviously also very important. The success of these massive construction efforts is shown by the fact that Nimitz felt comfortable in moving to Guam in February 1945 and occupying the new buildings constructed for the Advance Headquarters of the Pacific Fleet in the heights above Agana.

One historian of the Marianas campaign, perhaps to bolster the concept of interservice harmony, wrote that "the major construction effort on all three islands was of course laying out airfields and other facilities for the very long range bombers of the Army Air Force's B–29s."[21] A closer examination of the situation on Guam, Saipan, and Tinian during the last quarter of 1944 shows just how wrong is this statement. Actually the work on the projected air bases on Guam was given a very low priority by Island Command. When MajGen. Curtis LeMay arrived on Guam on 19 January 1945 to take command of the 20th Air Force, he found that construction was far behind schedule despite the earlier projections that Depot Field (later Harmon Field) would be operational by 15 October and North Field by 15 December. He discovered that Nimitz's headquarters had designated harbor improvement, CINCPOA Headquarters, Supply Facilities, and Medical Facilities all ahead of the completion of the B–29 fields. LeMay later related with some humor and much bitterness how on arrival he discovered:

> The Navy had been hard at work otherwise. They had built tennis courts for the Island Commander; they had built fleet recreation centers, Marine rehabilitation center, dockage facilities for inter-island surface craft, and every other damn thing in the world except subscribing to the original purpose in the occupation of those islands. The islands were attacked and taken and held because we needed them for air bases to strike against Japan. All along, that was the way it went. Guam, Tinian, Saipan, Iwo Jima, Okinawa—Thousands and thousands of young Americans died on those islands, in order to give us a base of operations against the Japanese homeland. And here people were, piddling around with all this other stuff, and not giving us anything to fly from or fight with.[22]

The problem on Guam which was not duplicated on Saipan or Tinian was that two branches of the service wanted to use the island as a major headquarters and no one in Washington apparently understood how the complex command relationships in the Central Pacific would impede the development of the large airfields. The 20th Air Force was not a part of Area Command. It was directly under the chief of staff of the Army Air Force, General Arnold. However, Island Command and all the supply and support activity was directly controlled by Admiral Nimitz and he had different priorities from the Air Force generals. Not until late autumn 1944 did the Navy give up its ideas of an invasion of Formosa. The completion of the Naval base and the construction of adequate headquarters and supply buildings for the Advanced Naval Base therefore took precedence over everything else. The Navy on Guam at first under the direct command of VAdm. J. H. Hoover was also very jealous of its prerogatives. The Air Force did not even have final approval of the plans for the three heavy bomber airfields proposed for Guam.[23]

The planning guide for the construction of the B–29 bases, the Frank Report, in May 1944 had envisioned five great airfields in the Marianas—two on Guam, two on Tinian, and one on Saipan—with the headquarters and general supply point for all being at Depot Field on Guam. The construction of the Air Force facilities at Depot Field was consistently behind even the revised schedule because of the continual rains and the attitude of Island Command. The revised date for completion of Depot Field was December, but it was not ready for use until 2 February 1945. Even then only the headquarters building and one quonset hut had been finished. Admiral Nimitz did not direct General Larsen to give priority to the airfields over roads and other projects on the island until March 1945. In reversing his position he was obviously responding to continuing pressures from Washington. During the winter months, work had also been progressing slowly on the two northern fields. Much of the work on Depot Field and North Field had fallen by default to the 854th Aviation Battalion which had arrived in Guam on 7 October. Within two weeks the battalion's entire engineering section went north with two D–8 dozers, two half-tracks, and heavily armed guards to give protection from the Japanese still hiding in the bush.[24] Roadways had to be cut through the heavy underbrush in areas which had never been mopped up and these had to be paved and given adequate drainage. Service buildings and barracks had to be constructed in addition to the 8,000–foot runways. Although LeMay and his staff were located on Guam, the first long-range missions against Japan were flown from the northern islands where, because of the easier terrain and relative lack of interservice bickering, North Field on Tinian was operational in late November. By contrast, the first mission flown from North Field on Guam was on 25 February 1945, and Northwest Field's one runway was not ready for service until 1 April.[25]

Despite all the difficulties, the B–29s did begin to operate from the Marianas early in 1945. Small-scale high-level precision bombing attacks against Japanese industry were launched first from Saipan, then Tinian, and later from Guam. By early March 1945, LeMay from his Guam headquarters was able to order over 300 of the huge bombers to attack various targeted cities. The results at first were not as satisfactory as expected, and then LeMay and his superiors in Washington decided on a radical alteration of the bombing policy. On many future raids the bombers would go in at low altitudes and most of them would be loaded with incendiaries. The most devastating of these attacks was launched against a twelve-square-mile area of Tokyo on the night of 9–10 March with 334 B–29s. This one raid, the most destructive of the war, wiped out one quarter of the city, killing 83,793, wounding 40,918, and destroying 267,171 buildings. As the official Air Force historian noted, "No other air attack of the war, either in Japan or Europe, was so destructive of life and property."[26] The bombing attacks continued with even greater frequency and were extended to every large city in Japan. It is probable that even without the use of the two atom bombs dropped on Hiroshima and Nagasaki in August 1945, there would have been few buildings left standing in all of Japan by the end of that year.

The capture of Guam, placed in the larger context of the conquest of the Marianas, was a part of the most significant events in the war in the Central Pacific. In retrospect, the securing of bases for the B–29s within striking distance of the Japanese homeland was the most important strategic result of the seizure of the Marianas. There were other factors as well which made most of the men in the Japanese government believe after the loss of the Marianas that there was no hope of ultimate victory. These feelings brought about the collapse of the inflexible Tojo regime which had directed the war during Japan's glory days. The Japanese had lost over thirty battalions, with more than 50,000 men killed in their attempt to hold the islands. Ultimately more than 18,000 Japanese were lost on Guam alone.[27]

The Japanese navy, although it made one last sortie during the Philippine campaign in October, was never the same after its defeat in the Philippine Sea battle in mid-June 1944. The "Marianas Turkey Shoot" not only destroyed hundreds of Japanese planes, but also the last significant cadre of relatively experienced pilots. From the newly improved naval bases, particularly on Guam, the United States fleet could more effectively block the transport of supplies and men to the thousands of Japanese troops stranded in the lands which they had earlier conquered, extending as far south as New Guinea and westward to Burma. They were now isolated without hope of support of any kind from the Imperial government. It is unlikely that enemies such as Admiral Nagano, chief of the Japanese naval staff, and General H. M. Smith would agree on much concerning the Pacific War. One point, however, reiterated at length by both was that the loss of the Marianas meant that Japan had irretrievably lost the war. Perhaps the most succinct expression of this was that stated later by Prince Naruhiko Higashikuni, Commander of Japan's Home Defense Headquarters, when he wrote:

The war was lost when the Marianas were taken away from Japan and when we heard the B–29s were coming out. . . . We had nothing in Japan that we could use against such a weapon. From the point of view of Home Defense Command, we felt that the war was lost and said so. If the B–29s could come over Japan there was nothing that could be done.[28]

There was much controversy in the years following World War II concerning the wisdom of some of the decisions made by senior Navy, Army, and Marine staff. It appears on the basis of the best evidence available now that the assault on Tarawa was probably unnecessary and certainly the seizure of Peleliu was not worth the cost in Marine and Army lives. Although there were tactical blunders and questionable decisions made by senior officers, particularly on Saipan, there has never been any serious criticism of the decision to seize the Marianas. By a fortunate set of circumstances, the Guam operation, the last of those directed at the Japanese in the Marianas, was postponed long enough to assure maximum naval and air support, and General Takashina was obliging enough to throw away much of his troop strength in his abortive *banzai* attacks. Nevertheless, the casualties in recapturing Guam were heavy. More than 1,700 men were killed or died of their wounds, while over 6,000 were wounded. Unlike some other areas in the Pacific theater, the positive results of these sacrifices could immediately be seen. By the spring of 1945 Guam had become the centrum for the complex command network of the Navy and the Strategic Air Force in the Pacific. Most of the destruction wrought on Japan during the last months of the war had its origins on Guam. By mid–1945 over $170 million had been spent on military improvements on the island and it had become what some far-sighted naval planners had envisioned forty years before—the chief American military bastion in the Central Pacific.

NOTES

CHAPTER I:

[1] The early history of Guam is taken from Paul Carona and Charles Bendsley, *Guam, Past and Present* (Tokyo and Rutland, Vt.: C. E. Tuttle, 1964); I. G. Edmonds, *Micronesia* (New York: Bobbs-Merrill & Co., 1974); and Laura Thompson, *Guam and Its People* (Princeton, N.J.: Princeton University Press, 1947).

[2] Edmonds, *Micronesia*, pp. 27–29.

[3] Thompson, *Guam*, p. 34.

[4] Edmonds, *Micronesia*, p. 33.

[5] Earl S. Pomeroy, *Pacific Outpost* (Stanford, Ca.: Stanford University Press, 1951), p. 4.

[6] Ibid., p. 5.

[7] Edmonds, *Micronesia*, p. 63.

[8] Pomeroy, *Pacific Outpost*, p. 9.

[9] Ibid., pp. 14–16.

[10] Ibid., p. 24.

[11] G. J. Rowcliff, "Guam," *U.S. Naval Institute Proceedings*, Vol. **71**, #509, July 1945, p. 781.

[12] Edmonds, *Micronesia*, pp. 81–84, and Tony Palomo, *An Island in Agony* (Agana, Guam: privately published, 1984), pp. 72–81.

[13] For a detailed examination of these many proposals, see Pomeroy, *Pacific Outpost*, Chapters IV and V.

[14] Ibid., p. 45.

[15] Ibid., p. 57.

[16] Ibid., pp. 79–80.

[17] Philip Crowl, *U.S. Army in World War II, The War in the Pacific, Campaign in the Marianas* (Washington, D.C.: Department of the Army, 1960), p. 3.

[18] "Report on Need for Additional Naval Bases . . . ," *House Documents*, 76th Congress, 1st Session, No. 65.

[19] As cited in Pomeroy, *Pacific Outpost*, p. 142.

[20] As cited in Ibid.

[21] Crowl, *Campaign in the Marianas*, pp. 3–4.

[22] Adm. Harold Stark to Adm. Husband Kimmel, 19 August 1941, as quoted in Pomeroy, *Pacific Outpost*, p. 151.

[23] *New York Times*, 1 December 1945, p. 3, cols. 2–3.

[24] Pomeroy, *Pacific Outpost,* pp. 100–101.

[25] Maj. Orlan R. Lodge, *The Recapture of Guam* (Washington, D.C., Historical Branch, Headquarters, U.S. Marine Corps, 1954), p. 8.

[26] Crowl, *Campaign in the Marianas,* pp. 3–4.

[27] Palomo, *Island in Agony,* p. 16.

[28] Diary of James O'Leary, entry of 10 December 1941, found in wreckage of Marine Barracks on 10 August 1944, now located in Personal Correspondence Section of Marine Corps Archives, Washington Navy Yard, Washington, D.C.

[29] Palomo, *Island in Agony,* p. 26.

[30] Ibid., p. 30.

[31] Ibid.

[32] Ibid.

CHAPTER II:

[1] Tweed's adventures on Guam are told in George Tweed and Blake Clark, *Robinson Crusoe, U.S.N., The Adventures of George Tweed, RM 1/C, U.S.N. on Jap Held Guam* (New York: McGraw Hill, 1945). For details of Guamanian actions in sheltering the escapees, see Palomo, *Island in Agony,* pp. 101–120.

[2] Entry of 18 December 1941 in Diary of James O'Leary.

[3] Henry Shaw, Bernard Nalty, and Edwin Turnbladh, *History of U.S. Marine Corps Operations in World War II,* Vol. III, *Central Pacific Drive* (Washington, D.C.: Historical Branch, Headquarters U.S. Marine Corps, 1966), p. 442.

[4] Palomo, *Island in Agony,* pp. 22–23.

[5] Geographic descriptions of Guam based upon personal observations and a close analysis of the eleven sheets of the 1:20,000 map and the 1:62,500 map of Guam in the Marine Corps Archives.

[6] Edmonds, *Micronesia,* p. 65.

[7] Palomo, *Island in Agony,* pp. 179–81.

[8] Pomeroy, *Pacific Outpost,* pp. 106–107.

[9] Lodge, *The Recapture of Guam,* pp. 10–11.

[10] Shaw, *Central Pacific Drive,* pp. 442–443.

[11] Reply by ex-staff officer Lt. Col. Hideyuki Takeda, 29th Division to BGen. J. C. McQueen, USMC, 20 Feb. 1952, Monograph and Comment File C7–1, Marine Corps Archives, Washington, D.C.

[12] Lodge, *The Recapture of Guam,* Appendix VII.

[13] Barney Tobyer, Pfc Hq. 2nd Bn, 307th Inf., "A History of the Guam Operation," p. 22, Record Group 407, Entry 427, Box 11712, 377 INF (307.0), National Archives, Suitland, Md.

[14] Palomo, *Island in Agony,* pp. 179–181.

[15] Ibid., pp. 186–187.

[16] Lt. Col. Hadeyuki Takeda, "The Outline of the Japanese Defense Plan and Battle of Guam Island," 4 Oct. 1946, File E1–2, Marine Corps Archives, Washington, D.C.

[17] Lodge, *The Recapture of Guam,* Appendix VII.

[18] III Marine Amphibious Corps, C–2 Periodic Report, No. 21, and 3rd Marine Division, Guam, Japanese Defenses published by D–2 Section, File C4–1, Marine Corps Archives, Washington, D.C.

[19] Task Force 56, G–2 Report, Appendix H., Marine Corps Archives, Washington, D.C.

[20] Shaw, *Central Pacific Drive,* p. 447.

[21] Ibid.

[22] Operations and Special Action Report, 1st Marine Provisional Brigade, 19 August 1944, Guam, File A18–1, pp. 8–9, Marine Corps Archives, Washington, D.C.

[23] CINCPAC–CINCPOA Item, Agana Garrison Order A27, 15 July 1944; see also Takeda, "Outline of Japanese Defense," p. 2.

CHAPTER III:

[1] As quoted in Rikihei Inoguchi, Tadashi Nakajima, and Roger Pineau, *The Divine Wind* (New York: Ballentine Books, 1958), p. xiv.

[2] This early decision to favor Europe is confirmed in many sources. See particularly Albert C. Wedemeyer, *Wedemeyer Reports* (New York: Henry Holt & Co., 1958), pp. 15–26; Winston Churchill, *The Grand Alliance* (Boston: Houghton Mifflin Co., 1950), pp. 543ff; and Robert Sherwood, *Roosevelt and Hopkins* (New York: Harper Brothers, 1948), pp. 230ff.

[3] E. B. Potter and FAdm. Chester Nimitz, eds., *Triumph in the Pacific* (Englewood Cliffs, N.J.: Prentice Hall, 1963), p. 48.

[4] Crowl, *Campaign in the Marianas,* p. 6.

[5] Ibid., pp. 10–11.

[6] Ibid., pp. 11–13, and H. H. Arnold, *Global Mission* (New York: Harper Brothers, 1949), pp. 476ff.

[7] Lodge, *The Recapture of Guam,* p. 17.

[8] Potter and Nimitz, *Triumph in the Pacific,* pp. 65–66.

[9] Shaw, *Central Pacific Drive,* pp. 181–219.

[10] Potter and Nimitz, *Triumph in the Pacific,* p. 73.

[11] Lodge, *The Recapture of Guam,* p. 18.

[12] Shaw, *Central Pacific Drive,* p. 240.

[13] Robert Aurthur, Kenneth Cohlmia and Robert Vance, *The Third Marine Division*, (Washington, D.C.: Infantry Journal Press, 1948), pp. 58–83, 136–39.

[14] Benis Frank, Interviewer, Oral Transcript, Gen. Lemuel Shepherd, Jr., 1967, pp. 191–193, Marine Corps Archives, Washington, D.C.

[15] Ibid., pp. 417–418.

[16] Lodge, *The Recapture of Guam*, pp. 18–19.

[17] TF56, G–3 Report, p. 2, Marine Corps Archives, Washington, D.C.

[18] TF53, Report of Amphibious Operations for the Capture of Guam, July-August 1944, File A05–1, pp. 4–6, Marine Corps Archives, Washington, D.C.

[19] Crowl, *Campaign in the Marianas*, p. 326.

[20] Intelligence annex to Special Action Reports, 17 August 1944, File 65A44556, Marine Corps Archives, Washington, D.C. and Lodge, *The Recapture of Guam*, pp. 24–25.

[21] Operations and Special Action Report, 1st Marine Provisional Brigade, 19 August 1944, Guam.

[22] III Marine Amphibious Corps Operations Plan 1–44, 11 May 1944, File C–2, Marine Corps Archives, Washington, D.C.

[23] A reinterpretation of this controversy is Harry A. Gailey, *Howlin' Mad vs. The Army* (Novato, Ca.: Presidio Press, 1986).

[24] Holland M. Smith and Percy Finch, *Coral and Brass* (New York: Charles Scribner's Sons, 1949), pp. 113, 117, 120, 149 and letter from Spruance to Col. Warren Hoover, 14 Jan. 1949, Miscellaneous Papers Adm. Raymond Spruance, 1937–1963, Hoover Institution Archives, Stanford, Ca.

[25] Smith, *Coral and Brass*, pp. 217–218.

[26] Benis Frank, Interviewer, Oral History Transcript Gen. Robert C. Hogaboom, 1972, pp. 196–217. Marine Corps Archives, Washington, D.C.

[27] Geiger's life is related in the laudatory biography Roger Willock, *Unaccustomed to Fear* (Princeton, N.J.: Haskins Press, 1968).

[28] Aurthur, et al., *The Third Marine Division*, pp. 48–50.

[29] Shaw, *Central Pacific Drive*, p. 435.

[30] Interview with Col. Joseph Coolidge, Saratoga, Ca., 6 November 1985.

[31] III Marine Amphibious Corps Operational Plan 1–44, 11 May 1944.

[32] Shaw, *Central Pacific Drive*, p. 444.

[33] Lodge, *The Recapture of Guam*, p. 29.

CHAPTER IV:

[1] III Marine Amphibious Corps Special Action Report, Supply Report.

[2] Ibid., and 3rd Marine Division Operational Plan, 2–44, File C4–1, 13 May 1944, Marine Corps Archives, Washington, D.C.

[3] TF53, Report of Amphibious Operations for the Capture of Guam, July-August 1944, Operations Plan A 162–44. 17 May 1944.

[4] Ibid., Enclosure B, Naval Gunfire Support Report.

[5] Lodge, *The Recapture of Guam*, p. 28.

[6] Ibid., p. 29.

[7] Smith, *Coral and Brass*, p. 181.

[8] For a discussion of the Saipan controversy see Gailey, *Howlin' Mad vs. The Army*.

[9] TF53, Report of Amphibious Operations for Capture of Guam, July-August 1944.

[10] The most detailed treatment of the Philippine Sea action is in Samuel Eliot Morison, *History of United States Naval Operations in World War II*, Vol. VII, *New Guinea and the Marianas* (Boston: Little Brown and Co., 1962), pp. 213–321, and also E. P. Forrestel, *Admiral Raymond A. Spruance* (Washington, D.C.: Office of Naval History, 1966), pp. 131–146.

[11] Smith, *Coral and Brass*, pp. 213–233.

[12] Benis Frank, interviewer, Oral History Transcript, LtGen. Mervin Silverthorn, 1973, p. 308.

[13] Lodge, *The Recapture of Guam*, p. 30.

[14] Tobyer, "A History of the Guam Operation," p. 1.

[15] Interview with Wilcie O'Bannon, Mariposa, Ca., 27 April 1986.

[16] Alvin M. Josephy, "They Lived Through Hell," in *Semper Fidelis, The U.S. Marines in the Pacific—1942–1945*, arranged by Patrick Sheel and Gene Cook (New York: William Sloan and Associates, 1947), p. 62.

[17] As quoted in Crowl, *Campaign in the Marianas*, p. 315.

[18] For the background of the 77th Division prior to the Guam operation, see Lt. Col Max Meyers, ed, *Ours to Hold High, The History of the 77th Division in World War II* (Washington, D.C.: Infantry Journal Press, 1947).

[19] Interview with MajGen. James Landrum, San Francisco, 23 December 1985.

[20] Ibid.

[21] TF56, Report on FORAGER Operation, Enclosure G, Transport

Quartermaster's Report, Enclosure B-B, Marine Corps Archives, Washington, D.C.

[22] Letters on operation forwarded by General Geiger, 23 July 1944, in Geiger Personal Papers, Personal Papers Section, PC 311, Box 5, Marine Corps Archives, Washington, D.C.

[23] Crowl, *Campaign in the Marianas*, p. 321.

[24] TF53, Report of Amphibious Operations for the Capture of Guam, July-August 1944, p. 7 and Appendix 4 to Enclosure C.

[25] Crowl, *Campaign in the Marianas*, p. 324.

[26] Palomo, *An Island in Agony*, p. 175.

[27] TF53, Report of Amphibious Operations for the Capture of Guam, July-August 1944, Enclosure B, Naval Gunfire Support, p. 11.

[28] Reply of LtCol. Hideyuki Takeda to BGen. J. C. McQueen, 24 January 1952, pp. 7–8.

[29] TG56.2, Prisoner of War Interrogation Reports, File C1–1, Marine Corps Archives, Washington, D.C.

[30] As quoted in Crowl, *Campaign in the Marianas*, p. 337.

CHAPTER V:

[1] TF53, Report of Amphibious Operations for the Capture of Guam, July-August 1944, p. 10.

[2] John Magruder, "Epitaph" in S. E. Smith, *The United States Marine Corps in World War II* (New York: Random House, 1969), p. 609.

[3] TF53, Report of Amphibious Operations for the Capture of Guam, July-August 1944, pp. 6–7.

[4] Robert Leckie, *Strong Men Armed* (New York: Random House, 1962), p. 360.

[5] Details of operations on Guam on W day based on Ibid. and TG53.2, Action Report, Guam, File A2–1; TG53.4, Action Report, File A3–1; III Marine Amphibious Corps, Periodic Report, File A11–2; 3rd Marine Division Periodic Report, File C4–1; 1st Marine Provisional Brigade Special Action Report, File A18–1 in Marine Corps Archives, Washington, D.C. See also Lodge, *The Recapture of Guam*, pp. 37–58; Shaw, *Central Pacific Drive*, pp. 457–484; and Crowl, *Campaign in the Marianas*, pp. 339–348.

[6] Aurthur and Cohlmia, *The Third Marine Division*, p. 147.

[7] Benis Frank, Interviewer, Oral History Transcript, LtGen. Pedro del Valle, 1973, pp. 169–170.

[8] Thomas O'Neil, "A Platoon in Battle," Personal Correspondence, File PC 453, Marine Corps Archives, Washington, D.C.

[9] 9th Marine Regiment Unit Report, Guam, 1800 Hours, 21 July 1944, File A23–1, Marine Corps Archives, Washington, D.C.

[10] Lodge, *The Recapture of Guam*, pp. 38–41.

[11] Cyril O'Brien, "Chonito Cliff," in *Semper Fidelis*, p. 186.

[12] Lodge, *The Recapture of Guam*, pp. 43–44.

[13] Takeda, "Outline of Japanese Defense Plan," pp. 3–4.

[14] Robert Martin, "Guam Finale" in S. E. Smith, *United States Marine Corps*, p. 617.

[15] Operations and Special Action Report, 1st Marine Provisional Brigade, p. 7.

[16] Takeda, "Outline of Japanese Defense Plan," p. 1.

[17] Shaw, *Central Pacific Drive*, p. 473.

[18] Ibid., pp. 475–476.

[19] Ibid., p. 480.

[20] Takeda, "Outline of Japanese Defense Plan," p. 3.

[21] Lodge, *The Recapture of Guam*, p. 54.

[22] Takeda, "Outline of Japanese Defense Plan," p. 3.

[23] Lodge, *The Recapture of Guam*, p. 55.

[24] Herman Kogan, "The Nips are Nuts," *Semper Fidelis*, p. 222.

[25] Lodge, *The Recapture of Guam*, p. 56.

[26] Palomo, *An Island in Agony*, p. 205.

[27] Citation for Medal of Honor in Aurthur and Cohlmia, *The Third Marine Division*, pp. 367ff.

[28] Lodge, *The Recapture of Guam*, p. 59.

[29] 305th RCT After Action Report, 18 June–9 August 1944, pp. 1–2, File 377.3.3, Record Group 407, National Archives, Suitland, Md.

[30] Lodge, *The Recapture of Guam*, p. 57.

[31] Interview with MajGen. James Landrum, 23 December 1985.

[32] Ibid.

[33] 305th RCT After Action Report, p. 2.

[34] Crowl, *Campaign in the Marianas*, p. 348.

[35] III Marine Amphibious Corps, C–3 Reports 1–24 Guam, Entry 21 July, File A11–2, Marine Corps Archives, Washington, D.C.

CHAPTER VI:

[1] For Medal of Honor citation see Aurthur and Cohlmia, *The Third Marine Division*, pp. 367ff.

[2] Details of the operations on Guam from W + 1 through W + 4 based on III Marine Amphibious Corps Periodic Report, File C–2; 3rd Marine Division Periodic Reports, File C–41; 1st Marine Provisional Brigade Special Action Reports, File A 18–1; 3rd Marine Regiment

Journal 21 July–12 Aug. 1944, File A 19–4; 9th Marine Regiment, Regimental Journal, 21 July–31 Aug. 1944, File A 23–3 in Marine Corps Archives, Washington, D.C. See also Lodge, *The Recapture of Guam*, pp. 58–87; Shaw, *Central Pacific Drive*, pp. 479–518.

[3] 9th Marine Regiment R–2 Journal, 21 July–31 Aug. 1944, File A 23–3, Marine Corps Archives, Washington, D.C.

[4] Lodge, *The Recapture of Guam*, p. 61.

[5] III Marine Amphibious Corps, Special Action Report, Operations Report, p. 2.

[6] 77th Infantry Division, G–3 Journal, Guam Operation, 6 June–10 Aug. 1944, Group 407, Entry 427, File 377.3.2, p. 35, National Archives, Suitland, Md.

[7] 1st Marine Provisional Brigade Journal, and Lodge, *The Recapture of Guam*, pp. 65–66.

[8] 77th Division, G–3 Journal, Guam Operation.

[9] Ibid., and *Guam, Operations of the 77th Division*, Washington, D.C., Historical Division, War Department, 1946, pp. 39–40.

[10] Interview with MajGen. Landrum, 23 December 1985.

[11] Lodge, *The Recapture of Guam*, pp. 67–69.

[12] 1st Marine Provisional Brigade, Operations and Special Action Reports, entry for 24 July 1944.

[13] III Marine Amphibious Corps, Periodic Reports, entry for 23 July 1944, Marine Corps Archives, Washington, D.C.

[14] 3rd Marine Division, C–3 Reports, 1–24 Guam, entry for 23 July 1944, File A11–2, Marine Corps Archives, Washington, D.C.

[15] 9th Marine Regiment, R–2 Journal, entry for 24 July 1944, File A 23–3, Marine Corps Archives, Washington, D.C.

[16] Smith, *Coral and Brass*, p. 217.

[17] 3rd Marine Division, Periodic Reports, entry for 25 July 1944, and interview with Wilcie O'Bannon, Mariposa, Ca., 27 April 1986.

[18] Benis Frank, interviewer, Oral History Transcript, LtGen. Pedro del Valle, 1973, p. 170.

[19] 1st Marine Provisional Brigade, Special Action Reports, entry for 25 July 1944.

[20] Shaw, *Central Pacific Drive*, pp. 517–518.

[21] Reply of LtCol. Takeda to BGen. McQueen, p. 11.

[22] Interview with Colonel Coolidge, 6 November 1985.

[23] Leckie, *Strong Men Armed*, p. 372.

[24] Reply of LtCol. Takeda to BGen. McQueen, p. 3.

[25] Frank O. Hough, *The Island War*, (New York: J. B. Lippincott & Co., 1947), pp. 279–280.

[26] Lodge, *The Recapture of Guam*, p. 79.
[27] O'Neil, "A Platoon in Battle," p. 14.
[28] Josephy, "They Lived Through Hell," *Semper Fidelis*, p. 62.
[29] Ibid., p. 65.
[30] Ibid., p. 68.
[31] Leckie, *Strong Men Armed*, p. 378.
[32] Lodge, *The Recapture of Guam*, pp. 84–85.
[33] 1st Marine Provisional Brigade, After Action Report, 26 July 1944, File A 25–2, Marine Corps Archives, Washington, D.C.
[34] Leckie, *Strong Men Armed*, p. 33.
[35] Lodge, *The Recapture of Guam*, p. 85.
[36] Interview with Col. Fraser West, Ione, Ca., 13 April 1986.
[37] For Medal of Honor citation, see Aurthur and Cohlmia, *The Third Marine Division*, pp. 367ff.
[38] Hough, *This Island War*, p. 274.
[39] 3rd Marine Division, C–3 Reports, 1–24 Guam, entry for 27 July 1944.
[40] Josephy, "They Lived Through Hell," p. 74.
[41] Reply of LtCol. Takeda to BGen. McQueen, pp. 11–12.

CHAPTER VII:

[1] Details of operations on Guam from W + 5 through W + 10 based on III Marine Amphibious Corps Periodic Report, File C–2, 3rd Marine Division Periodic Reports, File C–41, 1st Marine Provisional Brigade Special Action Reports, File A18–1 in Marine Corps Archives, Washington, D.C., and 77th Infantry Division, G–3 Journal; 305th, 306th, and 307th Infantry Operations Reports, G–3 Journals and Unit Histories, Group 407, entry 427, National Archives, Suitland, Md. See also Lodge, *The Recapture of Guam*, pp. 88–105; Shaw, *Central Pacific Drive*, pp. 517–538; Crowl, *Campaign in the Marianas*, pp. 366–386.
[2] O'Neil, "A Platoon in Battle," p. 16.
[3] 1st Marine Provisional Brigade Special Action Reports.
[4] As quoted in Lodge, *The Recapture of Guam*, p. 95.
[5] Smith, *Coral and Brass*, p. 218.
[6] Ibid.
[7] 3rd Marine Division Periodic Reports, entry for 29 July 1944.
[8] 9th Marine Regiment Unit Report, Guam, entry for 29 July 1944.
[9] Lodge, *The Recapture of Guam*, p. 102.
[10] Letter Gen. A. D. Bruce to Roberta Bruce, 28 July 1944, Andrew Bruce Collection, U.S. Military History Institute, Carlisle Barracks, Pa.

11 77th Infantry Division, G–3 Journal.
12 Ibid.
13 III Marine Amphibious Corps C–3 Reports, Guam, entry for 28 July 1944.
14 Leckie, *Strong Men Armed*, p. 380.
15 Reply of LtCol. Takeda to BGen. McQueen.
16 III Marine Amphibious Corps C–2 Reports, Guam.
17 Aurthur and Cohlmia, *The Third Marine Division*, p. 157.
18 Martin, "Guam Finale."
19 Lodge, *The Recapture of Guam*, p. 125.
20 Ibid., p. 130.
21 Interview with MajGen. Landrum, 23 December 1985.
22 Letter Gen. Bruce to Roberta Bruce, 3 August 1944, Andrew Bruce Collection, U.S. Military History Institute, Carlisle Barracks, Pa.
23 Interview with Colonel Coolidge, 6 November 1985.
24 Smith, *Coral and Brass*, p. 218.

CHAPTER VIII:
1 Interview with Colonel Coolidge, 6 November 1985.
2 Interview with MajGen. Landrum, 23 December 1985.
3 Ibid.
4 Takeda, "Outline of Japanese Defense Plan," p. 4.
5 As quoted in Lodge, *The Recapture of Guam*, p. 145.
6 Details of operations on Guam from W + 12 to the end of the campaign based on III Marine Amphibious Corps Periodic Report, File C–2; 3rd Marine Division Periodic Reports, File C–41; 1st Marine Provisional Brigade Special Action Reports, File A 18–1; 3rd Marine Regiment Journal 21 July–12 Aug. 1944, File A 19–4; 9th Marine Regiment, Regimental Journal, 21 July–31 Aug. 1944, File A 23–3, in Marine Corps Archives, Washington, D.C.; 77th Infantry Division, G–3 Journal, Guam Operation; 305th, 306th, and 307th Infantry Operations Reports, G–3 Journals, and Unit Histories, Group 407, entry 427 National Archives, Suitland, Md. See also Lodge, *The Recapture of Guam*, pp. 120–159; Shaw, *Central Pacific Drive*, pp. 545–567; and Crowl, *Campaign in the Marianas*, pp. 386–437.
7 Lodge, *The Recapture of Guam*, p. 136.
8 77th Division, G–3 Journal, Guam Operation.
9 Crowl, *Campaign in the Marianas*, p. 411.
10 *Ours to Hold High*, pp. 110–111.
11 Ibid., p. 112.

[12] Crowl, *Campaign in the Marianas,* p. 419.

[13] 307th Infantry Regiment, Unit History, National Archives, Suitland, Md., and Crowl, *Campaign in the Marianas,* pp. 418–426.

[14] 77th Division, G–3 Journal, 5–6 August 1944.

[15] *Ours to Hold High,* p. 119.

[16] 77th Division, G–1 Casualty Reports.

[17] Lodge, *The Recapture of Guam,* pp. 139–140.

[18] Ibid., pp. 128–129.

[19] Alvin M. Josephy, *The Long and the Short and the Tall* (New York: Alfred Knopf & Co., 1946), p. 69.

[20] For Medal of Honor citation, see Aurthur and Cohlmia, *The Third Marine Division,* pp. 367ff.

[21] 3rd Marine Division, D–3 Journal.

[22] 9th Marine Regiment Unit Report, entry 5 August 1944.

[23] 1st Marine Provisional Brigade, Operations and Special Action Reports.

[24] Ibid.

[25] Josephy, *The Long and the Short and the Tall,* p. 91.

[26] III Marine Amphibious Corps, C–2 Journal, Guam; and Palomo, *Island in Agony,* p. 216.

[27] Interview with Wilcie O'Bannon, Mariposa, Ca., 27 April 1986.

[28] III Marine Amphibious Corps, C–3 Reports, Guam.

[29] Lodge, *The Recapture of Guam,* p. 157.

[30] As quoted in Shaw, *Central Pacific Drive,* p. 567.

[31] Reply of LtCol. Takeda to BGen. McQueen, p. 7.

[32] There is some question over the number of casualties suffered through 10 August. Those given by Crowl, *Campaign in the Marianas,* p. 437, are obviously incorrect. Those given in III Marine Amphibious Corps C–3 Reports are flawed because at the time of issuance there had been no recheck. The best information appears to be those cited in Shaw, *Central Pacific Drive,* p. 568, and the figures given here duplicate his count. For a detailed breakdown of Marine casualties, see also Lodge, *The Recapture of Guam,* Appendix III.

CHAPTER IX:

[1] Harry A. Gailey, *Peleliu: 1944* (Annapolis, Md.: The Nautical and Aviation Publishing Co. of America, 1983), pp. 15–18.

[2] *Ours to Hold High,* p. 126.

[3] Ibid., pp. 141ff.

[4] Benis Frank, interviewer, Oral History Transcript, MajGen. Graves Erskine, 1975, pp. 354–355, Marine Corps Archives, Washington, D.C.

[5] Oral History Transcript, Gen. Robert Hogaboom, p. 223.

[6] Palomo, *Island in Agony*, pp. 223–224.

[7] Lodge, *The Recapture of Guam*, p. 162.

[8] Takeda, "Outline of Japanese Defense Plan," p. 4.

[9] Josephy, "Some Japs Surrendered," *Semper Fidelis*, p. 227.

[10] Island Command Guam, Estimates of Enemy Situation, 6 March 1945, File C 6–1, Marine Corps Archives, Washington, D.C.

[11] Oral History Transcript, Gen. Robert Hogaboom, p. 224.

[12] Aurthur and Cohlmia, *The Third Marine Division*, p. 167.

[13] Josephy, "Some Japs Surrendered," *Semper Fidelis*, p. 232.

[14] Lodge, *The Recapture of Guam*, p. 165.

[15] Tetsuro Morimoto, et al., *Twenty-Eight Years in the Guam Jungle* (Tokyo & San Francisco: Japan Publications, 1972).

[16] Josephy, *The Long and the Short and the Tall*, p. 76.

[17] Palomo, *Island in Agony*, pp. 224–227.

[18] Lodge, *The Recapture of Guam*, p. 163.

[19] Karl C. Dod, *The Corps of Engineers: The War Against Japan* (Washington, D.C.: Office of the Chief of Military History, 1966), pp. 504–505.

[20] Lodge, *The Recapture of Guam*, p. 95.

[21] Crowl, *Campaign in the Marianas*, p. 443.

[22] Curtis LeMay and MacKinlay Kantor, *Mission with LeMay* (Garden City, N.Y.: Doubleday & Co., 1965), p. 340.

[23] Wesley F. Craven and James L. Cate, *The Army Airforces in World War II*, Vol. V (Chicago: University of Chicago Press, 1953), pp. 514–519.

[24] Dod, *The Corps of Engineers*, p. 517.

[25] Craven and Cate, *The Army Airforces*, p. 520.

[26] Ibid., p. 617.

[27] Island Command Guam, Estimates of Enemy Situation, 6 March 1945.

[28] AC/AS Mission Accomplished: Interrogations of Japanese Industrial, Military, and Civil Leaders of World War II, p. 18 as cited in Crowl, *Campaign in the Marianas*, p. 445.

BIBLIOGRAPHY

Primary Sources

Marine Corps Historical Archives, Washington, D.C.
Task Force 53, Report of Amphibious Operations for the Capture of Guam, July-August 1944, File A05–1.
Task Force 56, G–3 Report, Guam, File A3–1.
Task Group 53.2, Action Report, Guam, File A2–1.
Task Group 53.4, Action Report, Transport Division 4, File A3–1.
Task Group 56.2, Prisoner of War Interrogation Reports, File C1–1.
III Marine Amphibious Corps, Guam, R–2 Journal, File A1–2.
III Marine Amphibious Corps, Operations Plan 1–44, Guam, 11 May 1944, File C–2.
III Marine Amphibious Corps, Guam, Periodic Reports, File A11–3.
III Marine Amphibious Corps, Guam, C–3 Reports, File A11–2.
3rd Marine Division, Guam, Japanese Defenses, published by D–2 Section, File C4–1.
3rd Marine Division, Summary of Enemy Contacts, 2 November 1944–8 April 1945, File A17–3.
1st Marine Provisional Brigade, Operations and Special Action Report, Guam, File A18–1.
3rd Marine Regiment, C–2 Journal, 21 July–31 August 1944, File A23–3.
9th Marine Regiment, Guam, Unit Reports, File A23–1.
Headquarters Island Command, Periodic Report, 27 August 1944–5 April 1945, Guam, File E2–1.
Lt. Colonel Hideyuki Takeda's "Outline of Japanese Defense Plan and Battle of Guam Island," File E1–2.
Lt. Colonel Hideyuki Takeda's Correspondence with BGen. J. C. McQueen, Guam, File C7–1.
Benis Frank (interviewer) Oral History Transcript, Gen. Lemuel Shepherd, Jr., 1967.
Benis Frank (interviewer), Gen. Robert Hogaboom, 1972.
Benis Frank (interviewer), Gen. Graves Erskine, 1975.
Benis Frank (interviewer), LtGen. Merwin Silverthorn, 1973.
Benis Frank (interviewer), LtGen. Pedro del Valle, 1973.
Benis Frank (interviewer), LtGen. John C. McQueen, 1973.

219

Thomas E. Donnelly (interviewer), LtGen. Alan Shapley, 1976.
O'Leary, James B., Diary, P.C. 102.
Geiger, General Roy, Papers, P.C. 311.
O'Neil, Thomas R., Journal, P.C. 453.

National Archives, Suitland, Maryland
Record Group 407, Entry 427, File 377–3.3.
Journal File, Guam Operations, 77th Infantry Division, 30 July–10 August 1944.
77th Infantry Division, Guam, Operations Report.
305th RCT, 77th Division, Unit History, Guam.
305th RCT After Action Reports, Guam.
306th RCT Operations Report, Guam.
306th RCT After Action Reports, Guam.
307th RCT, 77th Division Unit History.
307th RCT, 77th Division, Operations Report, 7 July–10 August 1944.
307th RCT, After Action Reports, Guam.
Tobyer, Pfc Barney, "A History of the Guam Operation" in Box 11712.

U.S. Military Institute, Carlisle Barracks, Pa.
Bruce, General Andrew D., Papers.

Interviews by author
MajGen. James Landrum, USA, San Francisco, Ca., 23 December 1985.
Col. Joseph Coolidge, Saratoga, Ca., 6 November 1985.
Capt. Wilcie O'Bannon, USMC, Mariposa, Ca., 27 April 1986.
Col. Fraser West, USMC, Ione, Ca., 13 April 1986.

Books
Arnold, H. H. *Global Mission.* New York: Harper Brothers, 1949.
Aurthur, Robert, Kenneth Cohlmia, and Robert Vance. *The Third Marine Division.* Washington, D.C.: Infantry Journal Press, 1948.
Carona, Paul and Charles Bendsley, *Guam, Past and Present.* Tokyo and Rutland, Vt: C. E. Tuttle, 1964.
Churchill, Winston S. *The Grand Alliance.* Boston: Houghton Mifflin Co., 1950.
Craven, Wesley F. and James L. Cate. *The Army Airforces in World War II,* Vol. V, *The Pacific: Matterhorn to Nagasaki.* Chicago: The University of Chicago Press, 1953.
Crowl, Philip. *U.S. Army in World War II, The War in the Pacific, Campaign*

in the Marianas. Washington, D.C.: Department of the Army, 1960.

Dod, Karl C. *The Corps of Engineers: The War Against Japan.* Washington, D.C.: Office of the Chief of Military History, 1966.

Dyer, George C. *The Amphibians Came to Conquer,* Vol. 2. Washington, D.C.: Navy Department, n.d.

Edmonds, I. G. *Micronesia.* New York: Bobbs-Merrill & Co., 1974.

Forrestel, E. P. *Admiral Raymond A. Spruance, USN.* Washington, D.C.: Navy Department, 1966.

Gailey, Harry A. *Howlin' Mad vs. The Army.* Novato, Ca.: Presidio Press, 1986.

Gailey, Harry A. *Peleliu: 1944.* Annapolis, Md.: The Nautical and Aviation Publishing Co. of America, 1983.

Historical Division, War Department. *Guam, Operations of the 77th Division (21 July–10 August 1944).* Washington, D.C.: Historical Division, War Department, 1946.

Hough, Frank O. *The Island War.* New York: J. B. Lippincott & Co., 1947.

Hoyt, Edwin P. *To the Marianas.* New York: Avon Books, 1983.

Inoguchi, Rikihei, Tadashi Nakajima and Roger Pineau. *The Divine Wind.* New York: Ballentine Books, 1958.

Josephy, Alvin M. *The Long and the Short and the Tall.* New York: Alfred Knopf & Co., 1946.

Leckie, Robert. *Strong Men Armed.* New York: Random House, 1962.

LeMay, Curtis and MacKinlay Kantor. *Mission With LeMay.* Garden City, N.Y.: Doubleday & Co., 1965.

Lodge, Orlan R. *The Recapture of Guam.* Washington, D.C., Historical Branch, G–3 Division, HQMC, 1954.

Meyers, LtCol. Max, USA, ed. *Ours to Hold High: The History of the 77th Division in World War II.* Washington, D.C.: Infantry Journal Press, 1947.

Morimoto, Tetsuro, et al. *Twenty-Eight Years in the Guam Jungle.* Tokyo and San Francisco: Japan Publications, 1972.

Morison, Samuel Eliot. *History of the United States Naval Operations in World War II,* Vol. VII, *New Guinea and the Marianas.* Boston: Little Brown & Co., 1962.

Morison, Samuel Eliot. *The Rising Sun in the Pacific, 1931–April 1942.* Boston: Little Brown & Co., 1948.

Palomo, Tony. *An Island in Agony.* Agana, Guam: privately published, 1984.

Pomeroy, Earl S. *Pacific Outpost, American Strategy in Guam & Micronesia.* Stanford, Ca.: Stanford University Press, 1951.

Potter, E. B. and FAdm. Chester Nimitz, eds. *Triumph in the Pacific.* Englewood Cliffs, N.J.: Prentice Hall, 1963.

Sanchez, Pedro. *A Complete History of Guam.* Tokyo: 1964.

Shaw, Henry, Bernard Nalty, and Edwin Turnbladh. *History of U.S. Marine Corps Operations in World War II,* Vol. III, *Central Pacific Drive.* Washington, D.C.: Historical Branch, Headquarters U.S. Marine Corps, 1966.

Sheek, Patrick and Gene Cook. *Semper Fidelis, The U.S. Marines in the Pacific—1942–1945.* New York: William Sloan and Associates, 1947.

Sherwood, Robert. *Roosevelt and Hopkins.* New York: Harper Brothers, 1948.

Simmons, Edwin H. *The United States Marines.* New York: The Viking Press, 1976.

Smith, Holland M. and Percy Finch. *Coral and Brass.* New York: Charles Scribner's Sons, 1949.

Smith, S. E. *The United States Marine Corps in World War II.* New York: Random House, 1969.

Thompson, Laura. *Guam and Its People.* Princeton, N.J.: Princeton University Press, 1947.

Tweed, George and Blake Clark. *Robinson Crusoe, USN, The Adventures of George Tweed, RM 1/C, USN on Jap Held Guam.* New York: 1945.

Wedemeyer, Albert C. *Wedemeyer Reports.* New York: Henry Holt & Co., 1958.

West, Charles O., et al., eds. *Second to None! The Story of the 305th Infantry in World War II.* Washington, D.C.: Infantry Journal Press, 1949.

Willock, Roger. *Unaccustomed to Fear.* Princeton, N.J.: Haskins Press, 1968.

Periodicals

Baldwin, Hanson. "Our New Long Shadow," *Foreign Affairs,* April 1939.

Johnson, Lucius W. "Guam, Before December 1941," *U.S. Naval Institute Proceedings,* Vol. 72, No. 3, March 1946.

"Peace and the Navy," *Atlantic Monthly,* April 1938.

Rowcliff, G. J. "Guam," *U.S. Naval Institute Proceedings,* Vol. 68, No. 473, July 1942.

Smith, H. E. "I Saw the Morning Break," *U.S. Naval Institute Proceedings,* Vol. 72, No. 3, March 1946.

Tweed, George R. "31 Months Behind Jap Lines," *American Magazine,* December 1944.

Index